Introduction · Jan Silberberger

Against *and* for Method
Revisiting Architectural Design as Research[1,2]

Can design processes constitute genuine forms of research? Of course they can. Architects, like natural scientists, consider the state of the art and research gaps when developing design proposals. They experiment with hypotheses, test theories, and analyse results. They rely on procedures which they rigidly bind to their objects of study. Like researchers, many architects proceed rationally while including acts of spontaneity. Their approaches are systematic and based on an immense amount of training, yet architects sometimes decide to override routines. And like scientific laboratories, studios often constitute sites which are characterized as much by systematizing, categorizing, and arranging knowledge as they are by a desire for knowledge.

Teaching studios indeed exhibit procedures that can be considered scientific. In fact, many studios use approaches which effectively fulfil the requirements of scientific conduct—even though the people involved would likely not make such a claim. The edited volume at hand provides examples of such methodologies and demonstrates their necessity. The contributions and interviews urge studio teachers to reflect on and enhance the traceability, coherency, and comprehensibility of the methods they impart. They also offer support

1 Editor: Jan Silberberger →→
2 Contributions by Bernhard Böhm, Johan De Walsche, Kim Helmersen, Adam Jasper, Monika Kurath, Claudia Mareis, Amy Perkins, Wolf Reuter, Hans-Jörg Rheinberger, Jeremy Waterfield, and Albena Yaneva plus interviews with Adam Caruso, Dietmar Eberle, Momoyo Kaijima, Anne Lacaton, and Elli Mosayebi.

for tackling the project of increasing transparency, accountability, and awareness of quality and teaching content.

Methodological and research-oriented teaching and practice are relevant to architecture schools now more than ever. Since the mid-1990s, the economization and emerging entrepreneurial management of higher education, or the 'new governance of science',[3] has increasingly put architecture schools under pressure. To date, most architecture schools struggle to assert their relevance in the ever-increasing competition for funding. Evaluated against the criteria of assessment systems such as the European Qualifications Framework,[4] the United Kingdom's Research Excellence Framework,[5] or the International Standard Classification of Education,[6] most architecture schools score badly. This is hardly surprising since publication in indexed scientific journals is the decisive factor for research performance—and most teachers at architecture schools rarely (if ever) publish in such journals.[7] Consequently, compared to other academic disciplines most architecture schools have a distinctive competitive disadvantage.[8]

So far, architecture schools have responded to this drawback with three basic strategies. The first relies on hiring scholars from related disciplines (such as sociology, material science, history, building technology, or robotics) who have the necessary expertise to produce the required quantities of scientific publications. The second strategy demands that architects produce textual reflections alongside their work as legitimate scientific publications.[9] The third aims to promote an understanding according to which constructed buildings are granted the same status as published scientific papers.[10]

Yet, all three strategies are problematic. The problem with the first is apparent: while influencing factors (such as cultural conditions, legal and economic framings, or technological developments that inform and predispose design projects) are systematized and analysed scientifically, the activity of designing itself remains relatively untouched but slides into the background. The second strategy simply imports modes of text production from the humanities. When acting on the premise that designers 'reflect-in-action',[11] that is, while and by means of drawing or making models, it seems inconsistent to demand lengthy written accounts in the style of social science. Most architects are not particularly interested

→ Jan Silberberger is a senior assistant at the Institute for the History and Theory of Architecture (gta) at the Department of Architecture, ETH Zurich.

3 Dietmar Braun and François-Xavier Merrien, eds., *Towards a New Model of Governance for Universities? A Comparative View* (London: Kingsley, 1999); Uwe Schimank, 'Ökonomisierung der Hochschulen: Eine Makro-Meso-Mikro-Perspektive', in Karl-Siegbert Rehberg, ed., *Die Natur der Gesellschaft-Verhandlungen des 33. Kongresses der DGS in Kassel 2006* (Frankfurt: Campus, 2008), 622–35.

4 See https://europa.eu/europass/en/european-qualifications-framework-eqf (accessed 20 January 2021).

5 See www.ref.ac.uk (accessed 20 January 2021).

6 This classification system is maintained by the United Nations Educational, Scientific and Cultural Organization (UNESCO). See https://web.archive.org/web/20170326010815/https://uis.unesco.org/en/topic/international-standard-classification-education-isced/ (accessed 20 January 2021).

7 Frank van der Hoeven from the Delft University of Technology has taken the initiative and begun to upgrade selected architecture magazines to an academic status while keeping them as original as possible. So far, however, these journals have only scarcely entered the awareness of design practitioners.

8 Priska Gisler and Monika Kurath, 'Architecture, design et arts visuels: Les transformations des disciplines après la Réforme de Bologne', in Adriana Gorga and Jean-Philippe Leresche, eds., *Disciplines académiques en transformation: Entre innovation et résistance* (Paris: Editions des Archives Contemporaines, 2015), 165–79.

9 The Bartlett School of Architecture, for example, is famously promoting this option.

10 Dietmar Eberle argued for this option in a keynote lecture at the 'Research Perspectives in Architecture' conference at the Technical University Munich, 4 July 2019.

11 See Donald A. Schön, *The Reflective Practitioner* (New York: Basic Books, 1983) and Donald A. Schön, *The Design Studio: An Exploration of Its Traditions and Potentials* (London: RIBA, 1985).

in training the skill of academic writing because it is incongruous with their 'epistemic culture'[12]: their strategies, empirical procedures, and modes of collaboration. The problem with the third strategy is that it has often served as an excuse for not reflecting and clarifying design processes methodically. The argument that potential insights are intricately woven into buildings (which, due to their complexity can only be adequately assessed by direct peers—if even by them) has too often been used to conceal an unwillingness or inability to relate to and incorporate the present state of research of the discipline, let alone create relevant knowledge for the field.

In relation to promoting the second strategy, the catchphrase 'research by design' has been circulating through architecture schools since the mid-1990s.[13] Rather self-explanatory, research by (or through) design accompanies the claim that knowledge can effectively be created by design projects and that the insights generated are, in their applicability, 'not restricted to the product on which research is being conducted.'[14] Interestingly, the term 'research by design' is primarily used by theoreticians and elaborated on by scholars.[15] In contrast, most architects who were appointed professors for their oeuvre of completed buildings disdain it. This may have to do with the fact that the largely theoretical discussion on research by design at times comes across as if its proponents understand their role as that of educating design professors to achieve a form of scientificity to which the latter never aspired. For many practising architects, the written accounts produced by 'design researchers' are disconnected from practice, are mere imitations of humanities papers, or are alien to the epistemic culture of architectural design, and hence they are devoid of actual relevance. Their argument is that research in architecture must be tested in 'real life'. For them, only realized building objects (and perhaps fully developed design proposals such as competition entries) count as research. Hence, they claim that the projects they realize within their private offices (which they run alongside their academic appointments) are to be considered equivalent to the publications of scientists, whereas the teaching studio (and the lecture hall) is where the findings of this research are passed on. While this outsourcing does not have to be problematic, it is prone to become so if there is only little formal accountability with respect to evidence of research activity. Despite the quarrelling between the proponents of strategies two and three, their claims are related. Equating design processes with research processes (strategy two) and realized buildings with scientific publications (strategy three) are both based on an understanding that knowledge is generated through design processes and inscribed into their outcomes.

As the volume at hand shows, a fourth strategy which combines aspects of the second and the third could be pursued to combine the best of both. It would keep the demand for an accurate reflection and description of the process from strategy two but abandon expectations for the description to resemble a humanities paper, instead accepting concise accounts. From strategy three, it would accept fleshed-out design proposals and the notion that a building can be compared to an academic article but abandon expectations that the building would be realized. The combination then,

---

12 Karin Knorr Cetina, *Epistemic Cultures: How the Sciences Make Knowledge* (Cambridge, MA: Harvard University Press, 1999).
13 The source of the term is often given as Christopher Frayling, 'Research in Art and Design', *Royal College of Art Research Papers* 1, no. 1 (1993/94), 1–5.
14 Beat Schneider, 'Design as Practice, Science and Research', in Ralf Michel, ed., *Design Research Now* (Basel: Birkhäuser, 2007), 207–18, here 216.
15 Daniel Gethmann and Susanne Hauser, eds., *Kulturtechnik Entwerfen: Praktiken, Konzepte und Medien in Architektur und Design Science* (Bielefeld: transcript, 2009); Sabine Ammon and Eva M. Froschauer, eds., *Wissenschaft entwerfen: Vom forschenden Entwerfen zur Entwurfsforschung der Architektur* (Paderborn: Wilhelm Fink, 2013); Murray Fraser, ed., *Design Research in Architecture: An Overview* (Farnham: Ashgate, 2013).

in line with the epistemic culture of architectural design, would focus both on the design process and the design proposal. What remains to be developed is the format of a document that would enable peer review by describing research questions, hypotheses, rationales, and findings.

Pursuing this fourth strategy will eventually increase chances of securing funding. First, though, it is crucial to understand that it would enable the academic discipline of architecture to unlock the full potential of its unique way of producing and imparting knowledge. When compared to other academic disciplines, architecture's studio approach is exemplary in connecting teaching and research. The teaching studio enables students to make profound and veritable experiences, as it allows far-reaching experimentation collaboratively run and analysed by teachers and students. The decisive question for architecture as an academic discipline is thus how systematic and conceptually coherent student experimentation is guided and supervised. The answer depends on how traceable, comprehensible, or even verifiable the methodological principles of experimentation are—in themselves and in relation to their objects of study.

While there are many exemplary cases, studio teaching too often involves avoidable obscurities and inadequacies. Three major deficiencies can be observed regularly. The first is when 'epistemic positions' (formulations of a problem, aims, and procedures) are replaced without reflection. Research processes, be they design-based or natural scientific, require assumptions, methods, and even objects of study to be adjusted or replaced. Without serious efforts to develop plausible interpretations that rationalize and give meaning to such revisions,[16] the whole process becomes erratic, and any possibility of traceability and comprehensibility is disabled. Second, studios now and then tend to show an unreadiness to translate tacit into propositional knowledge. At times, subjective, intuitive judgements that teachers make during student critiques (crits) are left completely unchallenged, with students only vaguely aware of the statement's meaning, applicability, and significance. What is missing is an aspiration to find more systematic ways of imparting such 'designerly ways of knowing'.[17] Third, many studios overstate the value of final results. Reviews (and not only final reviews) often radiate a trade show atmosphere: flawless design proposals are presented with equally polished sales pitches, where students conceal problematic aspects of their design. From an academic point of view, such project presentations are misguided. Instead, efforts should be made towards presentations that address the difficulties that have been encountered and disclose the limitations and omissions that are inscribed into the designs.

Against this background, the book at hand is an absolute plea for method. The book title, of course, is a nod to the work of philosopher of science Paul Feyerabend,[18] who elaborated how groundbreaking scientific discoveries (and paradigm shifts) are often caused by 'disloyalties' to prevalent methodological routines. With architectural design, though,

---

16 Karl E. Weick, *Sensemaking in Organizations* (Thousand Oaks, CA: Sage, 1995); Ileana Stigliani and Davide Ravasi, 'Organizing Thoughts and Connecting Brains: Material Practices and the Transition from Individual to Group-Level Prospective Sensemaking', *Academy of Management Journal* 55, no. 5 (2012), 1232–59; Sally Maitlis and Marlys Christianson, 'Sensemaking in Organizations: Taking Stock and Moving Forward', *The Academy of Management Annals* 8, no. 1 (2014), 57–125.

17 Nigel Cross, *Designerly Ways of Knowing* (Basel: Birkhäuser, 2007). Cross coined the term 'designerly ways of knowing' to describe the inadequacy of language to grasp the insights that designers gain from interacting with material. However, all architects that I interviewed for this book were adept at putting their projects and the experiences they made into words. I would even claim that most good architects are able to verbally convey the insights they gained through their practice.

18 Paul Feyerabend, *Against Method* (London: New Left Books, 1975). The bookmark within this book (if it is still there upon reading) shows a photo, taken by Grazia Borrini-Feyerabend, of Feyerabend scrubbing dishes.

there are hardly any compulsory methodological routines. On the contrary: the discipline is characterized by an immense diversity of methods, but the understanding of the conditions, limitations, and implications of these distinct methods is often scarce. Only a profound understanding of established methods and their application can breach routine practice to be 'against' method according to Feyerabend's perspective: deliberate violations of prevailing standards to enable new ways of thinking and open up a new space of possibilities. This does not mean that acts of spontaneity and intuition should be banned. Not at all. However, it calls for thorough reflection and making sense of these acts;[19] that is, serious attempts at speculating about their potential for generalization.

The statements I have made so far are based on and relate to an extensive ethnographic study on studio teaching that my colleague Kim Helmersen and I conducted between 2018 and 2020. With a focus on methodologies of architectural design as they become discernible in teaching, we examined selected studios at six leading European architecture schools, ranging from technical universities (ETH Zurich, Technical University of Munich, University of Stuttgart, Delft University of Technology) to art schools (Royal Danish Academy of Fine Arts in Copenhagen), and schools in between (the Architectural Association School of Architecture in London). At each of these schools, we followed two to four studio courses for one semester each. The studios in our sample exhibited a range of proposed approaches, assignments, and objectives. Our fieldwork primarily focused on public intermediate and final reviews. In addition, we observed a few desk crits (that is, informal, one-on-one assessments carried out at students' desks) and conducted interviews with teachers (professors and assistants) as well as students. During field research, Helmersen and I assumed a variety of roles, from 'observer-as-participant'[20] to active members of the jury panel. During most crits we took notes quietly[21] (and used breaks

Introduction · Jan Silberberger

to speak with teachers and students and discuss our observations), while in a few we acted as guest critics and were directly involved in judging students' projects.[22]

This edited volume arises from the intention to contextually embed this research and enriches our ethnographic study. Scholars reflect on the politico-economic processes that currently shape architecture schools and studio teaching, precursors of the scientification of architectural design, the relationship of science and design in general, and ethnographic accounts of knowledge production and crit assessment inside the studio. The various contributions have been specifically commissioned to compile not only a more nuanced but, primarily, a more complete view on studio teaching and the challenges it currently faces. Finally, these contributions are critically supplemented by interviews with five leading architects who are (or have been) professors at ETH Zurich.

The three contributions of the first part, 'Academizing Architecture', deal with the effects of the current economization and entrepreneurial management of higher education and the accompanying imperative to increase research activities at architecture schools. Monika Kurath is attentive to the strategies that selected European and US architecture schools have developed to implement measurable scientific structures and practices. With her description of

---

19 Karl E. Weick, Kathleen M. Sutcliffe, and David Obstfeld, 'Organizing and the Process of Sensemaking', *Organization Science* 16, no. 4 (2005), 409–21.
20 Raymond L. Gold, 'Roles in Sociological Field Observations', *Social Forces* 36, no. 3 (1958), 217–23.
21 Kathryn J. Fox, 'Self-Change and Resistance in Prison', in Jaber F. Gubrium and James A Holstein, eds., *Institutional Selves: Troubled Identities in the Postmodern World* (New York: Oxford University Press, 2001), 176–92.
22 Patricia A. Adler and Peter Adler, 'Observational Techniques', in Norman K. Denzin and Yvonna S. Lincoln, eds., *Handbook of Qualitative Research* (Thousand Oaks, CA: Sage, 1994), 377–92.

the political and economic framing of academia and how it shapes architecture schools on an institutional level, Kurath lays the ground for the edited volume at hand. Johan De Walsche asks how these developments affect 'the backbone of architectural education': the design studio. De Walsche's contribution is based on an extensive ethnography of administrations and teaching studios (as well as corresponding document analysis) of selected architecture schools in Flanders. De Walsche shows that there are significant discrepancies regarding how the political bodies that govern higher education define research, and he convincingly argues that the studio constitutes a potential role model for connecting teaching and research. Bernhard Böhm's chapter, also based on an ethnographic study, elaborates the intricate relationship between tacit and propositional knowledge and thematizes the bipolar nature of the concept of designbased research: on the one hand, a strategic invention aimed at fulfilling the politically enforced research obligations, on the other, an inclination and desire to further the discipline.

The second part, 'Systematizing Design', provides two analyses of historic attempts towards a scientification of design, essentially motivated from within the discipline. While Claudia Mareis elaborates political, economic, and societal conditions which engendered this scientification between the 1950s and early 1970s, Wolf Reuter focuses on one of its most prominent proponents: design theorist Horst W. Rittel. As Mareis shows, the efforts of the so-called design methods movement must be understood as part of a general trend towards incorporating promising 'outliers' (research fields like cybernetics or parapsychology, but also creativity techniques) into the science system, harnessing their potential within the technological race of the Cold War period. Reuter's contribution reveals striking resemblances between Rittel's understanding of design and the latest state of research in design and planning studies. Centring ambiguity and uncertainty while seeing problemframing, conduct, and (possible) solution proposals as mutually dependent, Rittel's conception of design, as Reuter shows, sits well alongside contemporary interpretations of complexity theory.[23] Mareis's and Reuter's chapters make evident that this 'scientification from within' (which was largely rejected and forgotten during the 1980s, 1990s, and 2000s) provides a valuable groundwork for current endeavours.

The two contributions of the third part, 'Design as Research', consider the relation between scientific research and architectural design: the first from a philosophy of science perspective, the second in close relation to ethnographic data. Hans-Jörg Rheinberger's chapter discusses the role of design within the natural sciences, in which he defines design as 'a directed shaping activity according to explicit goals.' While this may suggest that the sciences and design constitute two rather incongruous fields, Rheinberger then provides an overview of research as an area of human activity, indicating numerous parallels—provided that we widen our understanding of design. Kim Helmersen follows by providing a fine-grained analysis of four sharply different yet equally coherent instances of studio teaching. As part of his analysis, he develops a coordinate system to position and locate the varied approaches in architectural design along axes that represent philosophical position, manageability of problems, and institutional orientation. Directly referring to De Walsche, Helmersen demonstrates that it is not the position within this coordinate system—that is, neither the object of study nor the methodological conduct as such—which determines whether a design process may be seen as equivalent to research but how the two dimensions are bound to each other.

The fourth part, 'Knowledge Production in the Studio', comprises two contributions that provide an in-depth discussion of different yet equally systematic ways of knowledge production in studios. Albena Yaneva describes a studio

---

23 John Alford and Brian W. Head, 'Wicked and Less Wicked Problems: A Typology and a Contingency Framework', *Policy & Society* 36, no. 3 (2017), 397–413.

which imports tools from contemporary anthropological research, while I provide an ethnographic account of two cohesive ways of using references in architectural design. The course described by Yaneva takes place in a traditional studio setting, but students are asked to deploy mapping and cartography techniques taken from contemporary anthropology to examine an urban design problem. As Yaneva shows, the integration of these methods raises awareness and allows for a sharp analysis of the 'invisible' aspects of design,[24] such as funding, climatic effects, or public acceptance.[25] The two studios I present both engage in the well-established practice of referencing in architectural design. One uses buildings as references (which is very common), the other works of art (which is rarer but not completely unknown) to facilitate decision-making in developing design projects. As the chapter shows, both studios exhibit well-traceable rationales, hypotheses, problem definitions, various trials, assessable analyses, and reflections on attempts to rationalize decisions taken intuitively. In combination, this generates design processes that clearly qualify as research.

The two ethnographic contributions of the fifth part, 'Review Practice in the Studio', deal with crit assessment. Both contributions are based on the understanding that crits are typically cluttered with requirements: students must excel in salesmanship (and are often expected to present their work as 'infotainment'), they frequently have to act as technical experts (for example by providing rational and sober information on construction aspects), and they should exhibit the curiosity and inquisitiveness of researchers (that is, they should seek criticism to further their project). Above all, final reviews are oral exams. These requirements are not only overloaded; some are even contradictory. Furthermore, and maybe as a consequence, crits often exhibit a striking arbitrariness with regard to the combination of technical expertise, aesthetic judgements, hypotheses, and assumptions, which are often insufficiently substantiated.[26] Against this background, both chapters discuss crits as sites where principles of comprehensibility and aspects of accountability collide with strict hierarchies, subjective judgements, and subjective decision-making. And yet, both chapters also indicate that the crit format possesses the capacity for engendering a truly advanced learning environment. Combining a historical overview of crit assessment with an ethnographic account of current practice written from the point of view of 'complete participants' who directly engage in the settings they study,[27] the chapter by Adam Jasper, Amy Perkins, and Jeremy Waterfield raises awareness of the modifiability of the crit and makes suggestions for improving it. Tying in with their chapter, my chapter that follows draws on ethnographic data to develop a conceptual framework for rethinking and enhancing crit practice and the role it plays in architecture education.

Finally, to critically supplement these scholarly reflections, the sixth part, 'Practitioners' Views', comprises five interviews with leading architects who run successful offices and at the same time work (or have worked) as professors. Common to all these architects is that their practice shares striking similarities with scientific conduct and that their teaching is characterized by a high degree of comprehensibility.

---

24 Lucius Burckhardt, 'Invisible Design: Das unsichtbare Design', in Bazon Brock, ed., *Die Kinder fressen ihre Revolution* (Cologne: DuMont, 1985), 48–53; Lucius Burckhardt, '… in unseren Köpfen', in Lucius Burckhardt, ed., *Design der Zukunft: Architektur, Design, Technik, Ökologie* (Cologne: DuMont, 1987), 11–17.

25 Interestingly, many studios run by design architects have also begun to orient towards what, until now, has often been referred to as the framing (political, social, economic) conditions of design projects. Architect Arno Brandlhuber, for example, runs studios at ETH Zurich that explicitly focus on issues such as property and land law; see https://station.plus/ (accessed 20 January 2021).

26 Dietmar Eberle explicitly addresses this non-hierarchical, erratic manner of throwing information at students in the interview in the book at hand.

27 Michael Angrosino, *Doing Ethnographic and Observational Research* (London: SAGE, 2007), 55–6.

Even though Dietmar Eberle has published a range of scholarly books,[28] all clearly scientific publications, he always claims that he does architecture, not research. In the interview, he discusses his most recent book, *9× 9—A Method of Design*, which reflects on his teaching over the last twenty years.[29] The *9× 9* methodology proposes is simultaneously systematic and adaptive. It can be applied to a wide range of design problems—and, as Eberle explains, it generates design processes that are comprehensible, retraceable, and verifiable. This in turn allows for crits that are much more focused, precise, and meaningful, and hence more effective for knowledge transfer.

Elli Mosayebi is among the few design professors at ETH Zurich with a doctoral degree. Having written a doctoral thesis in architecture history,[30] she is familiar with both architectural design and scholarly publishing. Mosayebi discusses the relationship between historiography and design and her view on design-based research. The main point of departure for the interview, however, was her 'Twelve Theses on the Architecture of the Second Modernity', which she proclaimed in her inaugural lecture in the fall of 2018.[31] Especially her claim to strive for 'objectivity and rationality without neglecting the subjective' is of interest since it corresponds precisely with this book's claim for (and against) method.

Momoyo Kaijima's method of ethnographic drawing[32] plays a crucial role in her teaching. In her interview, she explains how this method is primarily oriented towards studying settlement spaces and the built environment. At the same time, the drawings reflect the studio's position towards its object of study and feed findings back to the persons concerned (which resonates well with contemporary anthropology). In a similar spirit to Yaneva, Kaijima translates a typical social scientific research method into an integral part of the design process.

Adam Caruso is an architect who is known not only for designing and realizing esteemed buildings but also for his writings in the field of architectural history and theory.[33] His scholarly reflections and practical work tangibly intertwine, as is reflected in his studio teaching. In the interview, he discusses the relationship between architectural design and scientific conduct, aspects of methodological rigour, attempts at objectifying the design process, and the foundations of judgements.

In the interview with Anne Lacaton, she discusses the book which she published together with Jean-Philippe Vassal[34] and her presentation at the conference 'The Future of Open Building' at ETH Zurich in 2015.[35] Lacaton and Vassal's famous claim, 'build almost nothing!', expresses

---

28 Dietmar Eberle and Eberhard Tröger, eds., *Density & Atmosphere: On Factors Relating to Building Density in the European City* (Basel: Birkhäuser, 2014); Dietmar Eberle and Florian Aicher, eds., *be 2226_Die Temperatur der Architektur: Portrait eines energieoptimierten Hauses / be 2226_The Temperature of Architecture: Portrait of an Energy-Optimized House* (Basel: Birkhäuser, 2015).
29 Dietmar Eberle and Florian Aicher, eds., *9×9: A Method of Design* (Basel: Birkhäuser, 2018).
30 Elli Mosayebi, 'Konstruktionen von Ambiente: Wohnungsbau von Luigi Caccia Dominioni in Mailand, 1945–1970'. DSc diss., ETH Zurich, 2014. Forthcoming in English (gta Verlag, 2022).
31 For Mosayebi's 'Twelve Theses on the Architecture of the Second Modernity', see https://mosayebi.arch.ethz.ch/en/twelve-theses/ (accessed 21 January 2021).
32 Atelier Bow-Wow, *Bow-Wow from Post Bubble City* (Tokyo: LIXIL, 2006); Atelier Bow-Wow, *Echo of Space / Space of Echo* (Tokyo: LIXIL, 2009).
33 Adam Caruso and Helen Thomas, eds., *The Stones of Fernand Pouillon: An Alternative Modernism in French Architecture* (Zurich: gta Verlag, 2013); Adam Caruso and Helen Thomas, eds., *Asnago Vender and the Construction of Modern Milan* (Zurich: gta Verlag, 2014); Adam Caruso and Helen Thomas, eds., *Rudolf Schwarz and the Monumental Order of Things* (Zurich: gta Verlag, 2016); Adam Caruso and Helen Thomas, eds., *Hopkins and the City* (Zurich: gta Verlag, 2019).
34 Anne Lacaton and Jean-Philippe Vassal, *Freedom of Use* (Berlin: Sternberg, 2015).
35 For this conference, see https://openbuilding2015.arch.ethz.ch/ (accessed 26 January 2021).

their distinct understanding of design processes. Their pronounced approach of designing buildings to be appropriated by their users was mentioned repeatedly in the studios that Helmersen and I observed. Lacaton and Vassal's somewhat counterintuitive but conceptually highly consistent method of creating affordable excess space to ensure a building's adaptability and hence longevity and sustainability constituted a key point of interest for the interview.

Taken together, the contributions and interviews in this book raise awareness of the importance of carefully conceptualized methods. As the book argues, such methods do not only increase the probability of meaningful design proposals; they also enable substantial, systematic, and thorough discussion, and enhance the traceability and verifiability of design processes. This constitutes a basic condition of academia. Moreover, the edited volume at hand demonstrates that framing design processes as research procedures that genuinely resonate with the epistemic culture of architectural design may not just be a strategic response to external pressure but, first and foremost,[36] an intrinsically motivated endeavour to further the discipline.

---

36 This book would not have been possible without Corinna Gröbner.

Part One
Academizing Architecture

Monika Kurath

Design, Context, and Profession: Three Research Cultures in Architecture[1,2]

Architecture as a discipline at research universities oscillates between aims of producing unique, genuine research and its roots as an applied, skill-oriented, artistic, and profession-based discipline that focuses mainly on education.[3] As has occurred several times in the history of the discipline, interest in the methodological aspects of architectural design has once again increased in recent years.[4] As in the design methods movement, studies have analysed architectural design as a specific research practice, focusing on the elaboration of theoretical concepts that allow for facilitating design-based modes of decision-making. In the same spirit, further studies have aimed at developing a specific theory of architectural design based on intrinsic specificities of architectural work, practices, and thinking.[5]

Further contributions have projected architecture's epistemic culture against the background of the academization of the field[6] and the trend towards a scientization of design practices.[7] Current research discourses in architecture have become more focused on its core skill of architectural design, thus contrasting it with research. Yet positioning architecture as a profession-based field has significant impact on knowledge production in that it fails to build its own distinct research tradition.[8] So far, research in architecture has mainly been conducted in related disciplines such as art history, architectural history and theory, social sciences, humanities, natural sciences, and engineering.[9] Establishing research in applied, artistic, and profession-based disciplines entails academizing epistemically and ontologically distinct knowledge production practices to make them compatible with audit-oriented criteria of traditional research disciplines.[10]

Based on studies at five architecture schools and departments in Switzerland, the United Kingdom, and the United States,[11] this article analyses research cultures in

---

[1] Monika Kurath is Dean of Research and Faculty at the University of St. Gallen.
[2] This article is based on research funded by the Swiss National Science Foundation (SNSF grant number 100016-143206) and ETH Zurich (ETH grant number 05 14-1).
[3] Sabine Ammon and Eva M. Froschauer, eds., *Wissenschaft entwerfen: Vom forschenden Entwerfen zur Entwurfsforschung der Architektur* (Paderborn: Wilhelm Fink, 2013); Monika Kurath, 'Architecture as a Science: Boundary Work and the Demarcation of Design Knowledge from Research', *Science & Technology Studies* 28, no. 3 (2015), 81–100.
[4] Claudia Mareis, *Design als Wissenskultur: Interferenzen zwischen Design- und Wissensdiskursen seit 1960* (Bielefeld: transcript, 2011); Claudia Mareis, Gesche Joost, and Kora Kimpel, eds., *Entwerfen – Wissen – Produzieren: Designforschung im Anwendungskontext* (Bielefeld: transcript, 2010); Daniel Gethmann and Susanne Hauser, eds., *Kulturtechnik Entwerfen: Praktiken, Konzepte und Medien in Architektur und Design Science* (Bielefeld: transcript, 2009).
[5] Elke Krasny and Gudrun Hausegger, eds., *Architektur beginnt im Kopf: The Making of Architecture* (Basel: Birkhäuser, 2008); Susanne Hauser, Christa Kamleithner, and Roland Meyer, eds., *Architekturwissen. Grundlagentexte aus den Kulturwissenschaften: Zur Ästhetik des sozialen Raumes* (Bielefeld: transcript, 2011); Peter Lorenz, *Entwerfen: 25 Architekten; 25 Standpunkte* (Munich: DVA, 2004); Paul Schoper, *Zur Identität von Architektur: Vier zentrale Konzeptionen architektonischer Gestaltung* (Bielefeld: transcript, 2010).
[6] Ammon and Froschauer, *Wissenschaft entwerfen* (see note 3); Kurath, 'Architecture as a Science' (see note 3).
[7] Gernot Weckherlin, 'Vom Betriebscharakter des Entwerfens: Konjunkturen der Verwissenschaftlichung in der Architektur', in Ammon and Froschauer, *Wissenschaft Entwerfen* (see note 3), 171–204.
[8] Ammon and Froschauer, *Wissenschaft entwerfen* (see note 3); Kurath, 'Architecture as a Science' (see note 3).
[9] Bettina Heintz, Martina Merz, and Christina Schumacher, *Wissenschaft, die Grenzen schafft: Geschlechterkonstellationen im disziplinären Vergleich* (Bielefeld: transcript, 2004).
[10] Kurath, 'Architecture as a Science' (see note 3).
[11] The analysed schools and departments consisted of ETH Zurich, Bartlett School of Architecture, Cambridge University, Columbia University, and Princeton University.

architecture that focus on the design process, the context in which architecture takes place, and the architectural building practice. For this analysis, architecture was studied through a cultural lens, using a socio-material approach to enquire about knowledge production in architecture by applying Karin Knorr Cetina's concept of epistemic cultures.[12] In her research, Knorr Cetina showed the differences between the two analysed fields in regard to their working practices, their interpretation of the objects they analysed, and their social organization.

Analysing research cultures means focusing on three dimensions of knowledge production: epistemic, material, and social.[13] Applied to the analysis of architecture, the first dimension focuses on the practices of knowledge production—on methods, theories, and hypotheses, as for example on disciplinary and academic constitutions[14]—and on the framings of design as a cultural technique,[15] as a visual practice, as epistemic objects, and in terms of aesthetic knowledge.[16] The second dimension focuses on the materiality of knowledge production: visual representations and objects in architecture like plans, drawings, models, pens, or computer-aided design programmes.[17] Finally, the third dimension focuses on social aspects of the disciplinary identity of architecture, for example its cohesive social community that produces knowledge through a mixture of close collaboration and intense competition with peers, and as a discipline that trains its students through ritualized passage points.[18]

Studying research in architecture as an epistemic phenomenon means to focus on research, methods, approaches, and theories taught in departments, through agreements shared schoolwide on form and content of distinct architecture research, and on codified references, theories, and form and content of publications. To study research in architecture as a material phenomenon is to focus on skills taught and materials used in research and teaching. Analysing research in architecture as a social phenomenon requires a meta-perspective to study the handling of tenure processes, peer review, career trajectory, and the relation of architecture schools to other departments and university administration. These dimensions are inseparable.[19]

In this article, I argue that research in architecture manifests itself in a variety of forms and appearances and that these multiple manifestations are mainly driven by two trends: first, the external driver of a new governance of science, and second, the specific epistemic culture of architecture. I will further show that three major research cultures in architecture can be subsumed under the categories of design, context, and profession. The following two sections

---

12 Karin Knorr Cetina, *Epistemic Cultures: How the Sciences Make Knowledge* (Cambridge, MA: Harvard University Press, 1999).

13 Knorr Cetina, *Epistemic Cultures* (see note 12).

14 Peter Galison, 'Aufbau/Bauhaus: Logical Positivism and Architectural Modernism', *Critical Inquiry* 16, no. 4 (1990), 709–52; Peter Galison and Emily Thompson, eds., *The Architecture of Science* (Cambridge, MA: MIT Press, 1999).

15 Sabine Ammon, 'Transforming Tacit Knowledge: The Example of Architectural Drawings', in Professur Theorie und Geschichte der modernen Architektur, ed., *Architecture in the Age of Empire / Die Architektur der neuen Weltordnung, 11th International Bauhaus-Colloquium Weimar* (Weimar: Verlag der Bauhausuniversität Weimar, 2010), 598–609.

16 Boris Ewenstein and Jennifer Whyte, 'Knowledge Practices in Design: The Role of Visual Representations as "Epistemic Objects"', *Organization Studies* 30, no. 1 (2009), 7–30.

17 Kathryn Henderson, *On Line and on Paper: Visual Representations, Visual Culture, and Computer Graphics in Design Engineering* (Cambridge, MA: MIT Press, 1999); Kathryn Henderson, 'The Role of Material Objects in the Design Process: A Comparison of Two Design Cultures and How They Contend with Automation', *Science, Technology & Human Values* 23, no. 2 (1999), 139–74; Boris Ewenstein and Jennifer Whyte, 'Visual Representations as "Artefacts of Knowing"', *Building Research & Information* 35, no. 1 (2007), 81–9.

18 Dana Cuff, *Architecture: The Story of Practice* (Cambridge, MA: MIT Press, 1991).

19 Kurath, 'Architecture as a Science' (see note 3).

will focus on the two drivers, while the last will discuss the three categories.

The new governance of science

One of the major drivers behind the multiple research cultures in architecture is a new governance of science that has led to a global trend of homogenizing research and pressure to establish clear, measurable, and traceable scientific structures and practices.[20] Since the 1990s, an increasing economization, politicization, and harmonization of higher education—subsumed under notions like the new public management of universities[21] or the new governance of science[22] can be observed. A prominent example for this trend is the Bologna Process, which has led to a profound top-down reformation of higher education in Europe.[23] Various studies have elaborated the processes of standardization that this reform has facilitated and have shown how these increasingly transform both research and higher education into globally marketable products in a 'commodification of academic research'.[24]

Dietmar Braun and François-Xavier Merrien identified a general shift in the belief systems of higher education organizations in continental Europe, the United Kingdom, and the United States from cultural to public service institutions.[25] Other scholars have described universities as self-steering organizations with a distinct entrepreneurial function[26] within a globalized market of competing research institutions.[27] This new role of higher education systems and new mode of governance is expressed through the introduction and implementation of policy-steering instruments such as:
- accreditations with clearly defined structural and performance indicators, such as governance system and funding structure of the university, faculty typologies, student/faculty ratios, research performance, teaching excellence, knowledge transfer, and international outreach indicators;
- evaluations that measure the performance of universities according to indicators in research, teaching, knowledge

20 Uwe Schimank, '"New Public Management" and the Academic Profession: Reflections on the German Situation', *Minerva* 43 (2005), 361–76; Uwe Schimank, 'Ökonomisierung der Hochschulen: Eine Makro-Meso-Mikro-Perspektive', in Karl-Siegbert Rehberg, ed., *Die Natur der Gesellschaft: Verhandlungen des 33. Kongresses der deutschen Gesellschaft für Soziologie in Kassel 2006* (Frankfurt: Campus, 2008), 622–35.
21 Schimank, '"New Public Management"' (see note 20); Schimank, 'Ökonomisierung der Hochschulen' (see note 20).
22 Dietmar Braun and François-Xavier Merrien, eds., *Towards a New Model of Governance for Universities? A Comparative View* (London: Kingsley, 1999); Ulrike Felt and Maximilian Fochler, 'Riskante Verwicklungen des Epistemischen, Strukturellen und Biographischen: Governance-Strukturen und deren mikropolitische Implikationen für das akademische Leben', in Peter Biegelbauer, ed., *Steuerung von Wissenschaft? Die Governance des österreichischen Innovationssystems: Innovationsmuster in der österreichischen Wirtschaftsgeschichte* (Innsbruck: Studienverlag, 2010), 297–327; Sabine Maasen and Peter Weingart, 'Unternehmerische Universität und neue Wissenschaftskultur', *die hochschule* 15, no. 1 (2006), 19–45.
23 Jens Maesse, *Die vielen Stimmen des Bologna-Prozesses: Zur diskursiven Logik eines Bildungspolitischen Programms* (Bielefeld: transcript, 2010); Franz Schultheis, Paul-Frantz Cousin, and Martha Roca i Escoda, eds., *Humboldts Albtraum: Der Bologna-Prozess und seine Folgen* (Constance: UVK, 2008).
24 Alfred Nordmann, Hans Radder, and Gregor Schiemann, eds., *Science Transformed? Debating Claims of an Epochal Break* (Pittsburgh: University of Pittsburgh Press, 2011). See also Hans-Werner Fuchs and Lutz R. Reuter, eds., *Internationalisierung der Hochschulsysteme: Der Bologna-Prozess und das Hochschulwesen der USA* (Hamburg: Universität der Bundeswehr, 2003); Jan Masschelein and Maarten Simons, *Globale Immunität oder eine kleine Kartographie des europäischen Bildungsraums* (Zurich: Diaphanes, 2012); Franziska Muche, ed., *Opening Up to the Wider World: The External Dimension of the Bologna Process* (Bonn: Lemmens, 2005).
25 Braun and Merrien, *New Model of Governance* (see note 22).
26 Maasen and Weingart, 'Unternehmerische Universität' (see note 22), 20.
27 Ewan Ferlie, Christine Musselin, and Gianluca Andresani, 'The Steering of Higher Education Systems: A Public Management Perspective', *Higher Education* 56, no. 3 (2008), 325–48; Maasen and Weingart, 'Unternehmerische Universität' (see note 22); Schimank, '"New Public Management"' (see note 20); Schimank, 'Ökonomisierung der Hochschulen' (see note 20); Richard Münch, *Akademischer Kapitalismus: Über die politische Ökonomie der Hochschulreform* (Berlin: Suhrkamp, 2011).

transfer, and funding, such as the number of articles in peer-reviewed journals, the volume of competitively acquired third party funds, professor/student ratios, or the number of prize winners (such as Nobel Prize laureates);
• rankings as a subgroup of evaluations and as international performance indicators with a strong competitive aspect and streamlining factors, again with regard to research performance and influence (numbers of citations or h-indexes), teaching excellence, knowledge transfer, industry cooperation, and international outreach;
• output-related reward systems which finance universities based on the number of graduated students and publications;
• newly established research centres of excellence aiming at differentiating the university landscape and fostering its competitiveness;
• grant systems providing resources based on the evaluation of research applications; and
• processes of harmonization of educational programmes as bachelor's, master's, and doctoral degree programmes.

The introduction and application of the above-listed instruments of new public management have produced diverse effects on both research and education. While Uwe Schimank observes a greater flexibility in appropriating funds and a more efficient allocation of resources. He argues that universities are faced with increased difficulties in persevering long-term lines of research. He also argues that mainstream research is privileged and that academic diversity is reduced.[28]

These tendencies of a new governance of science[29] have had a major influence on the understanding and appearance of research and higher education.[30] While Georg Bollenbeck and Waltraud Wende[31] see the humanities and cultural studies as being most strongly affected by the economization and new regimentation of higher educational institutions, I argue that the introduction of research evaluations and performance agreements between universities and science ministries also affects skill-oriented disciplines such as architecture,[32] particularly architecture schools which provide practice-oriented education at research universities.[33]

In the 1980s, governments (particularly in the United Kingdom but also in continental Europe and in the United States) started to distribute public money for universities based on their research performance. Since most of the architecture schools in these regions were places for professional education, they had no individual or genuine research culture and conducted less quantifiable research activities than established academic disciplines. In order not to lose public funding, these architecture schools started to increase their research activities and introduce new research-based education programmes.[34] At first sight, this academization of architecture seems to be only a gentle, gradual extension of architecture's periodic waves of scientization.[35]

---

28 Schimank, 'Ökonomisierung der Hochschulen' (see note 20). See also Felt and Fochler, 'Riskante Verwicklungen' (see note 22), Kurath, 'Architecture as a Science' (see note 3).
29 Braun and Merrien, *New Model of Governance* (see note 22).
30 Felt and Fochler, 'Riskante Verwicklungen' (see note 22); Maasen and Weingart, 'Unternehmerische Universität' (see note 22).
31 Georg Bollenbeck and Waltraud Wende, eds., *Der Bologna-Prozess und die Veränderung der Hochschullandschaft* (Heidelberg: Synchron, 2007).
32 Kurath, 'Architecture as a Science' (see note 3).
33 Priska Gisler and Monika Kurath, 'Réconfiguration de la comprehension des disciplines en architecture, design et arts visuels', in Adriana Gorga and Jean-Philippe Leresche, eds., *Transformations des disciplines académiques* (Paris: Editions des archives contemporaines, 2015), 165–79.
34 Monika Grubbauer and Silke Steets, 'The Making of Architects: Knowledge Production and Legitimation in Education, Professional Practice and International Networks', *Architectural Theory Review* 19, no. 1 (2014), 4–9; Philip Steadman and Bill Hillier, 'Research Assessment under the Microscope: Disturbing Findings and Distorting Effects', *Architectural Research Quarterly* 6, no. 3 (2002), 203–7; John Templer, 'Architectural Research', *Journal of Architectural Education* 44, no. 1 (1990), 3.
35 Weckherlin, 'Betriebscharakter des Entwerfens' (see note 7).

Yet, with the exception of the design methods movement in the 1960s,[36] such research had been primarily carried out within subdisciplines such as structural design, building physics, or construction technology, or within accompanying disciplines like material sciences, art history, sociology, or human geography.[37]

The epistemic culture of architecture

A second major driver behind the multiple research cultures in architecture is seen in the specific epistemic culture of architecture as an education of practice and traditionally as a field without its own, genuine research culture—specifically, the development of design knowledge from individual and multiple theoretical and methodological approaches, the tight connection with tacit knowledge forms, and the faculty's close relation to architectural practice.[38]

Established as an academic discipline during professionalization processes in the nineteenth century, architecture underwent a transformation from an informal craft to a formal applied science profession.[39] In particular, in the German-speaking world, architecture mainly became part of the engineering sciences at technical universities. Other institutional settings for training in architecture were art schools, universities, and architecture schools.[40] Mainly at technical universities in central Europe, the applied aspects of a professional education have been at the forefront. Anglophone institutions' Beaux-Arts-oriented approaches usually located architecture in dedicated schools or art schools, establishing a more academic branch of architecture.[41] In the polytechnical context, research in architecture has primarily been undertaken by neighbouring disciplines such as art history, sociology, human geography, material sciences, and engineering statics, rather than by the discipline itself.[42]

Nevertheless, architecture went through periodic waves of scientization, such as during the design methods movement in the 1950s to 1970s and the digitization of design in the 1990s.[43] This lack of disciplinary research in architecture itself has significantly changed since the late 1990s, when applied disciplines underwent academization and research activities were increased in those fields.[44] Design as a core skill of architecture particularly came into focus as a result of research controversies that surrounded it.

The ways and practices through which knowledge is produced in design can be characterized by a lack of a community-wide shared pool of codified references and a traditional orientation towards skills, handcraft, and artistic practice, and ideals like individuality, singularity, and non-reproducibility. Knowledge production in architecture often focuses more on developing individual solutions for a specific task than on generating reproducible, universally applicable products, insights, or theories. In architecture, knowledge production appears as being oriented towards multidisciplinarity, individual situations, and contexts.[45]

---

36 Nigel Cross, 'Science and Design Methodology: A Review', *Research in Engineering Design* 5, no. 2 (1993), 63–9; Jesko Fezer, 'A Non-sentimental Argument: Die Krisen des Design Methods Movement 1962–1972', in Daniel Gethmann and Susanne Hauser, eds., *Kulturtechnik Entwerfen: Praktiken, Konzepte und Medien in Architektur und Design Science* (Bielefeld: transcript, 2009), 287–304.
37 Heintz, Merz, and Schumacher, *Wissenschaft, die Grenzen schafft* (see note 9).
38 Kurath, 'Architecture as a Science' (see note 3).
39 Spiro Kostof, ed., *The Architect: Chapters in the History of the Profession* (Oxford: Oxford University Press, 1977).
40 See also Kurath, 'Architecture as a Science' (see note 3).
41 Kostof, *The Architect* (see note 39).
42 Heintz, Merz, and Schumacher, *Wissenschaft, die Grenzen schafft* (see note 9).
43 Denise Scott Brown, 'The Hounding of the Snark', in Peter Galison and Emily Thompson, eds., *The Architecture of Science* (Cambridge, MA: MIT Press, 1999), 375–84; Weckherlin, 'Betriebscharakter des Entwerfens' (see note 7); Mareis, *Design als Wissenskultur* (see note 4).
44 Gisler and Kurath, 'Réconfiguration' (see note 33).
45 See, e.g., Kurath, 'Architecture as a Science' (see note 3).

The epistemic culture of architecture can further be described as following ideals like individuality, singularity, and non-reproducibility and as being based on a variety of insights from different fields such as the arts, art history, social sciences, and physics. This specific, individual approach of architecture has been interpreted by social science disciplines as an absence of theoretical and methodological rigour. However, architectural literature identifies this approach as architecture's own method. Methodologically, architecture shows a particular orientation towards tacit knowledge forms and flexible, intuition-based, and non-linear working processes. These methods have been described in relation to scientific laboratories practices in terms of testing, probing, and scaling, as well as in terms of individual traits regarding a specific gaze, translation, circulating knowledge, and simultaneous thinking.

From a social perspective, architecture can be described as built upon a cohesive social community that produces its knowledge through a mixture of close collaboration and intense competition with peers.[46] The community educates its members through ritualized 'passage points' such as charrettes and critiques. The latter is established as a combination of a conference talk situation and peer review (albeit neither anonymous nor formalized). Much architectural training takes place outside academia, instead within professional elite circles. Once established, a professional architect may return to academia. The way students are taught with the design critique (established as the combination of a conference talk situation and a non-anonymous, informal, and directly addressed peer review as its key instrument) significantly differs from epistemic cultures in traditional research disciplines.[47]

To sum up, design knowledge has been developed from individual and multiple theoretical, methodological, and experimental approaches tightly connected with tacit knowledge forms.[48] Furthermore, the tradition in architecture of non-formalized tenure and peer-review processes points to a research culture that is hardly compatible with the formal and structural criteria of traditional research disciplines and their audit cultures. The next section will address the ways these two drivers manifest themselves in architectural research in the literature and schools we analysed.

Research cultures in architecture

First effects of an increased orientation towards research are already visible at architecture schools in the Western world, which have decisively responded to the economization and standardization of higher education by implementing distinct research structures.[49] These implementations are, however, accompanied by conflicts regarding curricula restructuring, increased rates of doctoral degrees being awarded, the establishment of graduate programmes, and publication strategies in peer-reviewed journals.[50] Further effects can be identified in discussions on theories, methods, and the empirical quality of architectural design as well as on form and content of genuine architectural research.[51]

---

46 Cuff, *Architecture* (see note 18).
47 Anna Flach and Monika Kurath, 'Die Architektur als Forschungsdisziplin: Spannungsfelder der Akademisierung in der schweizerischen Architekturausbildung', *archithese* 2 (2016), 72–80.
48 Ammon, 'Transforming Tacit Knowledge' (see note 15); Albena Yaneva, 'Scaling Up and Down: Extraction Trials in Architectural Design', *Social Studies of Science* 35, no. 6 (2005), 867–94; Ignacio Farias, 'Epistemic Dissonance: Reconfiguring Valuation in Architectural Practice', in Ariane Berthoin Antal, Michael Hutter, and David Stark, eds., *Moments of Valuation: Exploring Sites of Dissonance* (Oxford: Oxford University Press, 2015), 271–89.
49 Murray Fraser, ed., *Design Research in Architecture: An Overview* (Farnham: Ashgate, 2013).
50 Gisler and Kurath, 'Réconfiguration' (see note 33).
51 Ammon and Froschauer, *Wissenschaft entwerfen* (see note 3); Hauser, Kamleithner, and Meyer, *Architekturwissen* (see note 5); Anna-Lisa Müller and Werner Reichmann, eds., *Architecture, Materiality and Society: Connecting Sociology of Architecture with Science and Technology Studies* (London: Palgrave Macmillan, 2015).

A literature analysis, interviews, and participant observation at several architecture departments at Swiss, American, and British universities revealed differences of research in architecture based on design practice, the context of a design project, and the profession. Hence, they are not framed as distinct categories but as overlapping understandings of the epistemic basis of research in architecture and its ontologies.

Figure i summarizes core aspects of three research cultures in architecture. All three make clear, albeit different, demarcations between design and research. The first research culture, design-based research, focuses on demarcating design from design research. Here, design research adds a written reflection to the design process. The second, context-oriented research, demarcates disciplines; namely, architecture provides the design and a research discipline provides the theories, methods, and research approaches through which the context of a design project is analysed. The third, profession-based research, focuses on the institutional context. Research is linked to professional identities and organizational settings, linking office practice with university teaching design studios. Despite their differences, the three cultures I identify share concerns about what makes research in architecture, what good research might look like, how it can be detected and measured, and how to do research without losing sight of the importance of architectural practice.

Design-based research

Design-based research takes place within an epistemic perspective that frames the design process as a practice of knowledge production. This framing is based on a sociomaterial understanding of research. 'Architectural design research can be described as the processes and outcomes of inquiries and investigations in which architects use the creation of projects, or broader contributions towards design thinking, as the central constituent in a process which also involves i Three research cultures in architecture

	Design-based	Context-oriented	Practice-based
Research framing	Design is research	Research takes place in neighbouring disciplines	Research is an experimental practice
Disciplinary orientation	Disciplinary	Inter-disciplinary	Trans-disciplinary
Epistemic basis	Architecture methodologies, drawing, modelling	Design combined with methodologies of neighbouring disciplines	Experimental setting, links to professional practice
Research ontology	Translation of design process into a written research text	Combination of design and research output from another discipline	Combination of design practice, office project, and reflection
Output	Design and text	Design and text	References, design portfolios, professional projects, buildings, text, or publications
Role of material artefacts and tools	Artefacts and tools as part of research	Material and immaterial aspects as research focus	Artefacts and tools as part of experiments
Formal and methodological standards	Hypotheses, design, results, conclusions	Multi-disciplinary fieldwork, methods of respective discipline	Experimental design project, no formal standards
Relation between research and practice	Design research as design practice and written reflection	Clear separation of epistemes and ontology	Design research as experimental design practice

the more generalized research activities of thinking, writing, testing, verifying, debating, disseminating, performing, validating and so on.'[52] Thus, knowledge is produced by experimental practice—the design process—and expressed in both material objects and written texts.[53]

Methodologically, design-based research appears open concerning methods and approaches. Also, theories are only sparsely specified. As an overall framework, research consists of questions, hypotheses, research methods, results, and conclusions, reflected in a written text. Theories, often from the humanities, are included and referred to. A range of themes, topics, and projects are possible as long as they are design-based. Hence, the underlying conception of research is the understanding of design as an experimental practice combined with a written reflection on the design process, materials, and tools.[54]

Researchers frame design as a practice to test and further develop architectural assumptions. This framing is used as the formal and methodological standard for design research, yet framing design in terms of research practice is not necessarily an obvious approach. Research consists of questions, hypotheses, research methods, results, and conclusions, reflected in a written text. Design should be differentiated from design research. The schools observed used a threefold structural frame for design-oriented research by establishing diverse standards for design research, strictly demarcating design research from design, and integrating this understanding into their research and teaching activities.[55] In demarcating design from design research, design is understood as an open and intuitive practice, while design research is framed as a practice with research questions, a written text that reflects the design, and a research approach. In other words, design research is the product of both the design process and the written text. Ultimately, design-oriented research entails that practices of design are foundational to the conduct of research, research happens within the discipline of architecture, research is epistemically based on architecture methodologies such as acts of drawing and modelling, and design-based researchers are able to translate aspects of the design process into written text.

Context-oriented research

Opposite to design-oriented research, which frames a design project as research, context-oriented research analyses the design project through the lens of a traditional research discipline. Analysing the social, cultural, ethical, political, legal, scientific, and engineering contexts of a design project outside the studio is essential to this approach.[56] Such research projects apply methods, approaches, and theories according to the research discipline chosen for the particular project. As in the design-based approach, outputs consist of a design and a text documenting the design practice. Yet, within context-oriented research, the written text focuses on contextual aspects of the design project, for example on cultural, historic, legal, economic, and social aspects of the design project.[57]

---

52 Fraser, *Design Research* (see note 49), 1–2.
53 Fredrik Nilsson, 'Making, Thinking, Knowing Architecture: Notes on Architecture as a Making Discipline and Material Practice', in Jørgen Dehs, Martin Weihe Esbensen, and Claus Peder Pedersen, eds., *When Architects and Designers Write / Draw / Build / ?* (Aarhus: Arkitektskolens Forlag, 2013), 126–47.
54 Jonathan Hill, 'Design Research: The First 500 Years', in Fraser, *Design Research in Architecture* (see note 49), 25–34.
55 Fraser, *Design Research in Architecture* (see note 49).
56 Flach and Kurath, 'Architektur als Forschungsdisziplin' (see note 47).
57 Galen Cranz, *Ethnography for Designers* (New York: Routledge, 2016); Galen Cranz, Lusi Morhayim, Georgia Lindsay, and Hans Sagan, 'Teaching Semantic Ethnography to Architecture Students', *International Journal of Architectural Research* 8, no. 3 (2014), 6–19. On interdisciplinary cooperation on building material and building technologies see Patrick Fleming, Simon Smith, and Michael H. Ramage, 'Measuring-Up in Timber: A Critical Perspective on Mid- and High-Rise Timber Building Design', *Architectural Research Quarterly* 18, no. 1 (2014), 20–30.

Comparable to the design-based approach, context-oriented approaches also include a structural frame for conducting research. While research in the design-based approach takes place within the discipline of architecture and within the design process, research in the context-oriented approach is conducted in another field or discipline. From a formal and methodological perspective, the context-oriented approach frames design research as consisting of a practical part such as fieldwork or explorations on the social, cultural, ethical, historical, political, legal, scientific, or engineering context of a design project. This approach follows a different but also clear separation of both design and research. While design is framed as a practice, architectural research is understood as a project that combines both the design practice and a research perspective from another discipline. Context-oriented architectural research therefore uses tools from traditional research disciplines to analyse the architectural context. Its epistemological basis focuses on practices from side disciplines, and students are trained to adapt to and use these practices in their projects. Context-based research thus entails that research and design are two separate epistemic practices that are rooted in different academic disciplines, that research in architecture is an interdisciplinary project, that research is epistemically based on methodologies from traditional research disciplines, and that context-oriented researchers produce knowledge on the context of a specific design project that informs design decisions.

Profession-based research

Profession-based research is closely linked to a professional design project. Themes, topics, and projects of profession-based research are usually linked to a professional architecture task or a design studio project. In this research culture, design is understood as an experimental practice.[58]

At the core of a profession-based research approach lies a project, task, or question from professional practice or a design studio, often combined with a reflection, experiment, or theory. The theory is based in architectural theory or another academic discipline, or it is developed out of the design practice. Profession-based research mostly takes place in collaboration among practical and academic architects or faculty at architecture schools and researchers from neighbouring disciplines. Research happens in experimental settings in the office, in teaching projects in design studios, in collaborations among architects in which a practice project supplemented by a reflection, or between architects and side disciplines in which a practice project is supplemented by a research component.

A frequent aim of profession-based research is to develop new ideas for teaching in design studios, gain input for professional practice,[59] or design a building that will serve as a reference in architecture. This link between research and professional practice is particularly important. Only through research and further consideration of professional architecture and practice can new ideas be developed.[60] Because architecture is primarily framed as a profession rather than an academic discipline, research in architecture can be an experimental practice that not only takes place within universities and teaching design studios but also in the offices that most of the architecture faculty in professionally oriented schools run in addition to being actively engaged in academia.[61]

---

58 Yaneva, 'Scaling up and Down' (see note 48).
59 Flach and Kurath, 'Architektur als Forschungsdisziplin' (see note 47).
60 Dietmar Eberle and Florian Aicher, eds., *be 2226_Die Temperatur der Architektur / be 2226_The Temperature of Architecture* (Basel: Birkhäuser, 2015).
61 Michael U. Hensel and Fredrik Nilsson, eds., *The Changing Shape of Practice: Integrating Research and Design in Architecture* (London: Routledge, 2016); Michael Weinstock, 'Can Architectural Design Be Research?' *AD+ Unit Factor* 78, no. 3 (2008), 112–15; David Hinson, 'Design as Research: Learning from Doing in the Design Build Studio', *Journal of Architectural Education* 61, no. 1 (2007), 23–6.

Outputs of profession-based research are not clearly defined. They can consist of buildings, projects, and references. In contrast to the design and context-oriented approaches, the profession-based approach is unrelated to established formal or methodological standards for design research. Here, research is seen as an experimental professional practice closely linked to a design project.[62] There is no clear demarcation between design and design research. Rather, research is perceived as an experimental attitude and a dialectical practice to build, defend, and rectify arguments in architecture practice projects.

To sum up, a profession-based research culture entails that research is an experimental design project from the professional practice and based on the idea that architecture is rather a practice than an academic discipline, that it can take place within the discipline of architecture or in interdisciplinary and transdisciplinary settings, that it is epistemically based on experimental settings in design projects and linked to the professional practice, and that practice-based researchers can link academic and professional knowledge and further develop the discipline by producing references.

Conclusion

The increasing focus on research in architecture clashes with its practice-oriented, empirically and methodologically open epistemic culture to produce broad and multifaceted understandings of research. Nevertheless, these understandings can be related to three research approaches based on design, context, or the profession. While design-based research follows a disciplinary understanding and clearly frames design practice as research, context-oriented research combines the architectural design practice with research from an external research discipline. Profession-based research instead follows a transdisciplinary approach and includes research in experimental settings at universities and design studios, interdisciplinary collaborations, and professional work in architecture offices.

Design-based research sees design practices as foundational to the conduct of research. Research is understood as being based on genuine architectural epistemologies and methodologies such as acts of drawing, modelling, seeing, and developing singular and unique ideas towards a specific question. Based on the idea that research clearly takes place within the discipline of architecture, the core contribution of design-based research lies in the translation of tacit knowledge forms of the design practice into explicit knowledge of a written text.

Context-oriented research is led by the assumption that research and design are based in two different epistemic cultures, clearly separating research from practice. Architecture is framed as a discipline of practice so research takes place outside of architecture, namely within traditional research disciplines from the social sciences, the humanities, engineering, and science. Context-oriented architectural research uses concepts, methods, and theories from traditional research disciplines and aims to produce knowledge on the context of a specific architecture project that informs design decisions. The core contribution of context-oriented research lies in interdisciplinarity and combining architectural design with research output from another discipline, making research results productive for design-based decisions.

Profession-based research frames research as experimental design projects plus reflection to produce references. As a tendency, design practices performed in offices of professional architects who also teach design studios at universities count as research. This approach is led by a transdisciplinary perspective that combines a specific professional identity, a design process, and ideas from research disciplines and practitioners.

Further research could focus on developing these three research cultures in architecture to observe the research

62 Helene Furjan, 'Design Research', *Journal of Architectural Education* 61, no. 1 (2007), 62–8.

trajectories of each type and see if the individual forms become more different or if they converge. Given the trends of research in architecture, one could ask what this increased research orientation has to do with the epistemic culture of architecture. Does research-based architecture move away from the built form? Will this lead to reflective practitioners losing their practices?[63] What this means for architecture as both an academic discipline and professional practice remains to be seen.

---

[63] Pierre Bourdieu, *Outline of a Theory of Practice* (Cambridge: Cambridge University Press, 1977).

Johan De Walsche

Academic Research and the Design Studio[1]

Architectural education is supposed to be academic, leading to a master's degree level 7 in terms of the European Qualifications Framework.[2] This framework, a major outcome of the higher education reform of the Bologna Process,[3] postulates that higher education is academic when it is based upon research. A close connection between research and teaching has been conceptualized as the research-teaching nexus, understood in connection with formal scientific research conduct at the university. So, to be accredited as an academic degree programme, architecture education must demonstrate its foundation in scientific research.

Next to the European Qualifications Framework, architectural education is also regulated by the European Directive on Professional Qualifications, which requires that architectural education programmes 'shall maintain a balance between theoretical and practical aspects of architectural training'.[4] This requirement is implemented in curricula

---

1 Johan De Walsche is Professor of Architectural Research Methods at the University of Antwerp.
2 Commission of the European Communities, *Towards a European Qualifications Framework for Lifelong Learning*. Commission staff working document SEC (2005) 957 (Brussels, 8 July 2005).
3 The Bologna Process was an ambitious attempt of the European Union to harmonize higher education by 2010 in the so-called European Higher Education Area. It is remarkable that at the moment of writing, exactly ten years later, its impact is still not fully digested.
4 European Parliament and Council of the European Union, 'Directive 2013/55/EU of the European Parliament and of the council of 20 November 2013, amending Directive 2005/36/EC on the recognition of professional qualifications and Regulation (EU) No 1024/2012 on administrative cooperation through the Internal Market Information System ("the IMI Regulation")', *Official Journal of the European Union* (28 December 2013), L354/132–170. See especially 2013/55/EU, Art.46 §2.

that comprise about half of the credits related to architectural design; the other half of the credits required are a combination of technical and humanities courses.

It can thus be said that the architectural design studio is the backbone of the architectural education programme.[5] To claim to provide academic education under the European Qualifications Framework, however, it must demonstrate a research-teaching nexus—but in the architectural design studio, even links with formal scientific research conduct are usually scarce or inexistent. Instead of being research-based, the design studio is practice-based; instead of being taught by researching academics, it is taught by designing practitioners. Does this mean, then, that studio education is not academic? Or does it mean that the non-academic environment of the design studio is nonetheless able to provide academic education despite its scarce links to formal scientific research conduct, its practice-based approach, and its non-academic teaching practitioners?

To investigate these questions, I will first point to the uneasy relation between research and the design studio. Because I wonder to what extent this unease is inherent to the notion of a research-teaching nexus, I scrutinize its very concept, retracing the rationales behind it to reveal complications and misconceptions. With these new insights, I reapply the issue to architectural design education. Finally, based upon fieldwork that I undertook in architectural design studios in Flanders, I propose a new perspective for discussing the academic quality of architectural studio education, a perspective that might be taken into consideration for academic higher education in general.

Research and design education: fear and reluctance

For most architecture schools, the Bologna Process's emphasis on research as prerequisite for academic higher education implied a sudden pressure, not only for demonstrating the existence of a proper research-teaching nexus but even for architectural education to develop its own research activity—

a new endeavour that architectural schools had never had to worry about and that many felt was alien to the discipline. Such prioritization of research over design has caused unease, tension, and confusion.[6] At the occasion of their General Assembly of 2009, the Nordic Association for Architectural Research published a manifesto about the merits of architectural research, in which they aver:

> The best practitioners of architecture traditionally teach at the schools of architecture, while architectural researchers, are publishing their research in nationwide journals and books that are read by the whole profession of architects and by a large part of the surrounding society. This kind of dialogue between theory and practice is currently under threat. Rigid merit systems borrowed from the scientific world without close relations to architectural practice operate with very narrow definitions of research and research communication. By being forced to adapt to this, architectural research risks to be banned to an ivory tower and loose its meaning for both practice and society.[7]

Two years earlier, the Royal Institute of British Architects (RIBA) had published a memorandum in which Jeremy Till

---

5 This is confirmed by analysis of a Europe-wide survey of the European Association for Architectural Education about curricular structures of European architecture schools. For the survey, see Marco Bovati et al., eds. *Architectural Education Towards 2030: An Inquiry among European Architecture Schools* (Santarcangelo di Romagna: Maggioli Editore, 2015); for the analysis, see Johan De Walsche, 'Genus, Locus, Nexus: An Inquiry into the Nature of Research in Architectural Design Education' (PhD diss., University of Antwerp, 2018), 197–205, 336–41.

6 Priska Gisler and Monika Kurath, 'Architecture, design et arts visuels: Les transformations des disciplines après la réforme de Bologne', in Adriana Gorga and Jean-Philippe Leresche, eds., *Disciplines académiques en transformation: Entre innovation et résistance* (Paris: Editions des Archives Contemporaines, 2015), 165–79.

7 Nordic Association for Architectural Research, *Statement on Merits within Architectural Research*, adopted at the association's annual general meeting in Trondheim, 2009.

points to a similar concern about the increasing divergence between practitioners and academics:

> Architectural research may be seen to have two main contexts of its production, the academy and practice. Each has its own strengths and weaknesses, but it is vital that neither is privileged over the other as a superior form of research, and equally vital that neither is dismissed by the other for being irrelevant. 'You are all out of touch with reality', says the practitioner. 'You are muddied by the market and philistinism', says the academic. There is unnecessary antipathy of the one camp to the other, which means that in the end the worth of research in developing a sustainable knowledge base is devaluated.[8]

But despite such attempts for mediation, the emphasis on a research foundation has polarized architecture schools, particularly in the design studio. In 2012, the Architectural Association School of Architecture in London dedicated a whole issue of its school journal *AArchitecture* to the question of research in the design studio.[9] The journal provides an overview of opinions of academics and students across the school. In it, Pier Vittorio Aureli explains his resolute rejection of research when he studied at the Berlage Institute: 'At the time the Institute was heavily influenced by Koolhaas's AMO research style. Google search was still new and Wikipedia did not yet exist; it was still regarded as "cool" to grab a bunch of data from the internet and display it in fat books with countless 72dpi images. I stood against this total nonsense, instead, I did projects. ... No need for research'.[10] Chris Pierce also fulminates against the emphasis on research: 'The last thing that Chris [Matthews] and I would ever want is for one of our students to be "researching". ... We'd put "researching" on par with "rendering"—another self-delusional practice of grandeur or hypertrophic activity akin to poetry or pantomime. ... Neither Chris nor I could imagine two less compatible tasks than research and design.'[11] Research in the studio is seen as a highly reductive model of intellectual enquiry, one that is humourless, sexless, inarticulate and undiscerning, capable of presenting neither the seductiveness nor the engaging models of thinking which contemporary society need.[12] It is considered incapable of contributing to the necessary architectural knowledge that can only be induced by learning from and acting within the complexity of urban life.[13]

These disconcerting judgements illustrate just how contested research in the studio is. At the same time, they fuel the quest to investigate the controversy. But before diving into the question about the sense or nonsense of a research-teaching nexus in the architectural design studio, it is useful to unravel its very concept and origins because, as the following section will demonstrate, it is a complication in itself.

The idea of a research-teaching nexus: polysemic, complicated, and unproved

The idea that a close link between research and teaching is crucial, particularly at the higher levels of education, stems from the principle of a 'unity of teaching and research' (*Einheit von Lehre und Forschung*) that was launched with the founding of the University of Berlin in 1810. The founders—a group of Prussian reformers, among whom Wilhelm von Humboldt (1767–1835) is best known as the iconic pro-

---

8 Jeremy Till, 'What Is Architectural Research? Architectural Research: Three Myths and One Model', 2007, https://jeremytill.s3.amazonaws.com/uploads/post/attachment/34/2007_Three_Myths_and_One_Model.pdf (accessed 19 December 2020).
9 Eleanor Dodman, Remus Radu Macovei, and Roland Shaw, eds., 'Architecture as Research', special issue, *AArchitecture* 18 (2013).
10 Pier Vittorio Aureli, 'Learning from Architecture', in Dodman et al., 'Architecture as Research' (see note 9), 3.
11 Chris Pierce, 'A Flea in Our Ear', in Dodman et al., 'Architecture as Research' (see note 9), 2.
12 Thomas Weaver, 'Against Research', in Dodman et al., 'Architecture as Research' (see note 9), 9.
13 Lionel Eid, 'Engagement, not Research', in Dodman et al., 'Architecture as Research' (see note 9), 17.

tagonist—strongly believed in the edifying power of the process of doing research. Research was to develop not only the student but also the teacher and even society as a whole.[14] Ever since, this idea has broadly been embraced by academics.

The rhetoric of the Bologna Process refers to this Humboldtian ideal. It considers the research-teaching nexus as a prerequisite for developing 'critical thinking, analysing, arguing, independent working, learning to learn, problem-solving, decision-making, planning, co-ordinating and managing, co-operative working.'[15] And exactly these competencies, so the rhetoric goes, are key for achieving the dual goals of the Bologna Process, namely 'to create a European citizenship that promotes peace, mutual understanding and tolerance, and confidence among peoples and nations ... [and] to provide society with proficient graduates that have the necessary competences to face the challenges of our time'.[16]

Despite plenty of empirical studies about the research-teaching nexus, there is no clear evidence about its effective benefits. Based upon a meta-analysis of fifty-eight empirical studies, educationalists Hattie and Marsh conclude that at the university 'the common belief that research and teaching are inextricably entwined is an enduring myth. At best, research and teaching are very loosely coupled'.[17] They point to three reasons why the belief exists, namely 'because universities use research as an advertising lure, because academics use research output as market commodities, and because most academics would like it to be true'.[18]

There is even less insight into the process of how such a research-teaching nexus would effectively contribute to the development of the competencies to which the Bologna Process refers. A critical look at the nexus's very concept reveals three sets of complications.

A first set of complications is situated at policy level and stems from differences in what is understood as research. Differences can be found at institutional and national levels.[19] At the institutional level, the concept of a research-teaching nexus appears much more frequently at comprehensive universities than at research-intensive universities because of a broader understanding of research by the former in contrast to a more rigid interpretation by the latter.[20] At the national level, one can observe the impact of differences in definitions of research. Let us compare the definition of the *Frascati Manual*, the worldwide guide for research monitoring, with the one from the Research Excellence Framework adopted in the United Kingdom. The *Frascati Manual* defines research as 'creative and systematic work undertaken in order to increase the stock of knowledge'.[21] For the Research Excellence Framework, research is understood as 'the process of investigation leading to new insights, effectively shared'.[22] Its qualitative description refers to research as a practice that addresses and affects another human being as a knowing subject. This stance sharply contrasts with the quantitative description of the *Frascati Manual*, where research is described in terms of production—

14 Mitchell G. Ash, 'Bachelor of What, Master of Whom? The Humboldt Myth and Historical Transformations of Higher Education in German-Speaking Europe and the US', *European Journal of Education* 41, no. 2 (2006), 245–67.
15 Council of Europe, Convention on the Recognition of Qualifications Concerning Higher Education in the European Region (Lisbon, 11 April 1997).
16 European Ministers of Education, Bologna Declaration (Bologna, 19 June 1999).
17 John Hattie and Herbert W. Marsh, 'The Relationship between Research and Teaching: A Meta-Analysis', *Review of Educational Research* 66, no. 4 (1996), 507–42, here 529.
18 Hattie and Marsh, 'Relationship' (see note 17), 533.
19 Monica Kurath extensively describes the impact of research definitions in national policy on the discipline of architecture in the previous chapter of this volume.
20 Carol L. Colbeck, 'Merging in a Seamless Blend: How Faculty Integrate Teaching and Research', *Journal of Higher Education* 69, no. 6 (1998), 647–71.
21 OECD, *Frascati Manual 2015: Guidelines for Collecting and Reporting Data on Research and Experimental Development* (Paris: OECD Publications, 2015).
22 REF2014, *REF 02.2011: Assessment Framework and Guidance on Submissions* (Bristol, July 2011).

the term 'knowledge' is seen as a commodity detached from any mind.

University funding is based on such definitions: what counts as research is funded, but vice versa, what is funded is taken into account as research. Consequently, what is not funded will not be considered as research. In concrete terms, this coexistence of such diverse definitions of research in policy documents has led to the remarkable situation that in 2015, expert panels of the Research Excellence Framework evaluated 3,750 non-written artistic research outcomes (such as performances, musical compositions, design work, and visual media like drawings and video) to allocate research funding to the institutions that produced these outcomes. Yet in the same year the *Frascati Manual* firmly postulated that 'artistic performance is excluded from research ... [as it is] looking for a new expression, rather than for new knowledge'.[23] In the United Kingdom it is possible for higher education disciplines to claim research founded on artistic practices, but in countries that adopt the *Frascati Manual*, it is not. Thus, the nature of a research-teaching nexus in the United Kingdom might be fundamentally different from the one in a country that follows the *Frascati Manual*.

A second set of complications relates to the nature of research and is situated at a more philosophical level. The Humboldtian idea of a unity of teaching and research was related to the early nineteenth-century idea of a unity of science and scholarship (*Einheit der Wissenschaft*).[24] Today, science is splintered in subdisciplines, each with fundamentally distinct scopes, modes, and methods.[25] Each of these particular practices results from very particular ways of looking at specific pieces of the world and identifying distinct constituents, ranging from natural laws to spirituality, neurons, or politics. These practices respond to distinct sets of phenomena that constitute reality and operate under distinct ontologies.[26] For each way of looking at the world, there are other things to know about that piece of the world—and there are many ways of knowing. Assertions that result from formal deductive logic of mathematics have the status of absolute truth, while insights that result from ethnographic studies rely on hermeneutics and understanding limited to a particular moment, place, culture, and community. These two approaches illustrate that the word 'research' also covers distinct epistemologies.[27] If research is understood as a process of coming to know, then also the practices that are undertaken to do so will coherently depend on a particular ontology (what is seen in the world) and epistemology (what there is to know about what is seen in the world). Compare the nature of practices that the mathematician will undertake to formulate assertions with the nature of practices that the ethnographer will undertake to uncover unseen realities within a specific group. Both practices rely on fundamentally different competencies and dispositions of the researcher. Research thus also covers diversity and distinction at a praxeological level.[28] And finally,

---

23 OECD, *Frascati Manual 2015* (see note 21), 65.

24 Ash, 'Bachelor of What?' (see note 14), 246.

25 This argument has extensively been demonstrated in Karin Knorr Cetina, *Epistemic Cultures: How the Sciences Make Knowledge* (Cambridge, MA: Harvard University Press, 1999).

26 The formulations used in this ontological approach to research are inspired by Heidegger's notion of *Bindung*. See the essay 'Die Zeit des Weltbildes' in Martin Heidegger, *Holzwege* (Frankfurt: Klostermann, 1950), ch. 2. For an English translation, see Julian Young and Kenneth Haynes, trans., *Martin Heidegger: Off the Beaten Track* (Cambridge: Cambridge University Press, 2002).

27 For a foundational discussion about the relationship between knowledge and understanding, see Hans-Georg Gadamer, *Wahrheit und Methode: Grundzüge einer philosophischen Hermeneutik* (Tübingen: Mohr, 1960). For a more recent discussion about the relationship between truth and insight, see Jonathan I. Kvanvig, 'Truth Is Not the Primary Epistemic Goal', in Matthias Steup, John Turri, and Ernest Sosa, eds., *Contemporary Debates in Epistemology* (Hoboken: Wiley-Blackwell, 2014), 352–62.

28 Elucidating in this regard is John Dewey's distinction between the concepts of a spectator view of knowledge and a transactional view of knowing. (cont. on p. 49)

the goals and interests that are pursued across these practices largely differ. Research that is undertaken for composing formulas that allow for prediction and control operates under different modes and drivers than research that aspires for a better understanding of cultural phenomena, or than research that aims at emancipation and change. These are fundamental distinctions at a teleological level.[29] Considering the diversity of ontological, epistemological, praxeological, and teleological features that is united under the broad denominator of 'research', it is hard to attribute a single set of expectations and competencies to the concept of a research-teaching nexus. Moreover, it is hard to understand how and why such a polysemic concept, covering such a broad and distinct set of features, would be a valid and sufficient ground to reach those qualities that make higher education 'academic'.

A third set of complications is situated at a societal level and relates to the place of research. Since massification of higher education in the 1960s and the ascent of the knowledge society and knowledge economies since the 1970s, universities have delivered not only professionals as graduates, but also knowledge producers and research-active individuals. Yet only a fraction of these research graduates remains in academia—3.5 per cent, according to one study from the United Kingdom.[30] As a result, knowledge production is no longer the monopoly of the university. Gibbons and Nowotny have demonstrated that knowledge production sites outside the university operate under modes distinct from academia.[31] Evaluation tools of universities are inadequate for valuing the features and qualities of these types of 'non-academic' research.[32] The academic instruments are simply too narrow, particularly for research in the creative sectors.[33] While the concept of a research-teaching nexus is too broad to be meaningful amidst the splintering of science into fundamentally distinct practices, it is also too narrow due to the inadequacy of academic evaluation tools to identify non-academic types of research and to address them as instances of sound and rigorous knowledge production.

The research-teaching nexus applied to architectural design education: even more complications

Applied to the field of architectural education, and more particularly to the architectural design studio, these sets of complications are not only pertinent but also problematic. I illustrate each of them concisely.

Firstly, the lack of a univocal understanding of what to consider as research, and its dependency on national or institutional definitions, is particularly striking for the field of architectural design research. While the Research Excellence Framework is open to any type of research outcome, including design, the *Frascati Manual* adopts a view that 'design is not research and that it has to be kept distinct from research for any statistical purpose'.[34] This leads to the remarkable observation that in the United Kingdom, a building may be considered as a valid outcome of research—

(cont. from p. 47) A good summary is provided in Gert Biesta, 'Why "What Works" Still Won't Work: From Evidence-Based Education to Value-Based Education', *Studies in Philosophy and Education* 29, no. 5 (2010), 491–503.
29 This teleological categorization is inspired by Habermas's theory of cognitive interests. See Jürgen Habermas, *Erkenntnis und Interesse* (Frankfurt: Suhrkamp, 1968); English translation by Jürgen Habermas and Jeremy J. Shapiro, *Knowledge and Human Interests* (London: Heinemann Educational, 1972).
30 The Royal Society, *The Scientific Century: Securing Our Future Prosperity* (London: The Royal Society, 2010).
31 Michael Gibbons et al., *The New Production of Knowledge: The Dynamics of Science and Research in Contemporary Societies* (Thousand Oaks, CA: Sage, 1994).
32 Helga Nowotny, Peter Scott, and Michael Gibbons, *Re-thinking Science: Knowledge and the Public in an Age of Uncertainty* (Cambridge: Polity Press, 2001).
33 Sybille Reichert, *Institutional Diversity in European Higher Education: Tensions and Challenges for Policy Makers and Institutional Leaders* (Brussels: European University Association, 2009).
34 OECD, *Frascati Manual 2015* (see note 21), 63–4.

that is, it counts as empirical evidence of certain findings, and thus solid ground for a valid research-teaching nexus in architecture—while in most other European countries, the prevailing definition of the *Frascati Manual* prevents any acknowledgement of the same building as an outcome of research.[35] In the United Kingdom, the studio teacher who designed this particular building will be recognized and valued for producing knowledge in and about architecture. In contrast, this very same studio teacher, with the same competencies and inquisitive design practice will, in any place that adopts the Frascati definition of research, be considered only as an instructor training students for their professional lives, not as someone producing 'new knowledge'. Under UK regulations this faculty member provides income for the institution—namely research funding. In institutions adopting the Frascati definition of research, such an instructor will be a cost.

Secondly, the extreme specialization of scientific research sharply contrasts with the holistic, synthetic, and even transdisciplinary nature of architectural design.[36] A recent study about emerging approaches in architectural education has identified thirty-eight disciplines across five scientific fields—natural sciences, technical sciences, social sciences, humanities, medical sciences—that architectural design education actually integrates.[37] If narrow specialization is an indicator of good research, then the architectural design studio fails as a research environment in its own, as it falls apart into an amalgamation of diverse nexuses, entailing research findings from disciplines elsewhere.

Thirdly, the inadequacy of academic evaluation mechanisms for acknowledging and valuing knowledge production outside the university is particularly problematic for architecture, both from an institutional viewpoint and from the personal viewpoint of the studio teacher. From the institutional viewpoint, this inadequacy is problematic for ensuring a close and proper entanglement with the professional field, not only as a destination for graduates but as a field of knowledge production. The incapability of academia to identify and assess 'non-academic' research quality is particularly problematic when we take into account the recent ascent of research endeavours in professional practice—think of the AMO research division of OMA, MVRDV's Why Factory, research sections of architecture firms such as White and Snøhetta, the fifteen practice-based research cases in professional practices reported in Michael Hensel and Fredrik Nilsson's book *The Changing Shape of Practice*, or Anne Dye and Flora Samuel's attempt to guide architects and practices into research with their book *Demystifying Architectural Research*.[38] Undeserved unawareness of architectural practice as a potential locus for research conduct results in missed opportunities and a deficit in knowledge production to underpin studio teaching. From a studio teacher viewpoint, the narrowness of academic evaluation mechanisms is problematic simply because these mechanisms are ontologically blind to outcomes of architectural design research. Studio teachers feel pressures to accommodate to these 'rigid merit systems borrowed from the scientific world without close relations to architectural practice'.[39] Frank van der Hoeven, director of research at the Department of Architecture and the Built Environment

---

35 Good examples of how architecture practices and buildings are explained as research outcomes under the UK-wide research assessment of the REF2014 can be found at www.bartlettdesignresearchfolios.com.
36 Hyun-Kyung Lee and Mark Breitenberg, 'Education in the New Millennium: The Case for Design-Based Learning', *International Journal of Art & Design Education* 29, no. 1 (2010), 54–60.
37 Peter Staub, Vera Kaps, and Johan De Walsche, 'Challenging the Frontiers of Architectural Education: In Search of New Schools of Thought', *Archithese* 2 (2016), 60–7.
38 Michael Hensel and Fredrik Nilsson, *The Changing Shape of Practice: Integrating Research and Design in Architecture* (London: Routledge, 2016); Anne Dye and Flora Samuel, *Demystifying Architectural Research: Adding Value to Your Practice* (London: RIBA, 2015).
39 Nordic Association, *Statement on Merits* (see note 7).

at the Delft University of Technology, depicts the dilemma these studio teachers face: those who decide not to comply with the academic expectation of publishing fail to be viewed with academic esteem and as proficient, whereas those who do decide to publish face the dilemma of either publishing in unindexed periodicals (which are not counted as academic research) or publishing in indexed academic journals in their field and alienating themselves from their disciplinary peers.[40] This results in the uncomfortable observation that studio teachers are either invisible in academia, acknowledged but not counted, or seen and counted but alienated from the practical field. How to attract, appoint, and evaluate teachers within the context of academia when their merits and excellence remain invisible to academic frameworks because they lie outside the university?

The concept of a research-teaching nexus: meaningless and inapplicable or still valid?

Given the polysemy about what to consider as research plus the conceptual indeterminacy of research as an umbrella for a myriad of distinct practices and cultures, one may wonder why it would still be meaningful to claim the research-teaching nexus as a prerequisite for higher education to be considered academic. This is further complicated by the incompetence and ontological blindness of academic evaluation instruments to comprehensively assess research practices outside of academic settings. There is, furthermore, a lack of empirical evidence about benefits of a research-teaching nexus and how it would effectively induce intended learning. When none of its components—neither research nor the learning process that it might induce—are clear, the very concept of a research-teaching nexus seems to have become a panacea for a broad spectrum of higher education aspirations, at the risk of becoming meaningless.

Instead of further problematizing the concept of a research-teaching nexus, I will now scrutinize the idea that it has meaningful educational capacities, including for profession-oriented courses such as the architectural design studio, and that it effectively may serve as a sound basis and legitimation for the academic quality of these courses. By tracing the roots and initial rationales of a research-teaching nexus, I argue that although the prevailing advocacy of it as an indicator for academic education entails simplification and misconception, a careful reconsideration of its roots elicits a clear definition of what it is that makes higher education academic. This reveals how the architectural design studio turns out to be an exemplary case of such research-based academic higher education.

Towards a new approach: reconsidering origins to reframe the debate

As mentioned earlier, the origins of the concept of a research-teaching nexus trace back to a group of Prussian reformers who conceived a new model for the university, implemented in Berlin in 1810. The reform reacted on the one hand against the continuation of the medieval scholastic tradition in which universities were seen as gatekeepers of settled knowledge to be cultivated rather than challenged, and on the other hand against the French functionalist approach that had abolished universities as products of the Ancien Régime and replaced them with new and specialized institutions—*Grands Ecoles*, *Ecoles Polytechniques*, and *Ecoles Nationales Supérieures*—as instruments for the functioning of the new republic.[41] In contrast to the French concern for maintaining the machine, the Prussian reformers realized that a society must cope with fast and unexpected changes, resulting in a continuing appearance of new and unforeseen questions. In contrast to both the scholastic tradition of gatekeeping and

40 Frank van der Hoeven, 'Mind the Evaluation Gap: Reviewing the Assessment of Architectural Research in the Netherlands', *Architectural Research Quarterly* 15, no. 2 (2011), 177–87.
41 Hilde de Ridder-Symoens, 'Nieuwe Wijn in Oude Zakken, of Toch Niet?' in Patrick Loobuyck et al., eds., *Welke Universiteit Willen Wij (Niet)?* (Ghent: Academia Press, 2007).

the French functional/instrumental approach, they advocated for the university as a place for renewal and development.

In this regard, the Prussian reformers distinguished between education 'at the lower levels' and 'higher education'. At the 'lower levels', such as for vocational education, teaching can rely upon 'closed and settled bodies of knowledge'.[42] The role of the universities, however, is higher education to provide orientation regarding questions for which no closed and settled knowledge is available or for which this knowledge is inadequate. Facing such questions is the distinctive feature that makes higher education academic. The university is the place that secures the proper conditions that allow for dealing with higher-order questions. This requires but also results in institutional autonomy and academic freedom—two central principles of the Humboldtian legacy—to ensure that such questions can be studied independently from political, economic, or religious pressure.

This particular role and duty of the university implies a particular pedagogical perspective of the unity of teaching and research (*Einheit von Lehre und Forschung*): 'At the higher level [of education], the teacher does not exist for the sake of the student; both teacher and student have their justification in the common pursuit of knowledge. The teacher's performance depends on the students' presence and interest—without this, science and scholarship could not grow.'[43] When facing problems for which no closed and settled knowledge is available, borders of teaching and learning blur. The distinction between teacher and student, both learners, becomes irrelevant; both teacher and student are involved in a common quest to pursue new insights—'*Beide sind für die Wissenschaft da*' (both are there for science).[44]

In the Humboldtian view, research assumes that gradually, as ideas and insights emerge in the mind of the knower, the knower's moral character is simultaneously formed. The ultimate goal for the teacher and the learner is not knowledge and knowing but personal transformation. Knowledge is not an end for this quest but a resource to induce this transformation; research is seen as a practice that induces a process towards liberation of the individual (from religion and other pressures) by offering all-round development, general education, self-formation, self-cultivation, edification—*Bildung*.⁴⁵ And consequently, moral edification of the individual—both student and teacher— would eventually lead to emancipation of society as a whole.

The considerations above are helpful to identify what it is that makes higher education academic, how this is related to research, and what type of educational processes this connection with research aims to induce. Yet, two fundamental remarks help clarify the educational capacity that this discourse attributes to research. Firstly, for the Prussian reformers the concept of *Einheit von Lehre und Forschung* was fundamentally rooted in *Wissenschaft* ('science', roughly translated) and, more precisely, in the so-called *Grundwissenschaft* (basic science). When these Prussian academics referred to this *Grundwissenschaft*, however, they were referring to something we would call today philosophy rather than science. Philosophy was thus given the duty to supervise the so-called *Brotwissenschaften* (the 'bread' sciences, meaning the fundamental sciences of medicine, technology,

---

42 Wilhelm von Humboldt, 'University Reform in Germany: I. On the Spirit and the Organizational Framework of Intellectual Institutions in Berlin. II. The Reform of Courses of Study in West German Universities', *Minerva* 8, no. 2 (1970), 242–67.
43 Von Humboldt, 'University Reform in Germany' (see note 42), 243.
44 The original text of the translated quote can be found in Wilhelm von Humboldt, 'Über die Innere und Äussere Organisation der höheren wissenschaftlichen Anstalten in Berlin', in *Gründungstexte* (Berlin: Humboldt-Universität, 2010), 229–41, here 230.
45 The notion of *Bildung* is difficult to translate; it has been translated as liberal education, general edification, self-formation, and self-cultivation. See David Sorkin, 'Wilhelm Von Humboldt: The Theory and Practice of Self-Formation (Bildung), 1791–1810', *Journal of the History of Ideas* 44, no. 1 (1983), 55–73.

and law): it was *die Mutter aller Wissenschaften* (the mother of all sciences). From this foundational and supervising position, philosophy secured the unity of science.

Two obstinate misconceptions pervade today's references to von Humboldt as father of the research-teaching nexus. The first is in equating the term *Wissenschaft* with the contemporary notion of 'science', and, consequently, to interpret the concept of *Einheit von Lehre und Forschung* as an entanglement of teaching with scientific research conduct. The second is in assuming that the educational benefit of scientific research is to be found in its outcome, namely knowledge. In the Humboldtian ideal, however, the edifying capacity of research is situated in the process of research conduct rather than in its outcome. More particularly, it is situated in the process of asking what to think about and what to do with knowledge that results from the 'sciences'. A research-teaching nexus thus is edifying only to the extent that it normatively frames scientific research conduct. This is exactly what scientists today carefully avoid instead of promote. Scientific research is to be objective and abstain from any normativity.[46]

If we now return to the discourse of the Bologna Process that claims the research-teaching nexus as a prerequisite for higher education to be academic, underpinning this assertion with reference to von Humboldt's notion of the unity of teaching and research, we must conclude that this argumentation relies on simplification that reflects misunderstanding and eventually results in misconception. But this reconsideration of the roots of such a nexus not only reveals problems of the actual debates; it also provides ground for reorienting this debate: in contrast to the Bologna Process's educational technology of competencies, the Humboldtian goal is to develop a set of personal dispositions. In contrast to prioritizing professional qualification as a goal, it emphasizes the development of a habitus.[47] And finally, unlike the Bologna Process's focus on the student as 'the independent learner', the Humboldtian view puts the teacher at the centre of determining which issues are to be faced.[48]

RS_Wiki_Commons P02 2001125

852189

Despite the simplification, misunderstanding, and misconception of the ideas of the Prussian reformers, the Humboldtian notion has persisted. Interesting in this regard is the discourse that the German philosopher Jürgen Mittelstrass developed in parallel to the development of the Bologna Process.[49] Mittelstrass continues an enduring Humboldtian line of thought by building upon Helmut Jaspers's plea to reposition philosophy as the underlying desire and driver for knowledge and scientific thinking,[50] Helmut Schelsky's argument that the emancipatory agency that makes higher education academic is situated in critical self-reflection of the sciences,[51] and Jürgen Habermas's claim that the academic quality of research is to be found in its capacity to induce ongoing negotiation based upon scientific argumentation and aiming at provisionally establishing truth as an intersubjective consensus.[52]

---

46 Maarten Simons, '"Education through Research" at European Universities: Notes on the Orientation of Academic Research', *Journal of Philosophy of Education* 40, no. 1 (2006), 31–50.
47 The relation between the research-teaching nexus, competencies, dispositions, and habitus is extensively elaborated in Roeland van der Rijst, 'The Research-Teaching Nexus in the Sciences: Scientific Research Dispositions and Teaching Practice' (PhD diss., Leiden University, 2009).
48 Jan Masschelein and Maarten Simons, 'The University as Pedagogical Form: Public Study, Responsibility, Mondialisation', in Stefan Ramaekers and Naomi Hodgson, eds., *Past, Present, and Future Possibilities for Philosophy and History of Education* (Cham, Switzerland: Springer, 2018), 47–61.
49 Jürgen Mittelstrass, *Das Mass des Fortschritts: Mensch und Wissenschaft in der 'Leonardo-Welt'* (Cologne: Karl Rahner Akademie, 2003).
50 Hedwig Kopetz, *Forschung und Lehre: Die Idee der Universität bei Humboldt, Jaspers, Schelsky und Mittelstrass* (Vienna: Böhlau, 2002), 52–69.
51 Kopetz, *Forschung und Lehre* (see note 50), 70–9.
52 Jürgen Habermas and John R. Blazek, 'The Idea of the University: Learning Processes', *New German Critique* 41 (1987), 3–22.

Mittelstrass looks at the university's public role as to provide orientation rather than (in terms of the *Frascati Manual*) 'to increase the stock of knowledge' and prioritizes the edifying potential of meta-reflection about research over research outcomes as commodities. Thereby, he reaffirms the university as a place of research but at the same time acknowledges that it is no longer the exclusive place of scientific research conduct. If that is the case, what then is the distinctive feature that makes higher education academic? For Mittelstrass, the epithet 'academic' refers to the quality of the university and its community of researchers, of developing a rationality in which *Verfügungswissen* (a positive knowing of causal inference and problem-solving or knowledge about how things can become and be done) coincides with an *Orientierungswissen* (a regulative knowledge concerning what ought to be done; an orientation for thought). Mittelstrass thus aligns with the Humboldtian concept that the edifying potential of research is articulated in normative framing.[53] Edification—or in Humboldtian terms, *Bildung*—occurs from first knowing what can be done (*Verfügungswissen*) and then facing what ought to be done (*Orientierungswissen*).

> Inquisitive practice: the academic nature of
> research in the architectural design studio

The prevailing understanding of a research-teaching nexus in terms of connections with formal scientific research conduct at the university turns out to be confusing and problematic, with perverse effects on faculty who actively conduct research outside academia. Current understanding reflects a misconception of the original rationales behind the idea. But consequently, a closer reconsideration of these origins might shed new light on the educational capacities and potentials of a research-teaching nexus. This reconsideration, as well as the enduring legacy that the Humboldtian ideas have induced, emphasizes that the educational capacity of research, and what makes higher education academic, are not situated in formal connections with the industry of scientific research but rather situated in research as a personal process and practice, and negotiation and judgement as a common process and practice. Therefore, I suggest reframing the debate about the research foundation of academic higher education in terms of inquisitive practice instead of in terms of the establishment of a research-teaching nexus.

In 2012 and 2013 I undertook fieldwork in design studios to observe the architecture schools in Flanders. It was at a moment that, as a result of a decree, all non-university-based architecture programmes had to migrate into a university—it was called 'integration', and it was the final step of a so-called academization process. In interviews with studio teachers, I gathered insights into what they understood as academic education. I also studied their intentions regarding studio teaching at the first-year master's level.

The fieldwork revealed a faculty that aligns much more closely with the Humboldtian idea that higher education must produce graduates who are able to provide solutions for an ever-changing society than with functional approaches that aim at delivering professionals who proficiently apply 'settled bodies of knowledge'. I learned that, at least in their view, design studio teaching at the master's level should not be about problem-solving but about phrasing questions, formulating concepts, and provoking thought; not about applying knowledge produced elsewhere but about developing knowledge about architecture through design as critical enquiry; not about solving pragmatic concerns but about digressing, exploring, delineating theoretical considerations, and moving between these poles; not about developing arguments based upon personal ideas but about developing personal ideas based upon arguments of others, expanding the own cultural frame of reference, and creating awareness about how a project relates to other valid solutions; not about learning how to design as a skill but

---

53 Simons, 'Education through Research' (see note 46), 47.

about learning how to design as a way of exploring architectural concepts.[54]

Inspired by the findings of this fieldwork, I built a framework that would evoke further discussion of the academic quality of the architectural design studio, but based upon the notion of inquisitive practice instead of a research-teaching nexus. The structure of this framework and the wording I use are based on the work of the educational philosophers Jan Masschelein and Maarten Simons in an elaboration of the Greek concept of *scolè* (which, although the root word of 'school', literally means 'free time')—a model highly applicable to design studio education.[55]

The academic architectural design studio brings together a group of students and one or two teachers, though for the sake of clarity I will speak about only one teacher. The teacher decides upon a piece of the world and brings it to the table. The teacher is personally involved and cares about both that piece of the world and the students. The atmosphere is enthusiastic and positive—essential qualities for creative work. The piece of the world is interesting, challenging, and triggering because it addresses issues for which no tailor-made solutions are available and new insights are needed. Both the teacher and students are learners, and both are involved in a common quest to generate insight—*Beide sind für die Wissenschaft da* (both are there for science).

The duty to decide about which piece of the world to be brought to the table gives the teacher a central responsibility: not only as an educator but also towards society. In contrast to the Bologna Process's primacy of the student as an independent learner, leaving the university to be the provider of the education that the student demands, the academic design studio points to the central role of the teacher as an educator, who—as an academic—sets the agenda, hence firmly reaffirming the public role of the university as a provider of orientation for society.

The teacher takes the lead and induces a set of conditions in order to generate a process of inquisitive practice.

The teacher then piques student interest by inducing *interesse* and sharing the piece of the world amongst the participants. The teacher then directs the attention of the students, thereby opening up that piece of the world. By doing so, two processes take place. Firstly, a process which Masschelein and Simons refer to as 'profanation' is induced, making the piece of the world under consideration accessible and removing it from any preoccupation, prejudices, or external pressures so that it can be 'read', frankly and open-mindedly, allowing provocative or (until that point) unconceived viewpoints. This step is directly connected to the Humboldtian principle of academic freedom and institutional indenpendence. The academic studio frees up time and opens up issues and questions that remain closed under conditions requiring productivity. Secondly, the teacher induces a process of ontological unfolding. By 'reading' the piece of the world in a personal way and by sharing this reading with the students, the teacher reveals and articulates the world in terms of particular constituents and from particular viewpoints. Consequently and gradually, students will perform their own readings. Yet each reading will be specific, see the world through a specific lens and understanding, and discern specific features of the things that are seen. All readings are shared as a common quest among the participants.

The ontological unfolding leads to both an epistemological and a praxeological question. While the ontological level articulates 'what there is', the epistemological level addresses 'what there is to know about what there is'. In architectural design, this epistemological stage is explorative. For architectural design questions, there are always multiple valid solutions. The inquisitive design practice of the studio aims at outcomes that broaden the view and inspire rather than at establishing conclusive truths. It prefers speculation over facts.

---

54 De Walsche, 'Genus, Locus, Nexus' (see note 5), 399–401.
55 Jan Masschelein and Maarten Simons, *In Defence of the School: A Public Issue* (Leuven: E-ducation, Culture & Society Publishers, 2013).

The praxeological question relates to method. It consists of the observation that in the design studio each next act depends on the outcome of the previous, consciously, un-, or subconsciously. For the sake of brevity and clarity, I limit the analysis to the conscious conception of a next act.[56] Ontologically opening up what is brought to the table, followed by the epistemological stance of providing meaning and speculative suggestion in what is seen, determines how the process will unroll. If method is understood as the sequence of steps taken in a research process, then in the design studio method consists of careful decisions about each next step made by rigorously responding to the outcome of a previous step. Rigour thus is understood as coherence in the response to features of what is seen (ontology) and what it means (epistemology). Method is not an a priori; it is ontologically and epistemologically dependent on the process. Rigour is not a feature of method—as it is often understood—but the other way round: method is a result of rigour.[57] To give an example: if the student's reading discerns daylight as a significant constituent of the piece of the world under investigation, then rigour means that, instead of going to the library and reading a book, the student would make a model, carefully look at the model, and thus discern qualities of light—ultimately engaging rigorously with the features of the thing-in-itself under study. If a student 'reads' appropriation of public space by inhabitants, then it may be more rigorous not to make models but to go to inhabitants, talk with them, and observe how they live.

If the inquisitive practice of the academic design studio is so fundamentally driven by what emerges—that is, by a sequence of intermediate and sometimes unpredictable design outcomes—then a question arises about what and how these different steps are connected. Limiting the analysis to the consciously (and thus rigorously) conceived steps is an evaluative judgement. For architectural design, which is a cultural performance situated in contexts and traditions, this evaluative judgement will inescapably be culturally framed and ethically loaded—it can be, for instance, judgements relating to concepts about how we should live together, deal with energy, or use materials. At this point, we can refer to Mittelstrass's discourse. If a design proposal, intermediate or final, is an embodiment of knowledge about what can be done (*Verfügungswissen*), then the inquisitive design process consists of a series of confrontations of this design proposal with judgements about what ought to be done (*Orientierungswissen*): it is a possible solution, but is it the 'right' solution? It is in this ethically loaded process of normative judgement of available knowledge that the academic quality is to be found. It is also here where the edifying capacity of design enquiry is situated—in the call for making up the mind, taking a stance, acting correspondingly, and consequently taking the responsibility over the consequences of this act.

But studio education should not primarily be understood as a process of the individual student. The inquisitive practice of the design studio is a common practice, and this commonality is a crucial feature: the different ontological readings of teacher and students lead to a rich frame of references that is commonly shared, debates about what ought to be done are held within the group, and intermediate design proposals are exposed for all.[58] As a scene of exposure and a forum of debate, the design studio is a place that brings together many views, voices, options, and answers. It is a place of academic enquiry to the extent it triggers ongoing

---

56 For an interesting analysis about leaps, sudden flashes, and abductive process in design practice, see Jon Kolko, 'Abductive Thinking and Sensemaking: The Drivers of Design Synthesis', *Design Issues* 26, no. 1 (2010), 15–28.
57 Again, I refer to Heidegger's notion of *Bindung* (see note 26).
58 To some extents, the design studio can be considered as a community of practice as developed by Jean Lave and Etienne Wenger, *Situated Learning: Legitimate Peripheral Participation* (Cambridge: Cambridge University Press, 1991). See also Keith R. Sawyer, 'Teaching Creativity in Art and Design Studio Classes: A Systematic Literature Review', *Educational Research Review* 22 (2017), 99–113.

negotiation based on argumentation and aims to provisionally establish intersubjectively constructed understanding.[59]

This exposure is shared among the students and teachers, but the debate and negotiation that is induced by the academic architectural design studio reaches into society. Particular for the design studio is that the outcome is provided by design. This means that the orientation provided for society consists of new hypothetical constellations of the future as hopeful suggestions, inviting society to participate in a debate that could not have taken place before these constellations were available—thus fulfilling an academic duty.

The inquisitive design studio:
a model for academic higher education

Attempts to define the academic quality of architectural design education in terms of a research-teaching nexus that is understood as connections with formal scientific research conduct at the university have not been fruitful: firstly because in the design studio such links are scarce or absent, and secondly because the very notion of a research-teaching nexus is complicated and confusing, while its educational benefits are still unclear and unproven. Much more helpful is to look at the original rationales behind the concept of research-based education.

In line with the Humboldtian notion of academic enquiry, the academic design studio is a place where teacher and students actively and rigorously engage with a piece of the world in a common quest, uninhibited and open to what emerges, freed from economic, political, or religious pressure or preconceptions. It is where they deal with questions for which no tailor-made solutions are available but are nevertheless relevant as orientation for society. What emerges from such uninhibited processes is unpredictable but leads to new points of view and new insights.

The inquisitive practice in the academic design studio not only aims to edify the student and satisfy the teacher's interests. Academic higher education centred around enquiry in response to societal challenges and demands operates differently from increasing scientific specialization. Such future-oriented inquisitive design practice might call for more holistic approaches or interdisciplinarity and hence impact organizational structures of the university and its relationship with society. If the relationship between research, teaching, and society is to be recalibrated, then I suggest that the academic design studio, with its specific, normatively framed inquisitive practice, should serve as a model and an experimental playground.

59 Habermas and Blazek, 'The Idea of the University' (see note 52).

Bernhard Böhm

Tacit Knowledge and the Politics of Architectural Design Research[1,2]

Since the 1980s, many architecture schools have begun conducting and teaching design research. Today, architecture lecturers and professors realize design-centred research projects and supervise students who attend design research-based master's and doctoral programmes.[3] Beyond these research-based positions, projects, and programmes, new societies and networks have been established to promote design research in architecture on national and international scales.[4] Proponents of design research describe it as a form of investigation in which the realization of a design project is a constituent part of the research process. The outcomes of this kind of research range from architectural designs and material artefacts to publications which articulate novel perspectives on what architecture is or could be.

For architecture, this tendency towards research is not self-evident. Typically, research has played a marginal role within the discipline of architecture. Of course, architecture has seen various waves of scientification in the past which brought design and research into proximity. Yet, these waves were short-lived.[5] Since the institutionalization of the profession of architecture in the nineteenth century, architects have been the designers of the built environment and managers of building projects. The outcomes of their design work are considered to be cultural or artistic products, not the results of research. Architecture schools at universities have been mainly places of education for students to acquire the skills they need to enter the profession, where experienced designers, who often work for or run an architectural office, introduce students to the fundamentals of the discipline. Until recently, research at these architecture schools was conducted rarely by architects themselves but rather in disciplines such as the history and theory of architecture or the social, material, or technical sciences.[6]

Since the rise of design research, not much is left of research's marginal position within the discipline of architecture. One theoretical approach that architects utilize to conceptualize design work as research is tacit knowledge, introduced by chemist and philosopher of science Michael Polanyi in the 1960s.[7] He defined tacit knowledge as personal, pre-logical, and sensual knowledge—that is, part of all creative acts and new discoveries but a type of knowledge that can never be fully rationalized. According to Polanyi,

---

1 Bernhard Böhm is a doctoral researcher at the Department of Architecture and the Chair of Science Studies, ETH Zurich.
2 A shorter version of this text was published in German: Bernhard Böhm, 'Implizites Wissen und die Politik des Design Research in der Architektur', *IFKNow* 2 (2020), 6–7.
3 See Murray Fraser, ed., *Design Research in Architecture: An Overview* (Burlington: Ashgate, 2014). For education, see Fredrik Nilsson and Halina Dunin-Woyseth, 'Some Notes on Practice-Based Architectural Design Research: Four "Arrows" of Knowledge', *Reflections 7+* (2008), 138–47; and Marc Belderbos and Johan Verbeke, eds., *The Unthinkable Doctorate: Proceedings of the Colloquium 'The Unthinkable Doctorate'* (Brussels: Hogeschool voor Wetenschap & Kunst and School of Architecture Sint-Lucas, 2005).
4 For example, the Architectural Research Network (ARENA), the artistic and design PhD programmes at architecture schools, such as the Bartlett School of Architecture or University of Applied Arts Vienna, or the platform for architectural research 'Architecture in the Making'.
5 Gernot Weckherlin, 'Vom Betriebscharakter des Entwerfens: Konjunkturen der Verwissenschaftlichung der Architektur', in Sabine Ammon and Eva Maria Froschauer, eds., *Wissenschaft Entwerfen: Vom forschenden Entwerfen zur Entwurfsforschung der Architektur* (Paderborn: Wilhelm Fink, 2013), 171–204.
6 On the design orientation of the discipline of architecture, see Dana Cuff, *Architecture: The Story of Practice* (Cambridge, MA: MIT Press, 1992), 109–55; and Spiro Kostof, *The Architect: Chapters in the History of the Profession* (New York: Oxford University Press, 1977).
7 Michael Polanyi, *The Tacit Dimension* (Chicago: University of Chicago Press, 1966).

all explicit knowledge rests on tacit knowledge, which he famously expressed in the phrase 'we can know more than we can tell'.[8]

Within the realm of design research, architects use the work of Polanyi to describe design as a knowledge practice relying mostly upon tacit knowledge and design research as the field in which this knowledge is cultivated and produced. According to these scholars, the strong dependency on tacit knowledge differentiates design research in architecture from research conducted in the sciences. Drawing on Polanyi's approach, Nat Chard characterizes design knowledge as 'a form of knowledge that is too unreliable to depend on scientific methods (or even those of the social sciences) and as a consequence cannot be taught as a sequence of instructions, for instance as might be the case in mathematics. Instead it is a form of tacit knowledge, which Michael Polanyi describes as "knowledge that we might not be able to tell".'[9] Fredrik Nilsson provides another description: 'The verbal is often regarded as the most appropriate and legitimate way to produce and communicate scientific knowledge. Design knowledge is often "tacit" or articulated in other languages that are more implicit and contextual, and design also involves a special kind of thinking and a fundamental intellectual ability. ... This design ability relies fundamentally on non-verbal media of thought and communication.'[10] Taking these conceptions of design research as a point of departure, this article adds another perspective to the current discourse on design research. Instead of theorizing design research as a field based on tacit knowledge, I ask how architects who conduct design research employ the concept of tacit knowledge and why it is currently so well received within the discourse of design research.

Analysing design research through the lens of practice shows that architects use tacit knowledge not only to conceptualize architecture as a field based on tacit knowledge but also to communicate epistemic concerns they experience when conducting design research. Data collected during an ethnographic research stay at one of the United Kingdom's leading architecture schools for design research give examples of how this happens. In particular, I will describe how the conduct of design research has involved both design projects and publications, in which the research aspects and knowledge of these projects should be presented.

During my research, architects experienced this kind of design research as an uncertain and tense activity. Above all, the questions of how to describe their design activities as research and how the knowledge architects created while designing could be written down in these publications was a matter of concern to them. As will be shown in this article, architects used Polanyi's concept to communicate their struggles in converting design-based tacit knowledge into explicit knowledge in the form of research publications. Furthermore, I will highlight the political conditions within which tacit knowledge became a concept used to describe concerns. Polanyi himself developed his philosophical work in opposition to totalitarian regimes and relied on liberal economic ideas.[11] Commenting on the sciences in the Soviet Union from this perspective, Polanyi was especially critical of communist governments that organized the sciences in accordance with their five-year plans and political aims—the organization of science by politicians, rather than

8 Polanyi, *The Tacit Dimension* (see note 7), 4.
9 Nat Chard, 'Searching for Rigour While Drawing Uncertainty', in *Architectural Design Research Symposium 2014* (Wellington: University of Wellington, 2014), 18–22, here 18. Chard cites Polanyi, *The Tacit Dimension* (see note 7), 10.
10 Fredrik Nilsson, 'Making, Thinking, Knowing Architecture: Notes on Architecture as a Making Discipline and Material Practice', in Jørgen Dehs, Martin Weihe Esbensen, and Claus Peder Pedersen, eds., *When Architects and Designers Write / Draw / Build / ?* (Aarhus: Arkitektskolens Forlag, 2013), 126–47, here 133.
11 Mary Jo Nye, *Michael Polanyi and His Generation: Origins of the Social Construction of Science* (Chicago: University of Chicago Press, 2011), chs. 5, 6, and 8.

independent and self-governed scientists, is likely to lead to decisions harmful to science.

As I will show in this article, in the case of design research, a critique of communist central planning is not the driving force behind the integration of Polanyi's thinking into architectural reasoning. Instead, architects draw on the concept of tacit knowledge to articulate concerns that are related to market-driven reform. Asking why design and research publications had such a tense relation at the analysed architecture school helped me discover how current design research is shaped by science policy decisions that started to emerge in the 1980s. The argument I put forward in this article is that architects' concerns did not arrive out of any fundamental incongruousness of design and text but that they emerged from reforms that restructured universities and their architecture schools along market principles, thereby also institutionalizing design research at architecture schools in the United Kingdom.

This article is structured to first give an overview of the theories, methods, and materials I used to analyse design research in architecture. I then describe how architects use the concept of tacit knowledge to speak about their concerns when conducting design as research, and I give one example of how this concern is articulated. Thereafter, I reflect on the relations of science policymaking and design research and how this concern is related to current policy-induced changes at the analysed architecture school in the United Kingdom. I relate the different arguments I developed throughout the text and close with thoughts on the political dimension of the use of tacit knowledge in architecture and the future development of architectural design research.

Analytical background, materials, and methods

The analytical background against which I conduct this analysis is related to the recent turn of science and technology studies (STS) to architecture. In the 1970s STS was established as an interdisciplinary field studying the manifold relations of science, technology, and society. Although STS scholars have analysed the sciences from various perspectives, most shared the analytical aim of objecting and challenging a mainstream understanding of science.[12] In popular accounts, science was characterized as a purely rational endeavour. The results of scientific enquiry were imagined to be true knowledge about nature, society, or history. Drawing on approaches from the humanities and social sciences, STS scholars challenged this understanding of science in multiple ways. They identified different scientific cultures, described how the interests of different social groups shape research activities, and theorized science and society relations.[13] Since the 1990s, various STS scholars have applied this way of analysing science to architecture. In their investigations they drew attention to the different ways in which architects design and produce knowledge and the relationships architecture has to wider society.[14]

---

12 Sergio Sismondo, *An Introduction to Science and Technology Studies* (Chichester: Wiley-Blackwell, 2010), ch. 1.

13 For examples, see Bruno Latour and Steve Woolgar, *Laboratory Life: The Social Construction of Scientific Facts* (Beverly Hills: Sage, 1979); Karin Knorr Cetina, *Epistemic Cultures: How the Sciences Make Knowledge* (Cambridge, MA: Harvard University Press, 1999); Sheila Jasanoff, *Designs on Nature: Science and Democracy in Europe and the United States* (Princeton: Princeton University Press, 2005).

14 For examples, see Albena Yaneva, *The Making of a Building: A Pragmatist Approach to Architecture* (Oxford: Peter Lang, 2009); Albena Yaneva, *Mapping Controversies in Architecture* (Burlington: Ashgate, 2012); Sophie Houdart, 'Copying, Cutting and Pasting Social Spheres: Computer Designers' Participation in Architectural Projects', *Science & Technology Studies* 21, no. 1 (2008), 47–63; Jörg Potthast, 'Sollen wir mal ein Hochhaus bauen? Das Architekturbüro als Labor der Stadt', WZB Discussion Paper, Wissenschaftszentrum Berlin, 1998; Ignacio Farías, 'Epistemische Dissonanz: Zur Vervielfältigung von Entwurfsalternativen in der Architektur', in Ammon and Froschauer, *Wissenschaft Entwerfen* (see note 5), 46–77.

Inspired by this kind of research, I draw attention to the practices and knowledge of design research. However, my analysis differs from the mentioned STS studies in various ways. So far, almost all STS scholars have examined the work of professional architects. I, on the contrary, analyse why design research is a current topic in the field of architecture, and I trace the relationship between the practice of design research and the political conditions within which it takes place. In this regard, I see my research in line with the work of the cultural theorists Sabine Ammon and Eva Maria Froschauer and the science and STS researcher Monika Kurath, who belong to the few scholars who reflect on the conditions and consequences of the increase of design research activities at architecture departments. According to Ammon and Froschauer, this increase of design research is rooted in a growing desire to reflect on the design process.[15] Kurath, on the other hand, identifies a potential import of approaches from disciplines with a more established research tradition into architecture,[16] which could lead to a transformation of the discipline of architecture. In order to receive funding for research and to get research-based positions, architects need to engage with practices of disciplines adjacent to architecture, such as the social or material sciences.

Kurath and Anna Flach[17] identify main drivers behind the institutionalization of design research at architecture schools as the economization- and new governance of science, tightly connected to science policy initiatives. Since governments have increasingly tied the funding of universities and their departments to indicators such as publications, realized research projects, or numbers of doctoral graduates, architecture schools started adapting to this situation by increasing their research activities.

Relating to the research of Kurath, Flach, Ammon, and Froschauer, I investigated the transformation of the discipline of architecture at the university at an architecture school in the United Kingdom. In this text, I analyse the concerns that architects experienced when conducting design research. As studies on novel research fields have shown, analysing researchers' concerns is a way to explore research practice as well as their relation to political conditions and broader discourses.[18] In her examination of the realization of projects on the nexus of art, design, science, and engineering, for example, Kari Zacharias identified various concerns that accompanied researchers while working on the institutionalization of this kind of transdisciplinary research at a university in the United States to show how these concerns are related to different ideas of transdisciplinary research, to issues of sponsorship, and to matters of disciplinary belonging.[19] By tracing the ways in which architects utilize the concept of tacit knowledge to articulate uncertainties and tensions associated with their research activities, the chapter at hand highlights the transformation that the discipline of architecture is going

---

15 Sabine Ammon und Eva Maria Froschauer, 'Zur Einleitung: Wissenschaft Entwerfen: Perspektiven einer Reflexiven Entwurfsforschung', in Ammon and Froschauer, *Wissenschaft Entwerfen* (see note 5), 15–48.

16 Monika Kurath, 'Architecture as Science: Boundary Work and the Demarcation of Design Knowledge from Research', *Science & Technology Studies* 28, no. 3 (2015), 81–100, esp. 92–4.

17 Monika Kurath and Anna Flach, 'Architektur als Forschungsdisziplin: Ausbildung zwischen Akademisierung und Forschungsorientierung', *Archithese* 2 (2016), 72–80.

18 Latour was amongst the first scholars to suggest the analysis of concerns and denounced practices of critique that do not propose improvements: Bruno Latour, 'Why Has Critique Run Out of Steam? From Matters of Fact to Matters of Concern', *Critical Inquiry* 30, no. 2 (2004), 225–48. One example for the analysis of new research fields is Ulrike Felt et al., 'Growing into What? The (Un-)disciplined Socialisation of Early Stage Researchers in Transdisciplinary Research', *High Education* 65 (2013), 511–24.

19 Kari Zacharias, 'The Transdisciplinary Dilemma: Making SEAD in the Contemporary Research University', (PhD diss., Virginia Polytechnical Institute and State University, 2018).

through as well as the political conditions contributing to this change.

In terms of materials, this analysis is based on a three-month-long research stay at one architecture school in the United Kingdom during the first half of the year 2016. Back then this school was one of the largest higher education institutions for architecture in the United Kingdom and highly regarded for its design research activities. Most of the architectural professors and lecturers conducted design research, and, alongside its PhD by Design programme, this school offered design research-based master's degree programmes. During my research stay, I conducted qualitative interviews with architects and architecture students in which I asked about their design research activities and the outputs of their research. Additionally, I interviewed the director of the architecture school as well as science administrators, such as the head of the PhD by Design programme and the dean of research of the department of architecture. In semi-structured qualitative interviews, my interview partners reflected on their research activities and their understanding of design research, as well as the political conditions within which design research became a topic of interest for the architecture school.[20] Furthermore, I conducted ethnographic observations and took photos and field notes of research-based architecture education and design research work as conducted by the architects of the school.[21] Apart from the interviews and observations, I collected documents that were produced by design researchers, students, and funding and political bodies (for example theses, dissertations, publications, funding applications and guidelines, and research reports). The chosen methods for analysis were situational analysis[22] and grounded theory.[23]

Design knowledge and publications: a difficult relationship

During my time at the architecture school, I witnessed various ways in which design research was conducted. Some architects maintained time-based approaches to design research and collected archival data on city infrastructures or housing trends. In their design work they used this data to build relations between the past and future and, as they called it, 'speculated' about coming architectural developments by designing buildings we might inhabit in the future. Others had a more contemporary perspective. For example, I learned from a doctoral candidate how he analysed computer games by drawing them as cartographical maps and documenting images of the games' aesthetics and spatial construction. In an interview, he told me how his digital drawings and architectural games led him to develop a new design language. Others chose a more hands-on approach: they combined digital technology, robotics, and knowledge of local construction materials to invent novel architectural building products (such as walls or ornaments) and production techniques.

Despite all these differences in the approaches to design research, I could also identify elements that all the projects had in common. First, architects doing this kind of research all agreed that their practices of making sketches, building models, or drawing maps can be seen as research practices that produce new knowledge. Second, many architects I met during my research stay were concerned about how to best communicate the knowledge that they generated through design. In particular, they were uncertain about how to build relations between explicit knowledge that can be verbalized and written down and design-based knowledge that

20 James A. Holstein and Jaber F. Gubrium, *The Active Interview* (Thousand Oaks, CA: Sage, 1995).
21 Robert M. Emerson, Rachel I. Fretz, and Linda L. Shaw, *Writing Ethnographic Fieldnotes* (Chicago: Chicago University Press, 2011).
22 Kathy Charmatz, *Constructing Grounded Theory: A Practical Guide through Qualitative Analysis* (London: Sage, 2006).
23 Adele E. Clarke, *Situational Analysis: Grounded Theory after the Postmodern Turn* (Thousand Oaks, CA: Sage, 2005).

architects understand to be tacit. They considered the knowledge they generated in design research to be incorporated into objects they produce and as something personal. One of the architects explained it in an interview as, 'the knowledge is embodied in the object, but also in the way the designer interacts [with the object], and the shape that is given to [it]. And all that is very intimate and personal to the designer.'

The tension between tacit knowledge embodied in the designer and the design objects and explicit knowledge was rooted in the need to publish research. At this school of architecture professors, lecturers, and doctoral candidates were required to write about their research activities. On the one hand, these publications could take the form of a thesis or a book in which doctoral candidates and faculty describe their design activities, reflect on their approach to design, and/or locate their research in its historic context. On the other hand, research activities were expected to be published in a recently established journal for design research or in a booklet series edited and distributed by the school. Some of the work of the design researchers was published in journals of related fields, such as the humanities or technical sciences. Yet, due to the tacit nature of design research, architects frequently found it difficult to write these kinds of publications.

One observation that I made during a lecture series at the architecture school I visited shows how these concerns were articulated. This lecture series was organized by architecture students, who invited faculty and external guests to present their design research activities. As part of the audience, I attended presentations in which the speakers talked about how they used architectural approaches and tools to conduct research projects. The presentation that I found to be the most remarkable in regard to the articulation of concerns was by a senior lecturer of the school. In front of an audience of approximately fifty people, she talked about her use of architectural design practices as tools of analysis. Instead of using architectural models and drawings to design a building, she used these practices to come up with a new spatial reading and interpretation of artwork. Giving examples of her work, she showed how she rebuilt a film as an architectural model and reinterpreted an art installation by spatially drawing and modelling parts of this installation. In addition to the design-based analysis, the architect talked about how she read and wrote about the artwork she analysed. She described how she gathered information on the historical, technical, and cultural aspects of the artwork by collecting theoretical and art-historical literature as well as archival material about the movie and installation. In her writing she related the literature and archival material to her design-based work. Doing so, she learned more about the architectural construction of the artwork and how specific topics are expressed through their spatial arrangement. Her combination of design and text-based work led to various publications in which she reflected on her design activities, the literature she collected, and the new insights she generated through combining these activities. The largest publication was her doctoral thesis, which was released as a book. Beyond the book she worked on many smaller publications, such as booklets or journal articles. At the end of the presentation, she talked about two different ways of understanding that were present when she analysed artwork: first, the tacit understanding of artwork, which emerged while she did drawings and models; and second, in her words, the 'intellectual' way of understanding artwork, which is very much related to writing and reading. For her it was, as she said, 'impossible to negotiate' between these two ways of knowing, and she even identified a 'fight' between intellectual and tacit ways of knowing.

The concerns I witnessed about the relation of tacit and explicit forms of knowledge in observations like the one above and in interviews made me curious about the reason for this tense relationship. To me it was understandable and not much of a surprise that the architects identify different ways of knowing that are part of their design research activities, but I had not assumed that the different forms of knowledge had such a tense relationship as in the case of the researcher described above.

The marketization of the university and tacit knowledge in design research

To find out why these concerns about the relation of tacit and explicit knowledge were present, I focus on the political conditions that contributed to the rise of design research and the way it got institutionalized in the UK university system, which since the 1980s has undergone dramatic changes. British scholars commenting on these transformations describe higher education policies as leading towards a 'marketization'[24] of British universities: since the 1980s, universities have no longer received funding for teaching and research directly from the government, instead being expected to compete with each other for their financial resources. To establish this competition, the government reduced the amount of funding directly transmitted from ministries to the university and introduced new mechanisms for resource distribution. University research performance became an important factor for the allocation of money. Professionally oriented architecture schools, which typically conducted less research than other university departments, were pressured to become more research-oriented.

The market-oriented science steering instrument most directly related to the rise of design research and the concept of tacit knowledge within architecture is the research evaluations introduced in the 1980s. In order to assure that the government distributes money for research as 'effectively' as possible, subject-specific panels were created to evaluate each university's research performance approximately every six years. The better a university is ranked in this evaluation, the more money it gets.[25] As documented in various publications, many architects based at British universities did not see their work represented in these evaluations,[26] which emphasized published works such as papers or books and barely acknowledged work related to design. Since a lot of the activities at architecture schools are dedicated to design and design teaching, they were constantly evaluated as below average. Since the late 1990s, some universities have threatened to close their architecture schools if their evaluation results do not improve.[27] To avoid these types of consequences, some architecture schools increased their research performance by hiring people from publication-oriented disciplines such as the social or material sciences; others established innovative structures to support design-based investigations.

The architecture school that I researched belonged to the latter group. After the university administration announced its dissatisfaction with the evaluation results of 2001, the school administration decided to establish structures that allow faculty members to conduct research based on their speculative design activities which they have been developing already for decades, using design as medium

---

24 Andrew MacGettigan, *The Great University Gamble: Money Markets and the Future of Higher Education* (London: Pluto Press, 2013), ch. 2; Roger Brown and Helen Carasso, *Everything for Sale? The Marketisation of UK Higher Education* (London: Routledge, 2013).
25 Valerie Bence and Charles Oppenheim, 'The Evolution of the UK's Research Assessment Exercise: Publications, Performance and Perceptions', *Journal of Educational Administration and History* 37, no. 2 (2005), 137–55.
26 See Christine Hawley, 'Undermining the Profession', *arq: Architectural Research Quarterly* 6, no. 1 (2002), 5; Philip Steadman and Bill Hillier, 'Research Assessment under the Microscope: Disturbing Findings and Distorting Effects', *arq: Architectural Research Quarterly* 6, no. 3 (2002), 203–7; Jane Rendell, 'Architectural Research and Disciplinarity', *arq: Architectural Research Quarterly* 8, no. 2 (2004), 141–7.
27 Luke Layfield, 'Architecture under Threat in Cambridge', *The Guardian*, 29 October 2004, https://www.theguardian.com/education/2004/oct/29/highereducation.cutsandclosures (accessed 2 July 2020); 'Will Cambridge Fall Down?', *Independent*, 20 January 2005, https://www.independent.co.uk/news/education/higher/will-cambridge-fall-down-487332.html (accessed 2 July 2020).

to create and visualize possible scenarios of urban development or to invent new forms of spatial expression. To maintain these traditions within a political environment that demands ever more research from architecture schools, faculty members introduced new positions for research centred on speculative design and got involved in launching networks and societies to represent the interests of architectural design researchers. Furthermore, the architecture school also supported architects conducting design-based research financially by introducing grants in addition to a new mentoring system.

To understand why tensions between tacit knowledge and explicit knowledge started to emerge in relation to these developments, it is important to notice that design research and architectural design are not necessarily the same activity. Unlike architects developing and publishing design proposals, design researchers need to write texts in which they describe their research approach and the knowledge they generate and also reflect on their design activities from different perspectives. Of course, already before the introduction of design research, architects were involved in written reflections on their designs.[28] Yet, as far as I understood from my encounters with architects, these written reflections were optional before the establishment of design research at their university. Architects who were inclined to write could do so, but writing about design activities was not necessary. Since the institutionalization of design research at this architectural school, however, combining design and writing has become mandatory for all faculty members for two reasons. Firstly, the people involved in the institutionalization of design research considered it important to combine design with literature research and reflection in order to differentiate design research from design. Several of my interview partners considered it crucial that people who conduct research are capable of historically and socially contextualizing their design and have the skills necessary to write about the contribution that each design researcher makes to knowledge. Secondly, in order to be counted as research output by the evaluators, publications needed to be written which included more than 'just' sketches, drawings, and photos of models. To foster these types of publications, the architecture school introduced a booklet series, requiring contributions from all faculty members. The approximately fifty-page booklets include the classic components of research publications: aims and objectives, research questions, context, methods, and dissemination.

Altogether, this increase of design research at the architecture school meant that architects had to engage more with practices of literature research, reading, writing, and the formulation of research questions and methods. Yet, many of the architects I met during my time as ethnographer had little experience with that kind of work. Their education had focused on design, and literature research, the definition of research questions and, writing had played only a marginal role in the curricula. Without training, combining text and design was challenging and, for some architects, an undesired requirement. One faculty member described the writing she did for a design research project in the following way:

> I worried the whole time that I have to write something up about it. So, at some point, this idea will become words and that worries me. … That isn't a skill that [her design partner] or I have or want to have particularly. … But, because we have this constant mentoring system, there is always someone saying, 'This is really good for you, this helps you make international contacts, this is a really interesting vein of research, I can see how that fits something that the [name of architecture school] does not yet do.' And then someone on that panel would say, 'Do you think you could write a paper about that?'

---

28 For a history of design-related writing, see Jonathan Hill, 'Design Research: The First 500 Years', in Fraser, *Design Research in Architecture* (see note 3), 15–34.

> So they are always trying to get us to write papers about what it is to design. But I am not interested in unpicking that topic.

Although this is one of the more extreme positions that I encountered (and I also met architects who were eager to write about their design activities), I got the impression that building relations between design and text was something extraordinarily difficult for many architects. Considering the importance of publications and the political environment within which these publications have become essential, it was not surprising that concerns about the relation of text and design emerged, and I understood that architects found it difficult to write about what they considered to be their tacit form of design knowledge.

Conclusion

Against the background of the current discourse of design research, this article shows that the concept of tacit knowledge is not just used to describe architecture as a field of research. Instead, I show how architects use the concept of tacit knowledge to communicate about epistemic concerns. Drawing on data I collected during an ethnographic research stay at one of the United Kingdom's leading architecture schools for design research, I describe how design research involves both the realization of design projects and the publication of research results as text. Architects experienced the conduct of design research as an uncertain and tense activity in which it was not clear how to build relations between design and text. The architects considered the practice of design as leading to tacit knowledge embodied in the designer as well as the object the designer produces, but writing about research outcomes requires explicit knowledge. An example from a senior lecturer showed how architects find it difficult to build relations between design-based tacit knowledge and text-based explicit knowledge.

Science policymaking is one important reason for why design and text have such a tense relationship at the analysed architecture school. Architects' concerns did not arrive out of a fundamental incongruousness of design and text; they emerged from how design research has become institutionalized at architecture schools in the United Kingdom since the 1980s, when the British government began restructuring universities according to market principles and increasingly distributed funding according to university research performance. Publications are one of the most important measures of research performance. Since many activities at architecture schools were dedicated to design and design teaching, not the production of publications, the schools were considered to exhibit poor performance. In order to retain resources and to avoid consequences from dissatisfied university administrators, the architecture school that I analysed introduced new publication formats for combining design and text. Yet, many of the architects I met had little experience with writing, and they were concerned about how to bridge their design activities with the texts they needed to write.

Not to be misunderstood: I do not claim that the marketization of universities and design research are one and the same, nor do I intend to say that practices of design research were invented due to policymaking. Architects at the analysed school rather expanded and developed speculative approaches to architecture they had developed before university administrators asked for better research evaluation results. Furthermore, the content and knowledge of the design research projects I witnessed cannot simply be described as adhering to trends of economization and current political developments in the United Kingdom. If design research were only about maximizing economic profit, then the faculty at the analysed school could have pursued close ties to the building industry or teamed up with researchers from disciplines that publish prolifically. Considering the complexity of design research, this article rather showed how policy decisions shape the practice of design research, not how they determine it—much in line with conclusions by art historians Tom Holert[29] and Fiona Candlin.[30] According to both scholars, recent developments of design research cannot be understood without considering the effects of market-oriented reform, but they cannot be reduced to these reforms. Candlin and Holert both show that, as soon as one looks at the actual research work, design research can be a practice which subverts current logics of economization.

Reflecting on how architects utilize the concept of tacit knowledge from this perspective, this article also contributes to a better understanding of the current political dimension of Polanyi's concept of tacit knowledge. When developing his concept, Polanyi was influenced by liberal economic ideas and developed his philosophical work in opposition to totalitarian regimes, especially communism.[31] Ironically, in the case of design research, communist central planning was not the driving force behind the integration of tacit knowledge into architectural reasoning but rather market-driven reforms. Architects employ the concept of tacit knowledge to describe concerns that are (at least partly) rooted in policymaking, drawing on similar ideas to Polanyi. In that sense, not communism but capitalism is problematized through the lens of tacit knowledge.

Considering that design research in architecture is a rather young phenomenon in its current constitution, one lesson that can be learned from my research for the future development of design research is that the the structural dimension of architects' concerns about tacit knowledge should be taken seriously. Instead of simply describing architecture as a field based on tacit knowledge, as happens in the current discourse on design research, acknowledging the relationships between policymaking and the concerns present in design research makes it possible to find structural solutions for structural problems. In regard to the concerns about tacit and explicit knowledge, this could mean starting to develop modes of expression that allow for building more suitable interactions between design and the written word. However these may look, it is crucial to consider that architecture is a discipline in which design plays a fundamentally important role and produces meaningful knowledge.

29 Tom Holert, 'Artistic Research: Anatomy of an Ascent', *Texte zur Kunst* 82 (2011), 38–64.
30 Fiona Candlin, 'A Dual Inheritance: The Politics of Educational Reform and PhDs in Art and Design', *Journal of Art & Design Education* 20, no. 3 (2001), 302–10.
31 Nye, *Michael Polanyi and His Generation* (see note 11), esp. chs. 5, 6, and 8.

Part Two
Systematizing Design

Claudia Mareis

Decision-Making in the Face of Uncertainty: Encounters between Design and Science in the Post-war Period[1,2]

In the decades following the Second World War, there were many attempts in Europe and North America to understand the design process from the ground up and make it more manageable and scalable by applying systematic methods. Although there had been previous attempts (for example at the Bauhaus), only in the post-war period were these pursued vigorously and with a broad scope. Design methodology—the field which promoted the systematization of design processes from the mid-1950s onwards—was a wide-ranging, interdisciplinary undertaking which embraced social, technical, and aesthetic issues alike. Debates in the field revolved around creating bridges between different knowledge cultures and contexts of application in an attempt to strengthen design through science. This changed not only views of design but of science as well: it revealed possibilities and limitations in both.

In this chapter, two relevant scenes of post-war design methodology will be discussed: the Ulm School of Design in Germany (1953–1968) and the so-called design methods movement that started in Great Britain around 1960. The aim of this chapter is to better understand the background

---

[1] Claudia Mareis is Professor for Design and History of Knowledge at the Department of Cultural History and Theory, Humboldt-Universität zu Berlin.
[2] An earlier version of this text was presented at the 4S-Conference in New Orleans, 4–7 September 2019, in the panel Social Sciences of the Artificial: Interrupting and Interrogating the Meanings of Design. Parts of this text have been published in German in Claudia Mareis and Michael Rottmann, *Entwerfen mit System* (Hamburg: Adocs, 2020).

and motives that shaped the design methodology of the post-war period and led to the promotion of an intense and productive yet complicated dialogue between design and science. Design methodology is described as an expression of a disciplinary crisis generated by socio-technological change, new forms of collaboration, and a fear of uncertain futures. I focus on two important principles that, in my view, constitute the logic of post-war design methodology: design understood as a systemic-systematic approach and design as a response to 'ill-structured', 'wicked' problems.

Encounters between design and science, part one

The first scene is set in war-torn Germany. The Ulm School of Design was founded in 1953 through the initiative of the anti-fascist Geschwister-Scholl Foundation and with the financial support of US allies. It was closed in 1968 due to financial and political difficulties as well as internal differences.[3] It was an important venue for the encounter between design and science in the post-war period. Led by former Bauhaus student and architect Max Bill, the school saw itself as a successor to the famous Bauhaus, which had closed in 1933 under pressure from the Nazis. From the beginning, it wanted to be more than just another design school. Its declared aim was to convey democratic values through design education and aesthetic pedagogy. Through the 'right' (that is, the functional, objective, and rational) design of everyday objects and visual communication, democratic principles could be anchored in people's everyday lives: both in their living rooms and their minds.[4] The school was set up as 'an experiment' whose aim was to 'teach methods for promoting democratic life in Germany', as the US Commissioner John McCloy, one of the university's most important donors, put it.[5]

Under Bill's leadership, the school was initially still oriented towards an artistic ideal of design. However, the idea of insisting a scientific basis for design grew stronger over the years. In the fifteen years of its existence the school passed through various phases during which the relationship between design, science, and industry was intensively explored and controversially discussed. While some of the Ulm professors saw the future of design in close interaction with science, others feared the loss of the artistic qualities and traditions of the profession. Especially younger lecturers took a decidedly pro-science, even positivist position, in which science was regarded as the primary standard of design. They pressed for a systematic evaluation of the fundamental principles of design and wanted to establish information theory and methodological subjects in design education.[6]

After Bill left the school in 1957 due to irreconcilable differences on precisely this issue, his successors in the rectorate, including Tomás Maldonado, promoted the inclusion of scientific methods and principles to an unprecedented extent.[7] From 1958 to 1962, the occupation with scientific

---

3 On the history of the school, see Hartmut Seeling, 'Geschichte der Hochschule für Gestaltung Ulm 1953–1968: Ein Beitrag zur Entwicklung ihres Programms und der Arbeiten im Bereich der Visuellen Kommunikation' (PhD diss., Universität Köln, 1985); René Spitz, *HfG Ulm: Der Blick hinter den Vordergrund. Die politische Geschichte der Hochschule für Gestaltung, 1953–1968* (Stuttgart: Edition Axel Menges, 2002); Christiane Wachsmann, *Vom Bauhaus beflügelt: Menschen und Ideen an der Hochschule für Gestaltung Ulm* (Stuttgart: avedition, 2018).

4 On the relationship between design, domesticity, and social behaviour, see Robin Schuldenfrei, ed., *Atomic Dwelling: Anxiety, Domesticity, and Postwar Architecture* (London: Routledge, 2012).

5 'McCloy ehrt Geschwister Scholl', in *Stuttgarter Zeitung*, 2 June 1953, quoted in Brigitte Hausmann, 'Experiment 53/68', in Dagmar Rinker et al., eds., *Ulmer Modelle — Modelle nach Ulm: Hochschule für Gestaltung Ulm 1953–1968* (Ostfildern-Ruit: Hatje Cantz, 2003), 16–33, here 16 (my translation).

6 Otl Aicher, 'Die Hochschule für Gestaltung: Neun Stufen ihrer Entwicklung', *Archithese* 15 (1975), 12–16, here 14.

7 Dagmar Rinker, '"Produktgestaltung ist keine Kunst" — Tomás Maldonados Beitrag zur Entstehung eines neuen Berufsbilds', in Rinker et al., *Ulmer Modelle* (see note 5), 38–49, here 43f.

theories and methods increased significantly. With the appointment of new lecturers in 1957 and 1958, the pro-science group was strengthened.[8] Among the new appointments were sociologist Hanno Kesting and mathematician Horst Rittel and, in temporary positions, sociologist Lucius Burckhardt, cyberneticist Abraham Moles, and psychologist Mervyn W. Perrine. These new lecturers were to give the university a desired scientific edge.[9] Their aim, as stated in Ulm's first quarterly bulletin of 1958, was to teach prospective designers 'the technological and scientific expertise necessary to participate in today's industry. ... [to] grasp and consider the cultural and social consequences of their work.'[10]

The students of the Ulm School of Design attended numerous scientific subjects in addition to their design courses. One of the basic design methods taught by Rittel was the 'morphological box' (or 'morphological analysis'). This was a combinatorial method for the systematic, comprehensive generation of problem-solving variants that was popular among designers and architects at the time. The method goes back to the Swiss astrophysicist Fritz Zwicky (1898–1974), who was trained at ETH Zurich and taught at the California Institute of Technology from the 1940s until his retirement.[11] Besides his actual scientific field, astrophysics, in which he was very successful, Zwicky was interested in systematic methods of inventing and thinking.[12] He used the morphological method himself in order to work on a wide variety of problems, including the optimization of rocket engines, the systematic scanning of galaxies, the development of a logistics programme for war-damaged libraries, and the systematic discussion of legal issues in the space age.[13] Bill had already introduced this method at the Ulm School of Design as early as 1956 at the first German-Swiss Werkbund conference after the war. By applying it in the design process, he hoped to make design more scientific and to eliminate personal preferences.[14]

The aim of the morphological box is to systematically expand one's horizon of knowledge and to encounter new, unknown ideas in the wealth of combinatorially generated results. In concrete terms, the method works by combining discrete parameters and components to create a variety of solution combinations for a clearly defined problem. While the parameters represent certain properties and functions of a sought-after solution, the components describe various possibilities for implementing these properties and functions. In the sense of systematics, both the parameters and components as well as the problem need to be clearly defined before the combinatorial procedure is started. As far as the visual presentation of the method is concerned several options are suggested, depending on the number of

8 Wachsmann, *Vom Bauhaus beflügelt* (see note 3), 138; Seeling, 'Geschichte der Hochschule' (see note 3), 214ff.
9 See Wachsmann, *Vom Bauhaus beflügelt* (see note 3), 127–44; Joerg Crone, 'Die visuelle Kommunikation der Gesinnung: Zu den grafischen Arbeiten von Otl Aicher und der Entwicklungsgruppe 5 für die Deutsche Lufthansa 1962' (dissertation, Universität Freiburg im Breisgau, 1998), 62–9.
10 *Quarterly Bulletin of the Hochschule für Gestaltung, Ulm 1* (October 1958), 1–24, here 1 (my translation).
11 On the life and work of Fritz Zwicky, see Alfred Stöckli, Roland Müller, and Ian Gordon, *Fritz Zwicky: An Extraordinary Astrophysicist* (Cambridge, MA: Cambridge Scientific Publishers, 2011); John Johnson, *Zwicky: The Outcast Genius Who Unmasked the Universe* (Cambridge, MA: Harvard University Press, 2019).
12 See Fritz Zwicky, *The Morphological Method of Analysis and Construction* (Pasadena: California Institute of Technology, 1948); Fritz Zwicky, *Discovery, Invention, Research through the Morphological Approach* (Toronto: Macmillan, 1969).
13 See Claudia Mareis, 'Quadratisch, praktisch, gut: Zur Erfolgsgeschichte des morphologischen Kastens', in Christof Windgätter, ed., *Verpackungen des Wissens (Reihe Maske und Kothurn)* (Vienna: Böhlau, 2012), 109–21.
14 Max Bill, 'Umweltgestaltung nach Morphologischen Methoden (1956)', in Jakob Bill, ed., *Max Bill: Funktion und Funktionalismus; Schriften, 1945–1988* (Bern: Benteli, 2008), 103–8, here 104.

parameters to be processed: cases involving only two parameters can be presented using a simple chart (see figure i). For cases with three parameters, it is recommended to use a diagrammatic cube (hence the term 'box'). For four and more parameters, however, a mathematical matrix ('scheme') has to be used.

Following the scientific demand for repeatability, Zwicky defined a total of five operationalization steps for the correct execution of a morphological analysis: (1) precise description and generalization of the problem, (2) definition of all parameters determining the solution of the problem, (3) application of the combinatorial process, (4) evaluation of the generated solutions, and (5) choice of the optimal solution.[15] The steps can be repeated as required, and the results can be linked together. In this way, more knowledge about a problem is to be accumulated step by step, thus generating a more soundly based solution. Mathematically speaking, a 'successive approximation' takes place, which ideally should lead to a solution that is as comprehensive, objective, and unprejudiced as possible.[16] However, given the many subjective influences that are inevitably involved in the description of the problem, the definition of the parameters, and the selection of the solutions, in reality this ideal must be relativized.

Methods such as the morphological box promised to give design a touch of scientific objectivity and credibility. At the same time, however, they were open to creative impulses and ideas. In that sense, they perfectly met the diametric needs for both freedom and predictability in design. They allowed, as Bill noted, a synthesis of 'feeling *and* thinking', which seemed to be essential for the activity of design.[17]

Encounters between design and science, part two

Germany was not the only Western country in which the systematization of design was an urgent topic in the post-war period. While the trend towards a more scientific approach to design at the Ulm School of Design was interrupted due to the forced closure of the school in 1968, the corresponding debates outside Germany were only just beginning. Originating in Great Britain, an international, interdisciplinary movement to systematize design methods

i Formation of a morphological chart. Source: Ken W. Norris, 'The Morphological Approach to Engineering Design', in John Christopher Jones and Denis G. Thornley, eds., *Conference on Design Methods* (New York: Macmillan, 1963), 118.

Parameters	Parameter steps				Remarks
What the subject must 'be' or 'have'; i.e. its required 'characteristics'	The 'means' of achieving — or description of — what the subject must 'be' or 'have'				
Form	Circular cylinder	Rect. cylinder	Sphere		
Size	1 unit	2 units	3 units	4 units	Definition of unit required
Material	Metal	Wood	Plastic		
Orientation	x axis	y axis	z axis		Definition required
Quantity	1	2	3	4	
Speed	Low	Medium	High		Definition required
Etc.					

15 Fritz Zwicky, *Morphologische Forschung: Wesen und Wandel materieller und geistiger struktureller Zusammenhänge* (Glarus: Baeschlin, 1989), 17f.
16 Fritz Zwicky, *Entdecken, Erfinden, Forschen im Morphologischen Weltbild* (Munich: Knaur, 1971), 99.
17 Max Bill, 'Die mathematische Denkweise in der Kunst unserer Zeit', *Das Werk* 36 (1949), 86–91, here 88 (italics in the original, my translation).

was formed at the beginning of the 1960s which became known as the 'design methods movement'.[18] As was the case at Ulm, this movement called for the replacement of subjective empirical knowledge and individual solutions in design with systematic procedures. In this way the outcomes and consequences of design decisions and results could be better anticipated and controlled. Some former lecturers of the Ulm School of Design, such as Rittel and Bruce Archer, were involved in this new design and science movement. But there were also new players in the field, such as the architect Christopher Alexander, who in 1962 presented one of the first dissertations in the field,[19] or the designer John Christopher Jones, who had dedicated himself to the development of an all-encompassing manual on design methods.[20]

Like the Ulm School of Design, the design methods movement was confronted with the challenging question of how the activity of design could be systematically optimized to keep pace with the scientific, technological, and industrial developments of the time without losing its former artistic and aesthetic qualities.[21] However, unlike the Ulm School, which was committed to the democratization of post-war German society, this movement did not follow an explicitly formulated socio-political programme. Rather, the focus was on finding ways of working across disciplines in light of emerging technological and scientific possibilities and changing conditions. Those in the design methods movement were guided by the conviction that design and planning problems of all kinds and scales could only be overcome through coordinated, methodically structured forms of cooperation.

Interdisciplinary conferences provided a promising format for exchanging views on design methods. The first of its kind, the Conference on Design Methods, was held in September 1962 at the Faculty of Aeronautics at Imperial College London. The organizing committee included two former Ulm lecturers, Anthony Frøshaug and Archer, who had in the meantime returned to Great Britain and were now both working at the renowned Royal College of Art in London. They brought together experts from various disciplines, all of whom showed interest in the systematization of design activity. Participants included experts from the fields of architecture, product design, art, engineering, cybernetics, systems engineering, management, logic, psychology, and computer science.[22]

The contributions addressed different aspects of the conference topic in accordance with the diversity of disciplines gathered. Alexander, for instance, presented his system-theoretical thoughts on urban planning using the example of a six-hundred-person Indian village, for him 'a city in miniature'.[23] Alexander understood the city as an adaptive system, consisting of different social, material, infrastructural, and organizational components whose interactions had to be systematically identified and taken into account in urban planning. He numbered a variety of

---

18 For more on the design methods movement, see Alise Upitis, 'Nature Normative: The Design Methods Movement, 1944–1967' (PhD diss., Massachusetts Institute of Technology, 2008); Claudia Mareis, *Design als Wissenskultur* (Bielefeld: transcript, 2011), 34–54; Nigan Bayazit, 'Investigating Design: A Review of Forty Years of Design Research', *Design Issues* 20, no. 1 (2004), 16–29; Nigel Cross, 'Forty Years of Design Research', *Design Studies* 28, no. 1 (2007) 1–4.
19 Christopher Alexander, 'Notes on the Synthesis of Form' (PhD diss., Harvard University, 1962).
20 John Christopher Jones, *Design Methods: Seeds of Human Futures* (London: Wiley, 1972 [1970]).
21 Peter A. Slann, 'Foreword', in John Christopher Jones and Denis G. Thornley, eds., *Conference on Design Methods* (New York: Macmillan, 1963), i–xiii, here xi.
22 Derman Guy Christopherson, 'Opening Address: Discovering Designers', in Jones and Thornley, *Conference on Design Methods* (see note 21), 1–10, here 3.
23 Christopher Alexander, 'The Determination of Components for an Indian Village', in Jones and Thornley, *Conference on Design Methods* (see note 21), 83–114, here 83.

components (grouped by topics such as 'religion and caste', 'employment', and others)[24] from 1 to 141 to tabulate possible interactions. In order to manage the complexity of all these interactions, he finally introduced a series of mathematical, partly computerized arithmetical operations to identify patterns and structures. For Alexander, urban planning was, as the historian of architecture George Vrachliotis has pointed out, 'a topological space of structures'[25] that needed to be systematically analysed and mastered. The computer, with which he was already working at the time, served him as a tool to reduce complexity on the one hand and to find patterns of interaction on the other.

Jones, for his part, addressed the question of what a contemporary systematic design methodology should look like. In contrast to Alexander, who propagated the computer as a future-oriented working tool for architecture, Jones's contribution can be understood as an attempt to methodically reconcile human and machine-based problem-solving skills. Jones, who had specialized in industrial design and would go on to write a seminal design methods manual,[26] diagnosed in his contribution a trend since the 1950s towards systematic design methods due to the increasing computerization of the working world (computers, automatic controls, and systems) and the growing interest in the phenomenon of human imagination and creativity in design ('under such titles as "creative engineering" and "brainstorming"'[27]). A major goal of the design methods movement was thus to relate these two crucial aspects of contemporary communication and working processes: automation and computerization on the one hand and human creativity on the other. Design methodologists like Jones dreamed of integrating 'all such developments ... into a unified system of design'. They regarded the design process as an interface where mathematical calculation and human imagination could meet: 'primarily a means of resolving a conflict that exists between logical analysis and creative thought.'[28]

What was striking about the methods discussed in the design methods movement, however, was that, with a few exceptions, they had no roots in art and design—rather, they came from scientific, technical, or structural science disciplines and were adapted for design purposes.[29] Booming new approaches such as cybernetics, operations research, game theory, artificial intelligence research, and semiotics played an important role in shaping new ways of data processing, decision-making, and problem-solving and strongly influenced the design methodology of the post-war period. Moreover, methodological approaches from military research were adapted to civil design problems. For Rittel, the emergence of the design methods movement around 1960 was to be seen as the civil application of military research—an attempt to transfer problem-solving approaches that had been developed by NASA and the US military for complex technological problems, to civil application areas such as urban planning or environmental protection.[30]

---

24 Alexander, 'The Determination of Components' (see note 23), 89–93.
25 Georg Vrachliotis, 'So fing ich an von Mustern zu träumen … Über das Denken in Strukturen, das Entwerfen mit Mustern und den Wunsch nach Schönheit und Bedeutung in der Architektur', in Andrea Gleiniger and Georg Vrachliotis, eds., *Muster: Ornament, Struktur, Verhalten* (Berlin: Birkhäuser, 2009), 25–40, here 33.
26 Jones, *Design Methods* (see note 20).
27 John Christopher Jones, 'A Method for Systematic Design', in Jones and Thornley, *Conference on Design Methods* (see note 21), 53–73, here 53.
28 Jones, 'A Method for Systematic Design' (see note 27), 54.
29 An important impulse came from the engineering disciplines, whose own repertoire of scientific methods set them certain limits in terms of creativity and who for precisely this reason tried to integrate aspects of design more strongly into their activities. On this, see Upitis, *Nature Normative* (see note 18), 121.
30 Horst W. Rittel, 'Son of Rittelthink', interview with Horst Rittel by Jean-Pierre Protzen and Donald Grant, *The DMG 5th Anniversary Report, Occasional Paper* 1 (1972), 5–10, here 5.

The heterogeneity of the methods and techniques that were packed under the label 'design methods' was also a problem for the participants themselves. The spectrum of methods ranged from simple brainstorming to complex mathematical decision theory. It was therefore not easy to say what exactly was the common denominator of these new methods and how they differed from the old design methods, as Jones explained at a conference at MIT in 1968.[31] He speculated that it was not so much the methods themselves that were of interest to designers but rather the fact that they could provide clues to novel design principles and advanced understandings of design. According to Jones, the main goal of design methodology was thus to use methods to change traditional design ideas and better understand the thinking behind the activity of design.[32]

However, the theoretical debate on methods also had its appeal completely detached from practical goals or benefits. Geoffrey Broadbent, another actor in the design methods movement, pointed out that the intensive, even obsessive, study of methods had distracted from the actual goals of design, becoming 'fascinated by means, rather than with ends.'[33] The hype surrounding systematic design processes and methods led, in the view of many designers, to an excessive formalization and rigid scientification of design activity. In particular, actors like Jones who came from design practice complained that the findings and results of the design methodology had little in common with the lives of practising designers and that the welfare of society had also been neglected. Jones's conclusion sounded disappointed: 'We sought to be open minded, to make design processes that would be more sensitive to life. ... But the result was rigidity: a fixing of aims and methods to produce designs that everyone now feels to be insensitive to human needs.'[34] He noted that design methods had only become more theoretical, academic, and the language more abstract, thus 'los[ing] touch with how it feels to be a designer and how it feels to inhabit the systems being designed.'[35]

Similar to what had happened at the Ulm School of Design a few years earlier, there was a fear especially amongst practising designers and architects that the creative 'core' of the design activity could be lost through forced scientific over-systematization. Tensions over the question of how much scientificity design practice could tolerate led to controversy within the design methods movement and finally to its disintegration in the early 1970s. The debates did not end there, however; they continued in the field of design research,[36] where the question of the scientific nature of design is still a controversial issue today.[37]

Rethinking design methodology in response to crisis

It has been said that the effort to systematize the activity of design in the post-war period was accompanied by a disciplinary crisis. At least this was the view of Rittel, who after his appointment at the Ulm School of Design taught design science at the University of California, Berkeley and the University of Stuttgart. He believed that the 'occurrence of interest in methodology in a certain field is usually a sign of a crisis within that field.'[38] According to Rittel, the purpose of design methodology was therefore not only the development of efficient design methods but also the deeper

---

31 John Christopher Jones, 'The State of the Art in Design Methods', in Gary T. Moore, ed., *Emerging Methods in Environmental Design and Planning* (Cambridge, MA: MIT Press, 1970), 3–8, here 3.
32 Jones, 'The State of the Art' (see note 31).
33 Geoffrey H. Broadbent, 'Creativity', in Sydney A. Gregory, ed., *The Design Method* (London: Butterworths, 1966), 111–19, here 111.
34 John Christopher Jones, *Design Methods*, 2nd ed. (New York: Wiley, 1992), xi.
35 Jones, *Design Methods* (see note 34).
36 Bruce Archer, 'Whatever Became of Design Methodology?', *Design Studies* 1, no. 1 (July 1979), 17–20, here 17–18.
37 Cf. Nigel Cross, 'Designerly Ways of Knowing: Design Discipline Versus Design Science', *Design Issues* 17, no. 3 (2001), 49–55.
38 Rittel, 'Son of Rittelthink' (see note 30), 5.

understanding of the activity of design. It seemed as if one of the most traditional human activities, that of design, had to be completely relearned and re-understood under the changed auspices and conditions of the post-war period. At the centre of this learning process was a questionable relationship between man and environment that had become complicated by technology and human progress. The triggers and causes for the design crisis diagnosed by Rittel, and thus the emergence of design methodology in the post-war period, were certainly manifold. Without claiming to be exhaustive, I can highlight the following four aspects: *artificiality*, *post-industrial society*, *interdisciplinarity*, and *future as catastrophe*.

First, the diagnosis of *artificiality*, which became virulent in the context of artificial intelligence research and computational thinking in the 1960s, was central for both rethinking design and the relation between humans and the environment. Through the lens of this diagnosis, more and more of the human environment carried traces of artificial design, even claiming that the world today is more human-made than natural: 'Almost every element in our environment shows evidence of man's artifice.'[39] Built environments, technical systems, linguistic symbols, human behaviours, and more were, in the context of design and planning debates in the post-war period, understood as artificial, that is human-made artefacts. Otl Aicher, the famous Ulm School designer, summed up the precarious artificial constitution of the post-war present with the expression *'die welt als entwurf'* (the world as design).[40] The more things were regarded as artificial, the more there was to design. At the same time, however, this extended claim for design also entailed an enormous responsibility, since social and ecological problems—such as environmental pollution or urbanization—had emerged as the dark side of material culture, technological progress, and civilization. The diagnosis of artificiality was thus both an opportunity and a burden for design.

A second fundamental factor for promoting a new perspective on design was the way knowledge production and work were transformed in the post-war period. With the growth of the service sector and the spread of computer technologies in the 1950s and 1960s, the conditions of work started to change significantly: where once material commodities and goods were at the centre of production, there were now ideas, services, and communication. Accordingly, new resources were needed, namely creativity, knowledge, and information. Like many other areas of human labour at that time, design became subject to a double process of rationalization: it needed to become both more manageable and more efficient. There are many sociological terms that try to put the changes of the post-war working environment into words. We often refer to it as knowledge, the information society, or the post-industrial society, a term coined by French sociologist Alain Touraine.[41] His idea of societies being defined (or 'programmed') 'according to the nature of their production methods and economic organization'[42] is also expressed in the design methodology project, namely in the attempt to operationalize the design activity in such a way that it could be integrated with new communication and data processing technologies and become part of the emerging knowledge economy.

Third, a new awareness of the value of *interdisciplinarity* manifested itself in the design methodology of the post-war period. Already during the Second World War, new forms of cooperation between the military, industry, and universities had been established, which in the post-war period were transformed into civilian contexts of knowledge production.[43] As in other professional and scientific areas, the field

---

39 Herbert A. Simon, *The Sciences of the Artificial* (Cambridge, MA: MIT Press, 1969), 3.
40 Otl Aicher, *Die Welt als Entwurf* (Berlin: Ernst & Sohn, 1991).
41 Alain Touraine, *The Post-industrial Society* (New York: Random House, 1971).
42 Touraine, *The Post-industrial Society* (see note 41), 3.
43 In this context, there is often talk of a 'military-industrial-academic complex' (cont. on p. 103)

of design could benefit from this development, too. Besides new forms of cooperation, technological progress also contributed to the increased interest in interdisciplinarity. According to Herbert Simon, computers were the very foundation of the 'new intellectual free trade' between the many specialist scientific cultures as well as for the growing interest in design: 'The ability to communicate across fields … comes from the fact that all who use computers in complex ways are using computers to design, or to participate in the process of design.'[44] At the same time, *ex negativo*, the development of systematized design methods also referred to a profound mistrust of human problem-solving capabilities in the emerging age of the computer as 'the unreliability of the human operator'.[45] Nothing seemed to be more unpredictable than the 'human factor' when it came to controlling complex systems and solving ill-structured problems. Yet humans remained indispensable because of their ability to deal creatively with unforeseen situations. In this context, interdisciplinary cooperation and technological support provided a twofold assurance to successfully manage complex planning and decision-making processes.

This brings us to the fourth and final point of this attempt to explain the intensified interplay between design and science in the post-war period: the emergence of the design methodology around 1960 was accompanied not only by technical euphoria and progress but also by an elusive feeling of uncertainty and fear. Issues such as environmental degradation, population growth, and, most notably, the latent danger of a nuclear attack during the Cold War period fuelled fears of a future that was anything but predictable. Literary scholar Eva Horn described this collective emotional state in her book titled *Zukunft als Katastrophe* (*Future as Catastrophe*).[46] Against that background, the activity of design was defined as a process that was as controlled as possible, but with many sources of error and a partially uncertain outcome. Morris Asimow simply defined design as 'decision making in the face of uncertainty with high penalties for error'.[47] At the same time, particular emphasis was placed on the genuinely project-like nature of designing—in other words, the ability of designers to create novel things and to model unknown states and futures.[48] Cultural historian Wolfgang Schäffner has recently described the project-like nature of designing as a specific form of epistemic practice with 'the future as [its] basic point of reference.'[49] To conceive of design as a project therefore means engaging with forms of knowing and not knowing, with methods and heuristics that attempt to systematically address precarious interactions with future objects and with uncertainty and ambiguity. In this sense, the emergence of design methodology in the 1950s and 1960s can be understood both as an expression of a crisis and as an attempt to manage and overcome uncertainty.

Design as a systematic problem-solving activity

In addition to its project-like nature, design was increasingly understood in post-war design methodology as a systematic problem-solving activity. The idea of design became increasingly detached from the realm of arts, aesthetics, and

(cont. from p. 101) that developed during the Second World War. See Stuart W. Leslie, *The Cold War and American Science: The Military-Industrial-Academic Complex at MIT and Stanford* (New York: Columbia University Press, 1993); Everett Mendelsohn et al., eds., *Science, Technology, and the Military* (Dordrecht: Springer, 1988).
44 Simon, *The Sciences of the Artificial* (see note 39), 82f.
45 Broadbent, 'Creativity' (see note 33), 111.
46 Eva Horn, *Zukunft als Katastrophe* (Frankfurt: Fischer, 2014).
47 Morris Asimow quoted in John Christopher Jones, 'Design Methods Reviewed', in Gregory, *The Design Method* (see note 33), 295–309, here 296.
48 Archer, 'Design Methodology' (see note 36), 18–20.
49 Wolfgang Schäffner, 'Vom Wissen zum Entwurf: Das Projekt der Forschung', in Jürgen Weidinger, ed., *Entwurfsbasiert Forschen* (Berlin: Universitätsverlag TU Berlin, 2013), 55–64, here 56 (my translation). For further insights into the topic of projects, see Markus Krajewski, ed., *Projektemacher* (Berlin: Kadmos, 2004).

craftsmanship and became associated with scientific and organizational thoughts and procedures instead. Leading design scholars, such as Rittel, understood designing as a deliberated, planned activity, striving to control its consequences and to create alternatives and improvements to existing living conditions: designing, he believed, 'is hard intellectual work and requires careful informed judgement. It is not always primarily concerned with the appearance, but with all aspects of its consequences, such as production, handling, perception, but also the economic, social, cultural effects.'[50] Simon held a similar view, defining design as a problem-solving activity in an artificial environment created (and complicated) by human beings, a 'science of the artificial'.[51] For Simon, design was not defined by a specific object or task but rather by *how* problems are handled through the aim of 'changing existing situations into preferred ones'.[52] For him, it mattered not whether intellectual activity produced material artefacts or prescribed remedies: 'Design, so construed, is the core of all professional training; it is the principle mark that distinguishes the professions from the sciences.'[53]

The concept of design thus underwent a radical expansion. The scope of the design problems that design methodologists of the era had in mind was so extensive that they were believed to 'include nearly all public policy issues'.[54] In its essence, the process of designing was equated with that of a general 'goal-directed problem-solving activity'[55]— with the emphasis, however, that it could not only be about the analysis of a problem but rather about its anticipation and practical improvement in the form of a synthesis. The difference between science and design was thus defined by that of analysis and synthesis: the scientific method was considered a problem-solving behaviour, while the design was 'a pattern of behaviour employed in inventing things of value which do not yet exist. Science is analytic, design is constructive.'[56] However, the more objects were regarded as the task of design, the more generalist and abstract the idea of design processes became. The design process, as it was argued in the 1960s, seemed to follow the same pattern in different disciplines and areas.[57]

In this process, not only the definition of design but also the exclusive role of designers themselves was up for discussion. To Rittel it was obvious that planning and design issues not only concerned designers as such: 'Design is not the monopoly of those who call themselves "designers". ... designing is plan-making ... guided by the ambition to imagine a desirable state of the world, playing through alternative ways in which it might be accomplished, carefully tracing the consequences of contemplated actions.'[58] The approach of seeing design as a general problem-solving activity was thus accompanied by a broader understanding of the processes, tasks, and actors of design.

Systematics was one of the basic principles hoped to expand the understanding of design in both practice and theory. This principle refers on the one hand to a structured approach or a structured arrangement according to certain categories, and on the other hand to a system as a unity of

---

50 Horst W. Rittel, 'Das Erbe der HfG?', in Herbert Lindinger, ed., *Hochschule für Gestaltung Ulm: Die Moral der Gegenstände* (Berlin: Ernst & Sohn, 1987), 118–19, here 119 (my translation).
51 Simon, *The Sciences of the Artificial* (see note 39), 55.
52 Simon, *The Sciences of the Artificial* (see note 39), 55.
53 Simon, *The Sciences of the Artificial* (see note 39), 55f.
54 Horst W. Rittel and Melvin M. Webber, 'Dilemmas in a General Theory of Planning', *Policy Sciences* 4 (1973), 160.
55 Bruce Archer, 'The Structure of Design Processes' (doctoral thesis, Royal College of Art, London, 1968), §2.5.
56 Sydney A. Gregory, 'Design and the Design Method', in Gregory, *The Design Method* (see note 33), 3–10, here 6.
57 Gregory, 'Design and the Design Method' (see note 56), 3.
58 Horst W. Rittel, 'The Reasoning of Designers', working paper for the International Congress on Planning and Design Theory in Boston 1987, in *Schriftenreihe des Institut für Grundlagen der Planung* (Stuttgart: Universität Stuttgart, 1988), 1.

related elements and their relationship to each other.[59] In the design methodology debates of the post-war period, both of these meanings were closely interwoven, hence the *systemic-systematic* understanding of design to express the interlocking of systematic design methodology and regulatory systems thinking. This interlocking can be reconstructed on several levels.

First, the principle of systematics stands with regard to the post-war design methodology for a structured, goal- and purpose-oriented design approach, following a Cartesian-rationalist understanding of methodology.[60] Problem breakdown and iteration were two methodological principles central to this respect. By splitting complex design problems into smaller, easier to handle subproblems and solution steps, the design methodologist hoped to better understand and control the design process. Ideally, this process should be scientifically 'operationalized' and cybernetically 'automated'. Besides, certain recurring solution patterns, for example in architecture and urban planning, should be identified and standardized in this way.[61] The segmentation of design processes into certain phases, such as analysis, synthesis, and evaluation, was in that sense popular, too.[62] Based on cybernetic thinking,[63] the design process was imagined as a controlled loop defined by external and internal variables, in which input and output are directly related. Through iterative processes (the repetition of certain design phases and problem-solving steps), a targeted accumulation of knowledge about a design problem should be achieved and lead to the optimization of the result. Iterative process models, such as the 'design method' from 1966,[64] were thus based on a cybernetic understanding of design.

Second, the principle of systematics, in the sense of a modularization, also applies to the modular systems design emerging in the 1950s, as it was developed and propagated at the Ulm School of Design in particular. The systematization of design and manufacturing processes as well as the modularization of the resulting products went hand in hand. Exemplary for thinking in systems were the designs of Ulm School professor and architect Hans Gugelot, who designed pioneering minimalist electrical appliances for Braun and modular furniture systems, including the legendary M 125 cupboard and shelf system (1950/53), for Wohnbedarf AG in Zurich.[65] The starting point for modular system design was, on the one hand, the standardized conditions of serial mass production, which demanded elements that could be combined and produced as easily and inexpensively as possible, and, on the other hand, philosophical influences such as the cybernetic systems thinking of the time already mentioned. Behind systems design was thus not only technical and economic constraints and mass industrial rationalization thinking but also the desire to use systems to bring order to a world that was perceived as chaotic. This was reflected not least in the aesthetic formal language of the Ulm system design, which stood for clarity, objectivity, and functionality.

59 See Wolfgang Jonas, *Design, System, Theorie: Überlegungen zu einem systemtheoretischen Modell von Design-Theorie* (Essen: Blaue Eule, 1994), 74–111.
60 Bernhard E. Bürdek, *Design: Geschichte, Theorie und Praxis der Produktgestaltung*, 4th ed. (Basel: Birkhäuser, 2015), 110.
61 Christopher Alexander et al., *A Pattern Language: Towns, Buildings, Construction* (New York: Oxford University Press, 1977).
62 On process models, see Claudia Mareis, 'Zeitlichkeit des Entwerfens: Visuelle Prozessmodelle und ihre temporale Bedeutung', in Claudia Blümle, Claudia Mareis, and Christof Windgätter, eds., special issue 'Visuelle Zeitgestaltung', *Bildwelten des Wissens, Kunsthistorisches Jahrbuch für Bildkritik* 15 (2019), 114–23.
63 See Norbert Wiener, *Cybernetics or Control and Communication in the Animal and the Machine* (Paris: Hermann & Cie, 1948); Ludwig von Bertalanffy, 'An Outline of General System Theory', *The British Journal for the Philosophy of Science* 1, no. 2 (1950), 134–65.
64 Gregory, 'Design and the Design Method' (see note 56), 12.
65 Hans Wichmann, *System-Design Bahnbrecher: Hans Gugelot 1920–65* (Basel: Springer, 1987), 12–18.

In a broader conceptual sense, the principle of the systematic eventually stands for the relational location of systematic design methods and modular systems thinking within a superordinate whole, such as a technical or social system, an epistemology or ontology. It generally addresses the tension between subject, medium, and system as well as the interactive dynamics between the participating elements and actors of a system. Thinking the world of life in terms of systems meant not only knowing its elementary parts, but understanding them holistically in their complex dynamics and processuality. The design debates of the 1950s and 1960s were about systematically understanding and correlating the different aspects and dimensions of a problem to control the design of the entire whole, the 'total situation'.[66]

Design methodology and 'wicked' problems

Based on a systemic-systematic understanding of design, the post-war activity of design was thought far beyond traditional design objects and associated with the optimization of artificial systems and general problem-solving. In this context, a very specific problem term came under the focus of design methodology: that of 'ill-structured' problems, or even more specifically, that of 'wicked' problems.[67] Design theorist Kees Dorst stated in retrospect that the extensive literature on problem-solving approaches published since the 1960s has considerably influenced design research ever since, especially the hopes for 'considering design the solution to "ill-structured problems"'.[68]

The distinction between 'well-structured' problems and 'ill-structured' problems can be first found in a 1958 essay by Herbert Simon and Allen Newell.[69] The authors used the term 'ill-structured' problems in the context of operations research. They wanted to draw attention to a type of problem which, unlike 'well-structured' problems, could not be easily quantified and processed by computer technology (which they considered to be the case for most design and management problems).[70] Accordingly, Simon and Newell were concerned with the development of a heuristic, not strictly algorithmic problem-solving theory.[71]

In the late 1960s, the concept of 'ill-structured' problems was taken up by Churchman C. West, Rittel, and urban planner Melvin Webber and further developed for the realm of design and planning.[72] They believed that planning problems, in contrast to scientific problems, constituted specific kinds of problems, so-called 'wicked' problems, which are characterized by a lack of knowledge, uniqueness, the diversity of the stakeholders involved, and the associated risks when trying to solve them.[73] According to Rittel and Webber, the distinguishing characteristics of these kinds of problems include the fact that 'there is no definitive formulation of a wicked problem', as problem understanding and problem resolution are concomitant, or: 'The formulation of a wicked problem is the problem!'[74] They were also guided by the belief of design methodologists that science is based on analysis; design, on the contrary, on synthesis.

---

66 Jones, *Design Methods* (see note 20), xi. The word 'control' is used here in its English sense of 'to lead / rein', and less in the sense of the French *contrôler* meaning 'to monitor'. I owe this distinction to Michael Rottmann.
67 See Daniel Huppatz, 'Revisiting Herbert Simon's "Science of Design"', *Design Issues* 31, no. 2 (2015), 29–40.
68 Kees Dorst, 'Design Problems and Design Paradoxes', *Design Issues* 22, no. 3 (2006), 4–17, here 4.
69 Herbert Simon and Allen Newell, 'Heuristic Problem Solving: The Next Advance in Operations Research', *Operations Research* 6 (1958), 1–10.
70 Simon and Newell, 'Heuristic Problem Solving' (see note 69), 5.
71 Simon and Newell, 'Heuristic Problem Solving' (see note 69), 6.
72 C. West Churchman, 'Wicked Problems: Guest Editorial', *Management Science* 4 (1967), 141–2; Horst W. Rittel, 'On the Planning Crisis: System Analysis of the "First and Second Generations"', *Bedriftsøkonomen* 8 (1972), 390–6.
73 See Rittel and Webber, 'Dilemmas' (see note 54), 155–69.
74 Rittel and Webber, 'Dilemmas' (see note 54), 161. On the difference between 'tame' and 'wicked problems', see also Rittel, 'On the Planning Crisis' (see note 72), 392f.

The social problems handled by planners were, they argued, 'inherently wicked' and, as fundamentally different from the 'tame' problems handled by scientists, unsolvable through scientific solutions. Not only the definitions of the problems in the various areas raised questions but more urgently the questions of how to deal with them.

Rittel presented his problem-solving approach as a corrective against what he called the systems analysis approach of the 'first generation' in operations research, which followed a strict, even technocratic problem-solving procedure. In this first-generation approach, a problem was first defined and then simply processed step by step. In contrast, Rittel was much more interested in the problem definition itself, which in his view was anything but trivial and the actual problem of wicked problems. Furthermore, by analysing wicked problems and suggesting ways of handling them, he was interested in broadening the limits of scientific planning and technical rationality. He pursued the question of how systematic, responsible decisions can be taken in the absence of a secure knowledge base; and how to explicitly include subjective, off-hand judgement within design and planning processes. In his view, there were certain inherent limits to the attempt to approach uncertain, complex things only systematically and rationally: 'The more systematic you want to be the less intuitive or off-hand you want to proceed. But the terminals are always off-hand judgements. This means that the more systematic you want to be and the less you trust your off-hand judgement, the more off-hand judgements you have to make.'[75] He called this vicious circle of intuition and systematics 'the Paradoxes of Rationality'.[76]

To make planning processes more transparent, Rittel, who worked occasionally with philosopher Jürgen Habermas in the Studiengruppe für Systemforschung (Study Group for Systems Research),[77] called for the development of systematic methods that could identify the implicit values and moral concepts underlying planning and make them accessible to intersubjective argumentation. So, he was not interested in rationalizing these processes or in making them 'purely' scientific, but only as far as this was possible and meaningful. He focused on creating awareness that scientific planning and technical rationality have limits—which must be addressed and considered accordingly. With the concept of objectification, which he introduced as a contrast to the concept of scientific objectivity, he affirmed the necessity of being able to 'successfully exchange information about the foundations of our judgement'.[78] He thus not only strengthened the role of argumentation, exchange, and criticism within design methodology but also revealed the technocratic and positivistic tendencies that dominated the planning debates of the time. 'There is not that detached, scientific, objective attitude in planning', he concluded: 'Dealing with wicked problems is always political' due to the underlying moral judgements and subjective interests.[79] In this way, design and design methodology were implicitly defined as something that acted politically from the ground up.

Eventually, the question of the relationship between scientific expertise and societal participation was addressed with the concept of wicked problems. Rittel was convinced that there was no longer one specific expert for handling, or even solving, the unique and complicated problems that could be found in urban planning or environmental design. Rather, in his view the necessary expertise needed to be distributed among different people and stakeholders. 'The knowledge needed in a planning problem, a wicked problem, is not concentrated in any single head', he believed, 'for wicked problems there are no specialists. The expertise which you need in dealing with a wicked problem is usually distributed

---

75 Rittel, 'On the Planning Crisis' (see note 72), 396.
76 Rittel, 'On the Planning Crisis' (see note 72), 391.
77 See Andrea Brinckmann, *Wissenschaftliche Politikberatung in den 60er Jahren: Die Studiengruppe für Systemforschung, 1958 bis 1975* (Berlin: edition sigma, 2006).
78 Rittel, 'On the Planning Crisis' (see note 72), 394.
79 Rittel, 'On the Planning Crisis' (see note 72), 394.

over many people. Those people who are the best experts with the best knowledge, are usually those who are likely to be affected by your solution.'[80] The concept of wicked problems thus marked a sharpened awareness that design and planning problems were no longer to be located only in the narrow area of exclusive scientific problem-solving and technical rationality but also in the broader context of society and policymaking. This is a clear criticism of an elitist expert culture that makes decisions over the heads of those affected, that acts in an expertocratic rather than a participatory manner. Rittel and Webber concluded that 'planning is a component of politics. There is no escaping that truism.'[81]

It was due to its political but also open character that the concept of wicked problems proved to be so productive for the field of design methodology, planning, and beyond.[82] As a critique of overly rigid systems theory and technical rationality,[83] it promoted a critical perspective on knowledge production per se. What was promised instead was the hope for a systematic yet adaptive way of addressing problems that affect us all but for which we have no answers yet.

Management of uncertainty by design [84]

The encounters, or sometimes confrontations, between design and science did not leave the disciplines nor the actors involved unchanged. They not only made an effort to relearn the activity of design but to challenge the limits of knowing. The design methods project of the post-war period substantially questioned the relationship between objective and subjective procedures, expertocracy and participation, man and machine. Design methodologists worked towards a scientific systematization of design processes but, only seemingly in contradiction to this first aim, called concepts of scientific objectivity and technical rationality into question. Eventually, computer technologies in the post-industrial society increased the desire to delegate individual responsibility for design and planning processes to algorithms and, in so doing, reduce the risk of human error. But it turned out that both human and machine were prone to errors. Ultimately, the design method project was concerned with the synchronization of cooperation between human and technical knowledge systems. Its greatest achievement was opening a field of tension in which questions concerning the activity of design were made productive, especially in their contradictions and incommensurability. All the paradoxes and tensions that design methodology has had to contend with make it a contemporary endeavour to this day.

The post-war debates on design as a response to a society in transformation, wicked problems, and uncertain futures, as well as the attempt at encountering design and science, touched on far-reaching questions that have remained topical. The concept of wicked problems represents a specific category of 'complex, intractable, open-ended, unpredictable problems'[85] associated with the realm of social policy and planning. In recent years this concept has been used to address social and environmental problems that even transcend the realm of policy and planning.[86] Complex problems such as global warming, drug abuse, child protection, or

---

80 Rittel, 'On the Planning Crisis' (see note 72), 394.
81 Rittel and Webber, 'Dilemmas' (see note 54), 169.
82 Richard Buchanan, 'Wicked Problems in Design Thinking', *Design Issues* 8, no. 2 (1992), 5–21.
83 The term 'technical rationality' was most prominently coined by Donald A. Schön in the early 1980s. Although my use of the term is largely consistent with his, for chronological reasons I do not focus on Schön in this paper. See Donald A. Schön, *The Reflective Practitioner: How Professionals Think in Action* (New York: Basic Books, 1984).
84 I would like to thank Johannes Bruder, Kenny Cupers, Orit Halpern, and Chris Salter, with whom I have worked on the idea of design as a mode of 'management of uncertainty' during the last years. Their expertise in the social sciences, science research, and urban studies has enormously enriched my own reflections on design.
85 John Alford and Brian W. Head, 'Wicked and Less Wicked Problems: A Typology and a Contingency Framework', *Policy & Society* 36, no. 3 (July 2017), 397–413, here 397.
86 Alford and Head, 'Wicked and Less Wicked' (see note 85).

natural disasters are nowadays declared to be wicked problems and are tackled by the means of design.[87] Design, then, is best described as an effort 'to intervene in and adapt to a complex world from a position of necessarily partial knowledge' and is thus a requirement for resilience.[88]

It is important to historize, and even more to understand and problematize design as an epistemology in its own right, to appreciate how an expanded concept of design revealed design tasks in different areas and contexts of application. Design's ability to deal with wicked problems and uncertain futures has a dark side, however: the precarious normalization of uncertainty and crisis.[89] The more situations are projected as design problems, the greater might be the interest in maintaining uncertainty and crisis as economic 'resources' that can be managed and commercialized. The field of design methodology promoted a set of concepts and tools that underlie the current trend to frame dealings with uncertain futures, ecological crises, and societal transformations first and foremost as design problems.

[87] Kelly Levin et al., 'Overcoming the Tragedy of Super Wicked Problems: Constraining Our Future Selves to Ameliorate Global Climate Change', *Policy Sciences* 45, no. 2 (2012), 123–52.
[88] Kevin Grove, *Resilience* (London: Routledge, 2018), 5.
[89] Tony Fry and Adam Nocek, 'Design in Crisis, Introducing a Problematic', in Tony Fry and Adam Nocek, eds., *Design in Crisis: New Worlds, Philosophies and Practices* (London: Routledge, 2021), 1–15.

Wolf Reuter

Horst Rittel and the Discrete Identity of Design[1]

When Horst Rittel came to the University of California, Berkeley in 1963, he wanted to observe the phenomena of design to make true statements about it. He named his field of research 'Science of Design': a simple-sounding name that has long been misinterpreted as 'scientific design'. This confusion is influenced by the mistaken conviction that Rittel, who studied pure mathematics and theoretical physics, would handle design as a scientific domain. Yet he clearly specified their difference: 'The kind[s] of problems that planners deal with … are inherently different from the problems that scientists and perhaps some classes of engineers deal with.'[2]

Nevertheless, Rittel's early teaching seems to substantiate the suspicion. When he started in 1958 at the Hochschule für Gestaltung (HfG) in Ulm as a twenty-eight-year-old lecturer, his courses on methodology, mathematical operations analysis, logics, mathematics, and technical physics indicated that he would be concerned with scientific design. He also taught general mechanics for the Department of Product Design; courses on information theory for the Department for Visual Communication; and courses on methodology, theory of structures, combinatorics, topology, philosophy of science, cybernetics, operations research, group theory and theory of sets, statistics, standardization, and planning techniques for the Department of Building Production. Yet Rittel was committed to include production, use, and social (and other) consequences into the design process.[3] His concern was to

---

[1] Wolf Reuter is Professor Emeritus at the Faculty of Architecture and Urban Planning, University of Stuttgart.
[2] Horst W. Rittel and Melvin M. Webber, 'Dilemmas in a General Theory of Planning', *Policy Sciences* 4, no. 2 (1973), 155–69, here 160.
[3] Gerhard Curdes, 'Die Abteilung Bauen an der HfG Ulm: Eine Reflexion zur Entwicklung, Lehre, Programmatik', in Ralph Johannes, ed., *Entwerfen II:* (cont. on p. 117)

figure out how to use science for awareness of complexity and the ethical commitment regarding consequences. Without downgrading creativity, he represented systematic thinking as one part of the dialectics of any design process.

Despite Rittel's impressive teaching list, we must consider that a discourse about the relation of science and design was, meanwhile, on the agenda in Ulm. In his famous article 'Arabesques of Rationality', Hochschule für Gestaltung Ulm professor Gui Bonsiepe noted that there is no getting around it: 'the cold bath of scientification for the profession cannot be spared'.[4] The main reasons for this scientification had been to minimize the risk of deficiencies in the face of mass production and to boost acceptance of scientific argumentation. In addition, the zeitgeist supported this tendency. In that context, the designers at the Hochschule für Gestaltung Ulm expected scientific justification from their scientist colleagues.

But the scientist Rittel refused. As an accurate observer of the designer's activity, he saw that aesthetics is a discrete variable, independent from technical functionality; that the tasks of designers are to be solved in conflicts of diverging interests; and hence, that it is futile to strive for ideal form. Consequently, he differentiated between what is teachable (like factual knowledge, methods, skills) and what cannot be taught: 'the awareness of the scope of free decision must be unfolded.'[5] Here, in the early 1960s, we already can observe a difference he points out: on the one hand, we have science, techniques, and methods, including the rational comprehensive analysis of complex tasks; on the other hand, part of problem-solving has to do with interests, the pulse of time, aesthetic standards, design politics, 'positions which can be discussed', or free decisions.

At the very beginning of his career in the domain of design, Rittel was triggered to develop his first position on the relation of science and design, which remained stable until several years later when he elaborated it. At the University of California, Berkeley's College of Environmental Design, he developed his fundamental theoretical ideas. Six main topics, described in this chapter, structure his thoughts: deficiencies of the scientific model, paradoxes of rationality, wickedness of design problems, epistemological difference, basics of a second generation of planning theory, and the argumentative model.[6]

Deficiencies of the scientific model

In the 1950s, different streams of thought formed a leading paradigm known as scientific-instrumental rationality. One basis was the means-to-an-end relationship as one determinant of social acting.[7] Economical and technical calculi typically follow the principle of best minimal input of means leading to a maximum effect. In the field of planning, it provides—given predetermined goals—an optimal allocation of resources. In the frame of that instrument-oriented thinking was the notion that the existence of a means by itself already legitimates its application—neglecting the discourse whether the objective of acting is even desired. Decisions would be obsolete in the face of the so-called 'coercion of facts'. Scientific-instrumental rationality, at its core, was oriented to a technocratic ideology.

```
(cont. from p. 115) Architektenausbildung in Europa
seit Mitte des 20. Jahrhunderts bis zum 'Bologna-Prozess'
(Hamburg: Junius, 2018), 525-61.
4 Gui Bonsiepe, 'Arabesken der Rationalität: Anmerkungen zur
Methodologie des Design', Bauen und Wohnen 6 (1967), 2-10.
5 Horst W. Rittel, 'Zu den Arbeitshypothesen der
Hochschule für Gestaltung in Ulm', Das Werk 48, no. 8
(1961), 281-3, here 283.
6 Remark: the reader will recognize that the terms 'design'
and 'planning' are used without stressing a difference.
The reason is that, on the level of abstraction which is
taken here, they are exchangeable mainly under the
epistemological perspective and due to their similarity
as similar types of cognitive activity. Both aim at
inventing new things instead of exploring existing ones.
7 Max Weber, Wirtschaft und Gesellschaft: Grundriss
der verstehenden Soziologie, 5th rev. ed. (Tübingen: Mohr
Siebeck, 1980).
```

At the same time, a corresponding mindset prevailed in the United States. Techniques developed during the Second World War (to solve well-defined problems like supplying troops at the frontline with arms, food, or gas) had been adopted for the field of corporate management. There was no need to dispute goals; only the efficiency of techniques was of concern. Operations research became a field at universities, providing also planners with hard methods ordered along a scheme of phases. Intellectual forebears were scientists like Russel Ackoff[8] or C. West Churchman.[9] A prototype of a scheme of treating planning problems looked like this:[10] formulate the problem, form a model with defined objectives and changeable and non-changeable variables, derive alternative solutions, optimize one solution, test, control, and implement. This planning phase model was the reference frame for design theory, supported by theorists like Morris Asimow, John Christopher Jones, Christopher Alexander, and Bruce Archer. Their phase schemes were variations of the above one, introducing ideas of overlaps, feedback loops, or circular progress.

With reference to this leading concept, Rittel developed a fundamental critique, the starting point of a paradigmatic turn. Already the attempt to formulate the problem in a final, binding way, would require complete information about the factual situation, its undesired aspects, and a desired status. Rittel stresses that this completeness never exists. In addition, what is undesired and desired depends on the judgement of individuals, which is different in contemporary social contexts and may also change during the solution process. Since any optimization assumes that there could be a defined solution space, it would need a complete set of constraints. But for problems in the social context (all design problems are, after all, socially embedded), already the constraints are typically the object of doubt and discussion, leading to their change. Hence, Rittel pointed out that the solution space cannot be limited and there are no final, valid constricting conditions.

Rittel's critique mentioned the need for a fixed measure of performance to come to an optimum—a fixed measure that depends on an individual's preference system, something not homogeneous in pluralistic societies where individuals' judgements are different and neither fixed nor 'objective'. An 'optimum' for one aspect of a typically complex design object, like its economic performance, may hinder or conflict with the optimum of another aspect of a design, like its functionality or environmental compatibility. But sub-optima cannot be added to an overall optimum (which is an essential feature of complex problems).

To summarize Rittel's critique of the scientifically oriented phase model: it fails.

Paradoxes of rationality

One of the attempts of designers and planners to be part of the scientific domain even in their context of practical action is to follow the idea of rationality—an attempt that Rittel shows is in vain by revealing its inherent paradoxes.[11]

The immanent principle of designers or planners (and in fact of all professionals who deal with developing objects for the future) is their understanding of rational behaviour: one acts rationally if one anticipates the consequences of a considered action before acting—and then acts accordingly. (This does not exclude any kind of intuition but postulates rationality's priority in case of conflict.) In other words: first think, then act. If designers try to do so, Rittel states that they will run into any of four paradoxes.[12] One indicates that, if somebody

---

8 Russel L. Ackoff, *Scientific Method* (New York: John Wiley, 1962).
9 C. West Churchman, *Prediction and Optimal Decision: Philosophical Issues of a Science of Values* (Eaglewood Cliffs, NJ: Prentice Hall, 1961).
10 Ackoff, *Scientific Method* (see note 8).
11 Horst W. Rittel, 'On the Planning Crisis: System Analysis of the "First and Second Generations"', *Bedriftsøkonomen* 8 (1972), 390–6.
12 Rittel, 'On the Planning Crisis' (see note 11), 391.

starts to detect a consequence of a considered action, they will find a consequence of that first detected consequence. They will discover that each consequence causes another in a never-ending process of causal chains and their networked ramifications. Designers will end their attempt to be rational not by a logical reason but because they may run out of time, money, capacity, or motivation. Another paradox that could arise would be if one elaborates the ramifications of consequences of consequences. The farther one looks into the future, the greater the uncertainty about the relevance of each item and what to do. The more one knows, the less able one is to decide. The incapability of acting grows with accumulative knowledge. The other two paradoxes that Rittel identifies refer to the inability to start with the attempt to be rational, and to the logical impossibility that a model about future phenomena caused by a considered action can contain the causal model itself as a decisive factor.

These considerations may lead to the conclusion not to act if rationality is lacking. But Rittel proposes to coexist with the paradoxes—either a wise art of living or an existential-philosophical position to act despite unsolvable fundamental questions, but one that cautions planners and designers from being naive about the search for rationality.

Wickedness

The most explicit demarcation of design thinking from the scientific pattern of thinking is deliberated in Rittel's profiling of design and planning problems as 'wicked'. In contrast, 'tame' problems are typically those of scientists and engineers. As an example, consider a problem in mathematics, such as solving an equation; or the task of an organic chemist in analysing the structure of some unknown molecule; or that of a chess player attempting to accomplish checkmate in five moves. For each the mission is clear. It is also clear whether the problem has been solved. 'Wicked' problems, however, have neither of these clarifying traits. In the first- and second-generation systems approach discussed above and in 'Dilemmas in a General Theory of Planning', Rittel and Webber characterized wicked problems by the following ten features.[13]

First, there is no definitive formulation of a wicked problem. Although a tame problem can be phrased in an exhaustive and valid way, a wicked problem reveals new information which changes the way one looks at the problem. We can take the case of designing housing for the elderly as an example. The problem formulation depends on one's understanding of the direction of solution: either as closed specialized homes, mixed-generation housing, integrated urban housing (achieved by placing apartments throughout a city), or apartments equipped to be adapted to seniors' needs. Only by developing a solution concept will you be able to define the problem.

Second, wicked problems have no stopping rule. In chess, mathematics, or chemistry, the problem solver knows when the job is done. When J. F. Kennedy, for example, said that an American would be on the moon in ten years, and after ten years the first person was on the moon and was indeed an American, the job was done: a 'tame', not 'wicked', problem, albeit a difficult feat. Yet there are two reasons why design problems are different: first, the final best solution depends on judgements of different people, not on objective criteria; and second, there is no end to the causal chains within interactions in open systems. You could always try to do it better, to find a better solution. There is no logic in stopping—you stop because you run out of time, or money, or patience and must settle with 'that is good enough', 'that is the best I can do', or 'I just like it'. That is the praxis in every architectural or designer's office.

Third, solutions to 'wicked' problems are not true-or-false but good-or-bad. In science there are shared determined criteria for objectively deciding whether the offered solution, for example to an equation or to a structural formula

[13] Rittel and Webber, 'Dilemmas' (see note 2).

of a chemical compound, is correct or false. It can be checked by other qualified persons according to the rules of science. The answer will be unambiguous. For wicked design problems there is no true or false answer. Rather, there are different groups, persons, or parties who judge. Their judgements normally differ according to their interests, sets of values, or ideological preferences. Solutions can be judged to be good enough, bad, satisfying, or great. One never can say that an apartment is true or false—that does not make sense, because nobody can prove it. There are only individually differing judgements on a scale of good and bad.

Fourth, there is no immediate and no ultimate test to a wicked problem. For 'tame' problems in science, the community of the scientists can test the correctness of a hypothesis immediately according to fixed rules. With wicked problems any solution after being implemented, any house after being built, will generate waves of consequences over a long period of time. Maybe there are more undesired than intended consequences. Nobody can tell when the waves of repercussions have completely run out. In middle Europe, for instance, suburbs at urban peripheries during the 1960s were considered good. Around the 1980s, not only members of society but also the architects decided that the bad features outweighed the good ones. At the beginning of the 1990s, architects again recognized good aspects and attractiveness of some suburbs in eastern parts of Germany. Where is the ultimate test for whether a solution is good or bad?

Fifth, every solution is a 'one-shot-operation'; every attempt counts significantly. With design problems, every implemented solution is consequential. It leaves traces. One cannot build a school to see how it works and then correct it after the performance is not satisfying. It has an impact on many people's lives, and large amounts of money are spent. These are irreversible acts.

Sixth, wicked problems do not have an enumerable set of potential solutions, nor is there a well-described set of permissible operations. Tame problems are solved according to a fixed number of options inside fixed rules, like the opening of a chess game or within an experiment that follows the laws of chemistry. You are not allowed to change the setting during an experiment. But this is different with wicked problems. Any result of a design competition, for example, is different. Two hundred participants deliver two hundred solutions. Sometimes the winner even neglects a constraint formulated in the competition brief because the solution is so overwhelmingly good that the jury rescinds its own limits and widens the solution space. In such fields of ill-definable solutions, the set of feasible solution proposals relies on judgements, on the capability of 'exotic' ideas, and on the amount of trust and credibility between designers and clientele.

Seventh, every wicked problem is essentially unique. For any two design problems, at least one distinguishing property can be found. If there are two schools to be designed at the same time, they necessarily are at different places. So the physical context is different. If you design a school two years later, the time context—that is, the context of the pedagogical discussion and inner school organization—may have changed.

Eighth, very wicked problems can be considered symptomatic of other problems. 'Tame' scientific problems are exactly defined in such a way that other levels of treatment are excluded. But take the case of solving bad housing in slums in capital cities like Manila, Caracas, Mumbai, or Rio de Janeiro. Intelligent, simple, and nice constructions have been developed. But after deliberation and acquiring better understanding, architects recognized that a slum is not a problem of constructing housing. It is a symptom of poverty which demands improving inhabitants' economic prospects, which entails improving job prospects, education, the societal system and political power structure. This illustrates that a design problem often can be considered a symptom of a higher-level problem. It is difficult for designers to go beyond the limits of their professional competence. But in the face of the complexity of their problems and the limited focus of their solutions, they may and should think about strategies of interdisciplinary networked approaches.

Ninth, in the beginning there may be numerous explanations, and the choice of explanation determines the solution. The example of the slum problem above illuminates this property of wicked problems. One explanation of bad housing could be the economic situation, but another equally plausible one could be that urbanization puts pressure on the availability of housing. Other explanations, like those named in the eighth feature, would result in other solution strategies. The analyst's world view is the strongest determining factor in explaining a problem and consequently in solving it.

Tenth, the designer has no right to be wrong. In design, solutions to problems are not mere hypotheses but always 'built in stone' and will directly affect the everyday life of people.

These features reveal how design problems are wicked, both in their undefinable causal chains in an open networked system and in the difficulty in dealing with different judgements of different groups and people in the growing pluralism of contemporary society.

Epistemological difference

The kind of knowledge which designers and planners use reveals a specific profile. Designers create things that were non-existent before, new elements of reality. Processing knowledge concerning these not-yet-existing parts of reality is a fundamental difference to science. Science mainly produces knowledge or theories about the world (or universe) which exists—it refers mainly to facts, explanations, and models about how it generally has functioned in the past or might function in the future. All scientific knowledge is—according to Karl Popper[14]—preliminary, since it holds only as long as trials of refutation fail. Design adds objects to the world which exist until their destruction. Science minimizes the effects of possible interventions of an actor as observer as far as possible. Design maximizes intervention: where there is nothing, there should be something.

Already now we recognize that designing is a discrete cognitive activity, different from activities like communication (e.g. teaching), learning, discovery (research), or organization (management). It requires a different kind of knowledge. Since design forms new parts of reality, it makes decisions about how that reality should look. Even if scientists provide knowledge about facts, these facts do not necessarily and logically lead to a decision. Design decisions, however, cannot be derived only from facts; the so-called 'coercion of facts' does not exist.[15]

Scientists bear a certain responsibility based on who stated the facts and showed with a model what would happen without intervention. But concluding what to do based on scientific facts requires at least one superior deontic statement. For instance, it may be proven that pollution in a city has ill effects on the population. Creating a countermeasure like banning cars, however, needs a deontic statement that people's health is of higher value than unlimited car mobility and thus should be protected. Only then is restricting car mobility or limiting emissions possible.

Rittel dedicated himself to the question of what kind of knowledge planners and designers must hold. In information science, he revealed different kinds of knowledge of designers: factual, deontic, instrumental, explanatory, or conceptual knowledge. Factual knowledge is needed for true statements about the system, the environment in which designers intervene. It relates to the world as it is and relies upon scientific knowledge. But if designers want to add new things to the existing world, they will develop knowledge about how it should look: 'should-be' knowledge or, in

---

14 See, e.g., Karl R. Popper, 'Die Logik der Sozialwissenschaften', in Theodor W. Adorno et al., eds., *Der Positivismusstreit in der deutschen Soziologie* (Neuwied, Berlin: Luchterhand, 1969), 103–23, here 106.
15 Horst W. Rittel, 'Sachzwänge: Ausreden für Entscheidungsmüde', in Wolf Reuter, ed., *Planen, Entwerfen, Design: Ausgewählte Schriften zu Theorie und Methodik* (Stuttgart: Kohlhammer, 1992), 271–81.

philosophical terminology, deontic knowledge. Next, designers need the instrumental knowledge for the means, techniques, and procedures necessary for implementation, drawing on technical sciences. Yet if designers want to strengthen the effects of their intended intervention on the real world (on people, material, mental states, economic or ecological consequences), they require explanatory knowledge about which and why consequences occur: knowledge is offered by all natural and human sciences. Last, difficulties in communication often occur if terms are not clear, so design discourse needs knowledge of definitions, or conceptual knowledge, to ensure that terms like 'urbanity' or 'modernity' are understood.[16]

A second generation of design and planning theory and the argumentative model

After this counterargument against the attempt of scientification in design by introducing the concept of wicked problems and showing the discrete character of design by its epistemological difference, the question arises whether it is possible to develop a model which maps the newly identified 'wicked' features of designing. Rittel stated a list of twelve principles which should be taken as guideline or orientation.[17] (1) Do not rely on the limits of distinctive phases: designing has chaotic features, and, while creating solutions, designers may need to collect more information or even change the problem definition and from there move directly to the assessment of networked impacts. (2) Do not aim for scientific objectivity for design; rather, crystallize the deontic premises. In design, the statements depend on personal judgements; the deontic ('should-be') premises of the value systems of designers are the real basis of design decisions. (3) Accept the principle of 'symmetry of ignorance': relevant knowledge is not concentrated in a single mind. Nobody knows best, not by virtue of their degree or status, what is good for someone else. (4) Support 'objectification', or the explicit and transparent communication of judgements (instead of objectivity, which in the scientific sense is guaranteed by a procedure and rules). (5) Consider the unpredictable distribution of knowledge. 'Information scouting' is part of the job: relevant knowledge is constantly generated, and the quest for that knowledge must be a permanent part of a designer's activity. (6) Consider the non-disciplinary distribution of the wide range of knowledge relevant to design. Much knowledge needed for a specific design depends on the task, site, client, and context. Design requires knowledge about statics, building physics, energy systems, material, construction, aesthetics, psychology, economy, ecology, laws, supply systems, and more. (7) Support transparency, because the main decisions in design are not based on scientific expertise but on subjective judgement. At the same time, the design is for others who should know why decisions were made, what the result will look like, and the underlying preference system. (8) Be open to participation. The theory of knowledge questions what knowledge is best for making good and sound plans. Clients' outsourcing of important issues to experts risks differences in deontic knowledge, so participation is a means to bridge the gap. People concerned usually have inputs about what would be good for them or could enrich the discussion on consequences of specific design measures. (9) Avoid premature decision-making. In face of uncertainty, deciding something may provide false security, but a designer should stay open to influences, alternative ideas, iterative solutions, and more information. Preliminary fixation hinders creativity, change, and possibilities to ameliorate a design. (10) Consider the notorious controversy in design knowledge and the need to negotiate

---

16 Werner Kunz and Horst W. Rittel, 'Issues as Elements of Information Systems', Working Paper No. 131, Center for Planning and Development Research, University of California, Berkeley, 1970; Werner Kunz and Horst W. Rittel, *Die Informationswissenschaften: Ihre Ansätze, Probleme, Methoden und ihr Ausbau in der Bundesrepublik Deutschland* (Munich: Oldenbourg, 1972).

17 Rittel, 'Planning Crisis' (see note 11).

finances, materials, self-representation, and sustainability. Designers should be prepared to think of alternatives and to deal with controversial opinions. This could mean working in parallel on alternatives and systematically collecting controversial arguments for and against proposals. (11) Support argumentation and be open for arguments including those confronting designers' own positions. Designers should seek out criticism to engage with conflicts early on in a project. (12) Doubt is respectable, even if it hinders action and makes decisions more difficult. Nevertheless, doubt is the starting point for progress, improvement, and invention. It is a good technique to question existing routines and seek new ideas.

Rittel proposed to map the design process as an argumentative model based on these twelve principles and suggestions. He saw the design process as an ongoing debate in which 'an image of the problem and of the solution emerge gradually among the participants, as a product of an incessant judgement, subjected to critical argument.'[18] This shift in paradigm regarding the understanding of design processes is in line with German philosopher Jürgen Habermas's concept of the 'design' of societies. Instead of following a technocratic ideal of controlling societal developments by means of mobilizing instruments to reach a fixed goal, Habermas emphasized that it is the discourse about the guiding norms of societies that best reveals how to act together—even when facing conflicts. His conviction—or more explicitly, his postulation—was that the best argument will win by its power to convince.[19]

Argumentation is not just a normative demand. It is also a factual description of what occurs. Designers and planners may argue with others, but they also argue among and with themselves. The argumentative model maps the designer's process of reasoning.[20] It corresponds to their constant reformulations of drafts, sketches, or models. More apparent is the argumentative characteristic of design during communication between designers, partners, and numerous participants which often include office colleagues, engineers, clients, employees, opponents, administrative offices, city planning authorities, investors, contractors, and also potential users. All of these players introduce different types of questions, positions, answers, and arguments to the design process.

Developing the argumentative model of design, Rittel proposed issues according to the types of knowledge as key elements. The structure of argumentation in general follows the same pattern: 'one of raising questions and issues towards which one can assume different positions, with the evidence gathered and arguments built for and against these different positions. The various positions are discussed, and ... one proceeds until the next question arises.'[21] The connections in the web of questions, positions, and arguments are defined by qualified relations like content, temporal evolvement, and hierarchical order. If we link this kind of argumentation structure to the interconnected form of design knowledge, we can imagine a system composed of elements such as issues, positions, and arguments, all of these feeding the discourse process in designing. Werner Kunz and Rittel referred to it as an 'Issue-Based Information System'.[22] They thought it a planning tool, an instrumental form of the argumentative model.

Discourse, negotiation, and argumentation thus became fertile ground for design practice. This can be considered Rittel's most important contribution, approximately two decades before it became the leading concept in American

---

18 Rittel and Webber, 'Dilemmas' (see note 2).
19 Jürgen Habermas, *Technik und Wissenschaft als 'Ideologie'* (Frankfurt: Suhrkamp, 1968); Jürgen Habermas, *Theorie des kommunikativen Handelns* (Frankfurt: Suhrkamp, 1981).
20 Horst W. Rittel, 'The Reasoning of Designers', Working Paper A-88-4, Institute for the Foundations of Planning, University of Stuttgart, 1988.
21 Rittel, 'Planning Crisis' (see note 11), 395.
22 Kunz and Rittel, 'Information Systems' (see note 16).

planning theory.[23] Rittel's proposal was to structure the discourse stringently. Any communication would follow the rationality of that structure, which comprises the expression of different kinds of issues, taking positions or giving answers to them and developing or exchanging the arguments against and in favour of these positions. Exchanging positions and arguments helps deliberate upon an issue, improve decisions, and create mutual learning. It does not necessarily have to lead to a consensus.

The argumentative model is based on the general impossibility to deduct deontic statements from empirical findings. It poses the controversy of interpretations of facts, of positions regarding objectives' means, of explanations and concepts as a historically permanent status. It models design and planning as a socially responsible activity and—under the coercion to act in case of conflict—as basically political. Due to its dependence on judgements and deontic knowledge of a variety of actors in pluralistically structured societies, it is opposed to objectivistic-scientific models of design and planning.

---

[23] For example, see Patsy Healey, 'Planning through Debate: The Communicative Turn in Planning Theory', *The Town Planning Review* 63, no. 2 (1992), 143–62; Frank Fischer and John F. Forester, eds., *The Argumentative Turn in Policy Analysis and Planning* (Durham, NC: Duke University Press, 1993).

Part Three

Design as Research

Hans-Jörg Rheinberger

Can Scientific Research Be Designed?[1,2]

With the notion of design, we usually associate ideas of streamlining, giving a finishing touch, wrapping, or conveying shape by anticipation. Thus, the notion of design carries with it an idea of combining functionality and aesthetics, of affordance and teleology—and for that matter, of seduction and veneer. Talking about design in scientific research seems to be counter-indicated at first sight—design appears as a form of practice that is utterly uncharacteristic of research processes in science, the latter being endowed with a form of rationality that thoroughly follows other rules. Research processes, insofar as they are assumed to generate unprecedented novelty, appear as being characterized by non-teleology, bricolage, and an essential touch of preliminarity and precariousness.

This article will explore whether this basic feature of research is compatible with an idea of design, and if so, with what kind of design. My remarks proceed from a rather straightforward notion of design, with distinctions made as an incentive for discussion rather than as a final argument.

Epistemic things cannot be designed

In characterizing scientific research processes, I have had recourse to a fundamental distinction inherent in the material constitution of experimental systems, taken as units of research and at the same time as a concept allowing for its description: the distinction between epistemic things and technical things. Since this distinction may help clarify whether (and if so, in which sense) we can talk about design in scientific research, I begin with a brief exposé concerning these two categories of objects in scientific experimentation: an oscillation between things with fuzzy boundaries on the one hand and things with a relatively determined and stabilized structure on the other.

Let us start with the fuzzy, epistemic things. They stand at the centre of interest of an experimental system because they are the part in want of knowledge. Experimental systems are the arrangements for productively dealing with epistemic things by operating at the borderline between what we know and what we do not. They are expected to bring forth, through their enactment, knowledge that, at the time of their actual operation, does not yet exist. Sociologist Robert Merton has talked in this context about 'specified ignorance' and claimed that ignorance is a category central to characterizing science as a process of knowledge acquisition.[3] But we must sharpen this description by adding that, at the frontier of exploring the unknown, we frequently are confronted with ignorance at one remove—that is, a form of not knowing that can be characterized as 'unanticipated ignorance'[4]—in which one is unaware of imminent knowledge options, or at least it remains unclear what exactly one does not yet know. Accordingly, Robert Root-Bernstein has distinguished two ways of overcoming these two forms of ignorance: bringing about serendipitous events leads a scientist to formulate a way of seeing things impossible to anticipate beforehand; bringing about pseudo-serendipitous events leads to unexpected ways of solving a problem specified in advance but impossible to solve beforehand.[5]

---

1 Hans-Jörg Rheinberger is Director Emeritus at the Max Planck Institute for the History of Science, Berlin.
2 For an earlier version of this paper see Hans-Jörg Rheinberger, 'The Problem of Design in Research', in Gerhard M. Buurman and Marc Rölli, eds., *The Intrinsic Logic of Design* (Zurich: Niggli, 2016), 133–8.
3 Robert K. Merton, 'Three Fragments from a Sociologist's Notebooks: Establishing the Phenomenon, Specified Ignorance, and Strategic Research Materials', *Annual Review of Sociology* 13 (1987), 1–28.
4 Hans-Jörg Rheinberger, 'Ignorance Is at the Heart of Scientific Knowledge Production', *Journal of the History of Knowledge*, forthcoming.
5 Robert Scott Root-Bernstein, *Discovering: Inventing and Solving Problems at the Frontiers of Scientific Knowledge* (Cambridge, MA: Harvard University Press, 1989).

For epistemic things, intrinsically, certain aspects remain in the dark in what can be called epistemic uncertainty. To let them play out their load of knowledge-generation capacity, of knowledge-to-be-acquired, they must be handled in such a way that their potential for manifesting things unheard-of is not too restricted by expectations that otherwise must accompany their manipulation. Thus, with respect to epistemic things, design in the usual sense of a directed shaping activity according to explicit goals is just not what can and should be aimed at in an experimental research situation. It would, as a rule, lead one into unproductive idling or even in the wrong direction.

Michael Polanyi, an unduly forgotten philosopher of science and contemporary of Merton, expresses what we might call the research situation:

> We make sense of experience by relying on clues of which we are often aware only as pointers to their hidden meaning; this meaning is an aspect of a reality which as such can yet reveal itself in an indeterminate range of future discoveries. This is, in fact, my definition of external reality: reality is something that attracts our attention by clues which harass and beguile our minds into getting ever closer to it, and which, since it owes this attractive power to its independent existence, can always manifest itself in still unexpected ways ... if we have grasped a true and deep-seated aspect of reality, then its future manifestations will be unexpected confirmations of our present knowledge of it.[6]

This quotation has several remarkable features that together capture what one could call a poetology of research.[7] The first of these features is that it stresses the materiality of the research process: although research involves and challenges the mind, it does not proceed through the mind alone, not even predominantly. Rather, it binds the scientific spirit[8] into a peculiar constellation. There is matter, and its condensation into things of research is the condition for the peculiar structure of the research process that presupposes it—an out-there without which it would soon be idling in itself. The second feature is that it endows the things around which research revolves with a peculiar kind of agency: a capacity 'to reveal itself in an indeterminate range of future discoveries.'[9] They have the ability to surprise the researcher, to defeat expectations, to dwarf powers of anticipation with their own revelatory richness. The question of who is the actor becomes blurred, if not even reversed. The third feature is that the research situation implies resistance, recalcitrance on the part of the things under scrutiny. Their malleability is limited; one cannot do anything one wants with them. Therefore, I avoid talking about the research activity as an activity of construction, let alone of social construction. Research is rather about manifestation—it needs extended technical tools in the researcher's hands, but these hands must come to feel whereto the things are leading them: they are in need of their things. Fourth, things are epistemic things only as long as their potential of signification is not exhausted. The very essence of epistemicity consists in the fact that there is a promise of a very peculiar kind, an expectation that is not under the power of definition. It is what agitates the researcher, who is unable to tell what will show itself behind the next corner. It is the expectation of novelty which by definition cannot be anticipated. Lastly, this being-beyond-our-will and yet in the realm of our interaction with an epistemic thing not only leads back to the first point of this characterization,

---

6 Michael Polanyi, 'The Unaccountable Element in Science', in Marjorie Grene, ed., *Knowing and Being: Essays by Michael Polanyi* (Chicago: The University of Chicago Press, 1969), 105–20, here 119–20.

7 The following paragraphs rely on Hans-Jörg Rheinberger, 'On Epistemic Objects, and Around', in Defne Ayas and Adam Kleinman, eds., *Witte de With Review: Arts, Culture and Journalism in Revolt, Vol. 1 (2013–2016)* (Rotterdam: Witte de With Publishers, 2017), 376–81.

8 Gaston Bachelard, *The New Scientific Spirit* (1934), trans. Arthur Goldhammer (Boston: Beacon Press, 1984).

9 Polanyi, 'The Unaccountable Element' (see note 6), 119.

materiality, but it also lays the ground for one of the most basic second-order categories on which science rests: the category of reality. And it is the reason for the specific and essential future-orientation of research. It is research only as long as it is able to uphold this precarious suspension between the known from which it tries to get away and the unknown, inaccessible for the time span of such essential suspension.

We can describe the research situation in yet another way by looking at the individuals engaged in the process instead of the things involved in it. From the perspective of the researcher, this amounts to an act of delegation. Setting up an experimental system revolving around an epistemic thing and exploring some of the inexhaustible aspects of its thingness means to undercut the subject-object constellation in the sense of a direct relation between the observer and observed. In an experiment, the act of observing is delegated to a technical object that one brings into interaction with the epistemic thing. But this interaction has to be crafted in such a way that the outcome—the traces the interaction leaves behind—is not completely determined in advance. Were that the case, we would deal with an experimental demonstration rather than with a research experiment.

A research experiment must have the potential to engender unintended effects—that is, to generate unexpected outcomes. Such outcomes are not in the realm of the designable; they can only be approached indirectly. Therefore, dealing with the unexpected and the unintended requires a particular kind of attention from the experimenter. Again, Polanyi comes to help here with his distinction between two kinds of attention: focal, directed attention; and subsidiary, undirected attention. These correspond to two kinds of knowledge: explicit and tacit knowledge.[10] Paying focal attention to something means to fix the thing before one's eyes from the viewpoint of one particular aspect to the exclusion of others. Focal attention can bring this particular aspect under sharp relief, but it also tends to ossify. Subsidiary attention, on the other hand, suspends the focus in favour of a hovering attentiveness that covers and leaves room for a range of possible events, none of which can be expected with certainty—as any event that deserves this name cannot be expected with certainty. What can be deduced from the present state is not an event; it is simply a consequence of that state. In all likelihood, events will escape the focused mind and senses based on explicit knowledge. Under subsidiary conditions, however, they can be traced and reveal the unanticipated. Subsidiary awareness in its two forms—marginal and subliminal (which Polanyi discriminates as directed outward and inward)—helps to bring the unprecedented into the realm of the graspable.

Technical things can be designed

In contrast to the nature of epistemic things, the technical things that enter an experimental constellation are usually characterized by technical precision of a certain degree, a precision that can widely vary according to the research question at stake, however. Generically, technical things are subsumed under the notion of research technology. They are the pieces of apparatus needed to create a situation in which an epistemic thing can be handled in a potentially knowledge-generating manner. In contrast to epistemic things, for technical things it makes sense to consider design, in the common sense of the word, as being purposefully conceived. Thus, if there are several core aspects of the research process that are difficult to be recognized as design, we nevertheless should continue to look out for design features in scientific experimentation.

This search can be pursued by judging and expecting the design of a research instrument to function in accord with the theorem that it is supposed to reify—like the French philosopher of science Gaston Bachelard, one can claim that '*an instrument, in modern science, is veritably a reified*

10 Michael Polanyi, 'The Logic of Tacit Inference' (1964), in Grene, ed., *Knowing and Being* (see note 6), 138–58.

theorem.'[11] A design that hampers its expression can be qualified as suboptimal. There are, in this respect, evaluation criteria available for the design of technical objects—research technologies—that are transparent. Epistemic objects, in contrast, are opaque by nature.

Besides reifying a particular theorem, a research instrument must in addition be designed in view of the function it is supposed to fulfil; that is, in view of its envisaged interaction with a certain range of epistemic things with which it has to share a common interface.[12] Such clearance or matching between the technical conditions of experimentation and the epistemic things handled in them can be subsumed under the label of interface design. The interface between the epistemic and the technical in an experimental setting is usually a tricky sphere of action. Here, the decision lies in whether a particular epistemic entity and a research technology can be brought together in such a way that knowledge effects result from the interaction.

Let me give an example. Relatively early in the development of the electron microscope in the late 1930s, attempts were made to use it to make visible biological structures that are invisible to a light microscope (such as viruses). Their dimensions were so small that they pushed capabilities of the new instrument's resolution. This borderline situation initiated a process of mutual calibration and reconfiguration of sample preparation on the biological side and sample reception on the technical side: samples and their preparation had to be designed in such a way that they reflected the technical conditions of the instrument, and the sample environment of the instrument had to be designed in such a way that it respected the biological conditions of the sample in a negotiation between the hard and the soft, the dry and the wet, the stable and the unstable.

Although such mutual design processes are particularly critical in the case of biological epistemic things, they reflect a generic feature of experimentation. They are characteristic of the encounter between epistemic and technical things, and they can take very different forms according to the research technologies involved and the epistemic objects at stake.[13] As a rule, however, the problems arising at this boundary can be stated explicitly and thus subjected to design procedures. The realm and range of design, however, is functionally determined in a rather strict manner in terms of 'affordance'.[14] A research instrument thus oscillates between two directions of affordance: one towards its user, the other towards its sample.

Experimental context

A third aspect of the experimental process where design plays a role is in the overall arrangement of an experiment. Another notion is often used here as a synonym in laboratory shoptalk: the so-called planning of an experiment. Planning or design here comes less with connotations of efficiency or effectiveness but rather with a connotation of sophistication, care in the arrangement of parts, and placement of proper controls. What does that mean? To put it simply, it is impossible to hire an outsider to design an experiment within the context of a given experimental system. Designing an experiment according to the state of the art requires an intimate contextual knowledge from within. Karl Popper famously depicted the experimenter, with reference to Hermann Weyl, as follows: 'The experimenter tries to design the assay in such a way that it becomes "as

---

11 Gaston Bachelard, *Les intuitions atomistiques: Essai de classification* (Paris: Boivin, 1933), 140, (italics in the original).
12 See Hans-Jörg Rheinberger, *An Epistemology of the Concrete: Histories of Twentieth Century Biology* (Durham, NC: Duke University Press, 2010), ch. 11.
13 Rheinberger, *Epistemology of the Concrete* (see note 12), ch. 11.
14 For the concept of affordance, see James J. Gibson, *The Ecological Approach to Visual Perception* (Boston: Houghton Mifflin, 1979), ch. 8.

sensitive as possible" toward one and only one question.'[15] However, designing a good research experiment means more than that. It requires framing an experiment in such a way as to help answer a question that one can ask—the focus of Popper—but at the same time with the potential to generate questions that could not yet be asked. The clever design of an experiment tries to keep this possibility open. But here, design strikes also its limit.

In *Toward a History of Epistemic Things*, I formulated a few general rules or principles in which such experimental awareness finds its expression.[16] Among them are, first, a 'symmetry principle' which pertains to the arrangement of experimental controls to be built into the experiment. The second is a 'homogeneity principle' which states that the materials used need to be of a comparable quality in successive experiments. The third, an 'exhaustion principle', postulates that as many options that an experiment leaves for combining things should be tried as possible. The basic reason for observing all these rules is the processuality of experimentation as an ongoing activity. Popper's fantasy of a single experiment as a test instance with an ideally yes or no answer has been replaced by the notion of a stream of experimentation. It is an essential feature of research experimentation that it occurs in temporal series of experimental acts—another expression for experimental systems.

To conclude

Taken together, aspects of experimentation that lend themselves to design are biased towards the technical side of experimental systems: instrumentation, the interface between instruments and epistemic objects, and the configuration of the experimental context. At its core, however, there resides an unruly thing, the epistemic thing, which defies design. The tension between these two poles, the designable and the undesignable, grants experimentation its peculiar rationality—a rationality that is not to be captured by a logic of anticipation.

This rich field for reflection has been fathomed for understanding neither the sciences nor other areas of human knowledge production. In particular, it might leave room for discussing the problematic relations between the sciences and the arts. We have barely begun to explore the realm of an intersection between these two areas of human activity which, in their similarities and their dissimilarities, in their congruences and their incongruities, aim to produce unprecedented things.

---

15 Karl Popper, *Logik der Forschung: Zur Erkenntnistheorie der modernen Naturwissenschaft*, 6th ed. (Tübingen: J. C. B. Mohr (Paul Siebeck), 1971 [1935]), 72; Hermann Weyl, *Philosophie der Mathematik und Naturwissenschaft* (Darmstadt: Wissenschaftliche Buchgesellschaft, 1976 [1927]).

16 Hans-Jörg Rheinberger, *Toward a History of Epistemic Things: Synthesizing Proteins in the Test Tube* (Stanford: Stanford University Press, 1997), 78.

Contemporary Studio Teaching in Europe: Towards a Theoretical Framework[1]

Since the Bologna Declaration of 1999, architecture schools in Europe have been undergoing far-reaching changes to establish architectural education as an academic discipline—that is, one based upon research.[2] This academization has brought the relationship between theory and practice under pressure and caused tensions and emotional stress within architecture schools, not least in relation to the design studio—the backbone of architectural education.[3] Resting on practice-based knowledge, studio teaching has struggled to fit into the Bologna scheme, which implies a natural-science perspective of research and its relation to teaching.

In this context, an increased interest in architectural design as a research practice has motivated new scholarship, connected to a turn to materiality and practice in literature on knowledge production.[4] These studies focus on the concrete proceedings, transactions, and instructions by which knowledge is produced in the form of material artefacts, insisting on material agency and contributing a vocabulary that challenges perceptions of studio education as a form of acculturation.[5]

Literature has now linked research to studio teaching but lacks specificity in descriptions of variations in the nature and use of socio-material references between different studios and perceptions of good practice. In particular, the literature fails to consider potential connections between micro-studies of the concrete research practices in design studios[6] and the more macro-scale historical and contemporary studies of institutional traditions.[7] Taking a step to bridge this gap, I suggest several relational and ideal-type philosophical positions underpinning research-based teaching in studios in varying national and institutional contexts. Identifying these positions, I develop a theoretical framework based on an ongoing synthesis of data from fieldwork in design studios in four European architecture schools with philosophy of science perspectives. I apply this framework to the fieldwork data to describe the methods used in student projects for redeveloping Køge Harbour near Copenhagen, densifying Anneberg Park on the Danish island of Zealand, constructing a new tower for Notre Dame in Paris after the fire in 2019, and regenerating parts of the Klybeck district of Basel.

1 Kim Helmersen is a doctoral researcher at the Institute for the History and Theory of Architecture (gta) at the Department of Architecture, ETH Zurich.
2 Joan Ockman, *Architecture School: Three Centuries of Educating Architects in North America* (Boston: MIT Press, 2012).
3 Johan De Walsche, 'Genus, Locus, Nexus: An Inquiry into the Nature of Research in Architectural Design Education' (PhD diss., University of Antwerp, 2018); Monika Kurath, 'Architecture as a Science: Boundary Work and the Demarcation of Design Knowledge from Research', *Science & Technology Studies* 28, no. 3 (2015).
4 Jörg Potthast, *'Sollen wir mal ein Hochhaus bauen?' Das Architekturbüro als Labor der Stadt* (Berlin: Wissenschaftszentrum Berlin, 1998); Albena Yaneva, 'Scaling Up and Down: Extraction Trials in Architectural Design', *Social Studies of Science* 35, no. 6 (2005), 867–94; Monika Kurath and Priska Gisler, 'Architecture, design et arts visuels: Les transformations des disciplines après la Réforme de Bologne', in Adriana Gorga and Jean-Philippe Leresche, eds., *Disciplines académiques en transformation: Entre innovation et résistance* (Paris: Editions des Archives Contemporaines, 2015), 165–79; Kurath, 'Architecture as a Science' (see note 3); De Walsche, 'Genus, Locus, Nexus' (see note 3).
5 Helena Webster, 'The Architectural Review: A Study of Ritual, Acculturation and Reproduction in Architectural Education', *Arts and Humanities in Higher Education* 4 (2005), 265–82.
6 Donald Schön, *The Design Studio: An Exploration of Its Traditions and Potentials* (Portland: RIBA, 1985); Kurath, 'Architecture as a Science' (see note 3); De Walsche, 'Genus, Locus, Nexus' (see note 3).
7 Ockman, *Architecture School* (see note 2).

Part Three · Design as Research

Design studios as research cultures

What is style? This question was the topic of a panel debate gathering architecture teachers and students at the Royal Academy of Fine Arts in Copenhagen in November 2017. The question of style in relation to architecture is provocative since architectural design is typically considered to rely on intuition, ideas, ideology, and individual personalities.[8] Making knowledge by architectural design, it has been argued, has a specific rather than general integrity, as it manifests in the specific relation between the researcher and the phenomenon of study.[9] In this way, a unified epistemic culture of architecture has been identified in opposition to the natural sciences. This culture has been characterized by subjective reasoning and singularity,[10] reflection in action,[11] personal epistemology, context dependency, and situated and tacit knowledge.[12]

When asserting architecture's status as an academic research discipline with reference to the radical specificity characteristic of its epistemic culture, the question of style potentially challenges its research base: if the different knowledge products in a studio look the same even to an architecture professor, how can the individual projects then assert their research recognition with reference to novelty, specificity, singularity, and subjectivity?

In this regard, a lecturer at the panel in Copenhagen presented some images comparing student projects from two schools in the United Kingdom and the United States, arguing that design projects tend to carry a style typical of the specific studio's teaching and its institutional context. The identification of such architectural styles potentially points to studios' reproductive mechanisms and activities. However, to explain similarity and variation between the designs as knowledge products, one must enquire about the knowledge-making from within the space of production—for example, in the design studio.[13] Much research has investigated knowledge production in design studios,[14] but these studies did not reflect further on the question of reproduction and the relation to the institutional context.[15] In other words, while previous research investigated individual cases, it did not compare multiple cases as part of a single research study. What is needed is a further exploration of the entanglement of the research teaching practices in the design studio with the wider networks of knowledge that inform the values and justifications of the teaching aims and the knowledge directing the use of a specific methodological tool or set of tools.

I build this argument on the basic assumption that the activities in the design studio can be viewed as research-based and that they assert academic standards (from the epistemic point of view of architecture). This assumption relies on recent scholarship on design studios as research cultures, tracing back to a number of laboratory studies regarding the social construction of scientific facts.[16] The

---

8 Kurath, 'Architecture as a Science' (see note 3).
9 De Walsche, 'Genus, Locus, Nexus' (see note 3).
10 Kurath, 'Architecture as a Science' (see note 3).
11 De Walsche, 'Genus, Locus, Nexus' (see note 3).
12 Karin Knorr Cetina, *Epistemic Cultures: How the Sciences Make Knowledge* (Cambridge, MA: Harvard University Press, 1999).
13 Schön, *Design Studio* (see note 6); Donald Schön, *The Reflective Practitioner: How Professionals Think in Action* (New York: Basic Books, 1983), 42; Yaneva, 'Scaling Up and Down' (see note 4); Kurath, 'Architecture as a Science' (see note 3); De Walsche, 'Genus, Locus, Nexus' (see note 3).
14 Bruno Latour and Steve Woolgar, *Laboratory Life: The Construction of Scientific Facts* (Beverly Hills: Sage, 1979); Karin Knorr Cetina, *The Manufacture of Knowledge: An Essay on the Constructivist and Contextual Nature of Science* (Oxford: Pergamon Press, 1981).
15 For example, Schön's description of a master-apprenticeship design teaching situation did not consider the context of the teaching, the character and network of the socio-material references, nor teaching in different design studios. Schön, *Reflective Practitioner* (see note 13).
16 Michael Callon, 'Le travail de la conception en architecture', *Situations Les Cahiers de la recherché architecturale* 37 (1996), 25–35; Potthast, 'Sollen wir mal ein Hochhaus bauen?' (see note 4); (cont. on p. 147)

methodological approach of these laboratory studies was later transferred to studies of architecture, its working practices, and its ways of producing knowledge.[17] These studies had a strong influence on recent studies of design (research) teaching activities in architecture schools. It was Johan De Walsche who finally connected research to studio teaching, but he built his argument on Monika Kurath's application of Karin Knorr Cetina's constructionist framework for studies of epistemic cultures to the field of architecture.[18] Kurath argued that architecture forms a distinctive epistemic culture different to those of the science disciplines. With this argument it was possible to understand and describe research in architecture in its own terms and thus identify a research base in the teaching of architectural design.

De Walsche found that the label 'research-based' inaccurately describes how research and teaching are entangled in the context of studio education. Rather than the unidirectional relation implied by the notion of being research-based, a research-teaching nexus can be found in the reciprocal process of learning in the design studio: the design object is shaped and worked on by both student and teacher together in a collaboration characterized by equity and mutual agency.[19] In this way, research not only informs teaching but also can be generated through teaching situations. It is an outcome of teaching rather than an input. In continuation of this argument, a study of a research-teaching nexus in architecture does not just enquire about the relation between department research and teaching but also about the research potential of the material knowledge produced in teaching situations in the design studios and the rationalities guiding these epistemic practices. However, I question the belief that teaching practices should per se be characterized by such openness to the design object and equity in the learning process.[20] The presence of architectural styles in studio education challenges us to question the teaching process that guides the objects in their making. Could it be that the knowledge inhabiting these teaching practices has a formative or even reproductive influence on the making of these objects? And could it be that certain epistemic communities inform this knowledge? If that is the case, would it be unfair to assume considerable variance in regard to the ways of knowledge-making across different epistemic contexts?

Contexts of studio teaching

It is noteworthy that architectural design is currently being taught within institutional contexts as different as technical universities, research universities, universities of applied arts and applied sciences, art academies, and independent architecture schools—all leading to the same professional degree. In this regard, Joan Ockman argues that architecture's syncretic nature is what most distinguishes architectural education.[21] She describes how the development of architectural education has been defined largely by three traditions: the polytechnic tradition, with its particular scientific focus; the Beaux-Arts tradition, with an emphasis

---

(cont. from p. 145) Peter Galison and Emily Thompson, *The Architecture of Science* (Cambridge, MA: MIT Press, 1999); Bettina Heintz, Martina Merz, and Christina Schumacher, *Wissenschaft, die Grenzen schafft: Geschlechterkonstellationen im disziplinären Vergleich* (Bielefeld: transcript, 2004); Albena Yaneva and Simon Guy, 'Understanding Architecture, Accounting Society: A Dialogue of Architectural Studies and Science and Technology Studies', *Science Studies* 21, no. 1 (2008), 3–7; Ignacio Farias and Alex Wilkie, *Studio Studies: Operations, Topologies & Displacements* (London: Routledge, 2015).
17 De Walsche, 'Genus, Locus, Nexus' (see note 3).
18 De Walsche, 'Genus, Locus, Nexus' (see note 3); Kurath, 'Architecture as a Science' (see note 3); Cetina, *Epistemic Cultures* (see note 12).
19 Inger Eriksson and Viveca Lindberg, 'Enriching "Learning Activity" with "Epistemic Practices": Enhancing Students' Epistemic Agency and Authority', *Nordic Journal of Studies in Educational Policy* 1 (2016), 7.
20 Ockman, *Architecture School* (see note 2), 6.
21 Eriksson and Lindberg, 'Enriching "Learning Activity"' (see note 19), 7.

on artistic creativity; and vocational education, with an attention to craftsmanship.

Since Ockman's categories reflect historical traditions of education rather than philosophical positions which can inform concrete teaching practices in the design studios, the categories of Beaux-Arts and polytechnical need further elaboration to work as analytical categories for investigating teaching in design studios. In addition, it is important to acknowledge that historical teaching traditions might have changed. The traditional Beaux-Arts education was generally characterized by a master-apprentice pedagogical approach and a use of reproduction, where the studio master had a clear vision of the trajectories of students' projects. In comparison, architecture teaching in contemporary art academies seems to operate more in line with Knorr Cetina's concept of epistemic practices, where neither the teacher nor the students can say in advance what learning, in a narrow sense, should be accomplished.[22] As a consequence, the epistemology would have changed from one where the individual human mind was the source of knowledge-making to one where the students, the teachers, and the design objects co-create knowledge. Rather than the kind of subjectivism that could be ascribed to Beaux-Arts education, perhaps the research in a contemporary art school could be better described as underpinned by a form of constructivism.

Figure i suggests ideal-type positions in contemporary design education as a conceptual framework to provide a context and starting point for further and more detailed observations. The figure reflects an intermediate stage of an ongoing analysis of fieldwork data through a philosophy of science perspective. The vertical axis refers to different philosophical positions,[23] and the horizontal axis refers to the orientation of the institution as focusing on applied research or on developing new research.[24] The vertical axis of philosophical positions is differentiated with regard to the character of (and relation to) the problem in the making of knowledge, spanning from constructivism to phenomenology to positivism as three ideal ways of coming to know about a particular problem or phenomenon. As an ideal type, the positivist researcher takes on problems which can be approached through expert knowledge, and the research often relates to fields of expertise which rely on research methods of hard science disciplines, such as building construction and engineering. Such problems are typically concrete rather than abstract. The positivist study thus employs more general and exact methods, and design decisions are underpinned by exact knowledge obtained in preliminary studies of the problem's 'objective features' before bringing this knowledge to the studio, where it is played with.

In contrast, the constructivist researcher takes on the kinds of problems which are abstract at the outset and require material translation. The researcher approaches the phenomenon by constructing it in a process that heavily relies on the researcher's own practical knowledge and ability

i Philosophical positions and institutional context

Philosophical position	Insitutional orientation	
	Problem-solving (Application)	Problem-framing (Development)
Constructivism	● ● ● ● ● ●	● ● ● ● ● ● ● ● ● ● ● ● ● ● ● ● ● ●
Phenomenology	● ● ● ● ● ● ● ● ●	● ● ● ● ● ● ●
Positivism	● ● ● ● ● ● ● ● ● ● ● ● ●	● ● ●

22 Monica Ponce Leon, 'Research, Practice, and the Making of Architecture', *Technology | Architecture + Design* 4, no. 1 (2020), 5–8; Ockman, *Architecture School* (see note 2).
23 Marijn van de Weijer, Koenraad Van Cleempoel, and Hilde Heynen, 'Positioning Research and Design in Academia and Practice: A Contribution to a Continuing Debate', *Design Issues* 30, no. 2 (2014), 17–29.
24 De Walsche, 'Genus, Locus, Nexus' (see note 3).

to engage with the unfamiliar through trials of experimentation in the studio, framing and reframing the phenomenon as it is coming into being. Thus, the constructivist research tends to follow a hunch rather than relate to an existing or established field of knowledge or methods, and the process is highlighted by unforeseeable 'events' where the objects 'talk back' to the researcher, who is ideally more guided by the objects than vice versa.

In between the positivist and constructivist positions, phenomenology here refers to activities which move back and forth between the two extremes as the researcher tries to connect with the object through experience. Like the positivist approach, the problem in phenomenological research tends to be concrete rather than abstract. The problem often relates to a specific site, and the research departs from both exact and experience-based registrations of the site and its context to dig out something essential about the specific place. While these preliminary studies carry an exact component, they are abstract in comparison to the positivist approach in the sense that the sought-after 'essence' is not available in any concrete form. Like the concept of atmosphere, which has been particularly resourceful for phenomenological research, this 'essence' is indeterminate in regard to its ontological status. It can be described as a kind of omnipresence which is impossible to assign to the place from which it proceeds or to the subjects who experience it.[25]

The three ideal-type approaches relate to knowledge and ways of coming to know about a phenomenon of study, but also to ways of learning in architectural design education. The categories operate not as absolutes, and elements from each of them could occur within a semester project as well as in multiple research applications: as problem-solving and problem-framing. This also means that constructivism in this context does not refer to a more active form of learning than phenomenology and positivism. The categories refer to philosophical underpinnings of the learning and research environment, not to full-blown pedagogical approaches.

With regards to the horizontal axis, I am aware of the difficulties in trying to relate practical applications of research teaching to institutional context. Studios and institutions sometimes relate in decentralized ways, with studios operating more as satellites which can have more in common with studios in other institutions, in other countries, than the one next door or down the hallway. In addition, demarcations between applied and fine arts in architectural education have become more blurred as political reforms have streamlined education and design practice has gained research status. Owing in large part to literature on practice and materiality in knowledge production, design practice has been identified as a knowing-in-action and reflection-in-action, which connects skills to knowledge through practice and thus to research. At the same time, craft has been depicted as an idea[26] and craftsmanship as a knowledge-constructive form of engagement with materials akin to the way I described constructivist research.[27] As a result of these developments, institutional identities in architectural education have shifted and their borders of definition become opaquer. By and large, with the exception of art academies and a small number of independent architecture schools, architectural education has now been adopted by universities of various profiles. In practice the activities of these universities overlap, and while in the German-speaking part of Europe the distinction between *Fachhochschule* (universities of applied arts and sciences) and *Universitäten* (universities) is still clear on a symbolic level (and, to an extent, on a policy level), in other parts of Europe distinctions are less clear. Thus, I argue that the distinction

---

25 Gernot Böhme, 'Atmosphere as a Fundamental Concept of a New Aesthetics', *Thesis Eleven* 36 (1993), 113–16, here 114.
26 Glenn Adamson, *Thinking through Craft* (Oxford: Berg Publishers, 2007).
27 Tim Ingold, *Making: Anthropology, Archaeology, Art and Architecture* (Oxford: Routledge, 2013); Richard Sennett, *The Craftsman* (New Haven: Yale University Press, 2008).

between applied research applications and developmental research applications refers to a distinction between design-as-process and design-as-product: to a difference in focus and aim rather than the ontology of the practice. For this reason, I differentiate between the focus of the research as problem-framing and problem-solving.

The influence of philosophical position on the design process

In what follows, I suggest how the design process might be influenced by wider networks of knowledge, potentially linking the macro-perspective with the micro-perspective. In doing this, I draw on De Walsche's reading of Martin Heidegger, whereby De Walsche describes the way in which a researcher tries to open up a specific phenomenon of study by responding to it.[28] The core of this established relationship between the research and the phenomenon of study is referred to by Heidegger as the *Bindung* (the bind/binding): 'The nature of the established relationship—*Bindung*—with the piece of the world under study—*Gegenstandsbezirk*—is determinative for the nature of knowing. One can also state that the nature of phenomena dictates the *Bindung*, and thus determines the type of relationship that is established. Consequently, it dictates how and in which terms research will be conducted.'[29]

Rigour is found in the *Bindung* and is a matter of the research coherently responding to the features of the constitutive elements of the specific phenomenon of study. Rigour thus refers to coherence between the features of the phenomenon of study and the framework that is built to open it up. Rigorous research means that this coherence is acknowledged and respected. Rigour thus is a form of ideal type whose role in research could be comparable to the role of the solution to a mathematical problem; the answer is given but the journey is not. When the nature of the research responds coherently with the nature of the phenomenon studied in the research, then that research is rigorous. This does not mean that there is only one way for research to become rigorous, since most phenomena are complex and multifaceted.

De Walsche argues that research in Heideggerian terms 'is not to be understood from methodological ground, but primarily from ontological ground'.[30] I agree with this reading but argue that the process of responding coherently with the features of the constitutive elements of the specific phenomenon of study is indeed a methodological issue. This is because the selection of methodological tools, by which the researcher constructs *Bindung* in relation to the phenomenon of study, is key to the strength of the *Bindung*, which I refer to as the guiding design principle.

The design principle for a specific project is constructed through the application of selected methodological tools which have been applied to open a specific phenomenon of study. The selection of methodological tools often relates to the philosophical position of the researcher, but not directly. It is more of an indirect influence, operating from the background. Methodological choice often follows an intuitive or implicit rather than explicit logic, with the methods engaged in ad hoc manner. For this reason, the influencing philosophical position is often tacit and therefore not immediately available for enquiry—not even by the architect, who often draws on embodied ways of knowing. I suggest, however, that observations of discussions of design proposals and their rigour during design reviews can help bring the teaching aims, their values, and justifications to the surface.

A design principle (such as a phenomenological site description or the construction of a new material), thus, is the specific result of the methodological activities put in action to open up the phenomenon of study. The design principle, in general terms, is a construct that focuses the design process, and its character and relation to the design project can vary. The construction of the design principle

---

28 De Walsche, 'Genus, Locus, Nexus' (see note 3), 92–6; Martin Heidegger, *Off the Beaten Track* (Cambridge: Cambridge University Press, 2002).
29 Heidegger, *Off the Beaten Track* (see note 28), 98.
30 Heidegger, *Off the Beaten Track* (see note 28), 98.

involves a process of continuous experimentation, with the aim that the employed methodological tools respond coherently to the nature of the phenomenon of study. As an ideal type, this is achieved with a design principle that merges the (analytically separated) ontology of the phenomenon of study and the research method.

The making of the design principle is not entirely individual, since the researcher draws on a knowledge, which is informed—directly or indirectly—by wider networks of knowledge. Returning to a previous argument, I suggest that an identification of distinctive architectural styles could be due to a relative coherence in philosophical positions, leading to a relative consistency in the composition of design principles. This does not mean that singularity and novelty cannot exist; it rather points to how design research might be informed by wider networks of knowledge and locates a potential source of reproduction that may explain in part why architectural styles occur in studio teaching.

Three distinctive philosophical positions emerged during my fieldwork research on studio teaching at four European architecture schools. The argument is that these approaches differ with regard to their ontological and epistemological orientation and the methodological activities that follow from this orientation. I describe the approaches as methods, since I observed them in their applied form in the design studio: concretized, materialized, and contextualized in relation to the phenomenon of study. In other words, they presented themselves as methods, their philosophical underpinnings more quietly operating in the background.

Constructivist method: redeveloping Køge Harbour through the lens of negotiation and change

During my fieldwork at the Royal Danish Academy of Fine Arts from 2017 to 2018, I followed a research-oriented urban design studio, which was going to raise, frame, and concretize problems to provide a possible point of departure for the bachelor's degree project studio. The studio found its departure point with the concept of negotiation and the redevelopment of a harbour area in the town of Køge, south of Copenhagen, and the problem field was further inspired by the concept of assemblages.[31] However, the urban design studio did not depart from any explicit theoretical or methodological position, instead establishing the studio as a form of experimentation with the concept of negotiation by design.[32]

The concept of negotiation became an entry point into the understanding of the urban site as a field of negotiation, raising the question of how this field could be simultaneously explored and constructed through design. In constructing the site as a negotiation field, four major impact factors on the site were introduced as selected and defined by the teachers: wasteland, transformation, flood, and heavy industry.[33] Students were divided into four groups, each of which dealt with one influencing factor. In this way, each factor was explored, mapped out, and represented in the harbour area, which led to the collective creation of one overarching model of a potential urban structure. The four different impact factors each operated in specific ways, and it was the first task of students to investigate the behaviour of these factors before trying to translate them into operative architectural typologies.

Based on these on-site studies, students built several models as instruments that represented the character of each of the four impact factors and the ways in which they shape space. Essentially, the students realized that to understand the concept of negotiation from a material point of view, by design, one must democratize the negotiation process to include non-human actors. The question was: how can non-human actors be included in the negotiation process?

---

31 Jane Bennett, *Vibrant Matter: A Political Ecology of Things* (Durham: Duke University Press, 2010).
32 Alberte Winther, Aniella Goldinger, Andrea Ougaard, and Kristin Vaagslid, *Om at udvikle by: 5. semester: Forhandlingens konstruktion* (Copenhagen: KADK, 2018).
33 Winther et al., *Om at udvikle* (see note 32).

At this point, the students took matters into their own hands and decided to deviate from the original direction of the brief and design the field of negotiation as a board game, thus rewriting the assignment in collaboration with the design teachers. Building a board game as a design research instrument became the answer, activating the identified impact factors as players in the negotiation of the future of the urban site and introducing the factor of chance. Besides structuring the negotiation process, students found that developing the board game could be a productive way of working with the concept of negotiation. The board game thus became the guiding principle for the urban design research itself.

Although it was not initially the idea that the studio should unfold as a board game, that development brought the investigation closer to its problem field than the teachers initially thought possible. As the concept of negotiation was explored through negotiations the students realized that chance plays an important role in urban construction in addition to negotiation, and that the invention of a board game to operationalize and mobilize the impact factors as active players in the negotiation was a better way of approaching the phenomenon being studied. To the principal teacher, the most thrilling part of this discovery was not the competency of the board game as a design research instrument but the simple fact that it was invented by the students themselves in negotiation with the teachers in a studio that was investigating negotiation: 'It was more this didactical process that the students bring a suggestion, which then becomes the project. That is what I think has been the important and the successful thing with it—that it was on their own terms; that they developed this game, by being in these different teams. In a future project you could then ask, which kind of game? This round was about imaging urban development as a board game with material players.'

Thus, from a methodological point of view, the important lesson was how the brief, which was about negotiations, turned into a negotiation itself involving both teachers and students. In other words, the phenomenon of study—negotiation—translated into a method helping to open up knowledge about its own constitutive elements. In this way, the method changed along the way, starting with a teacher's hunch, before gradually developing into a specific method. As the teacher argued, 'this is also what I encourage the students to do: when they work with other types of projects, their method mirrors [the phenomenon] they investigate. ... on a simple, practical level.'

In this way, the design principle was the board game, but what was the philosophical position underpinning the method? I argue that the method encountered in this studio can be described as constructivist in that it changes along with the changing of the phenomenon of study through the design process. Hence, knowledge is performative and rigour is found in an immersion into the connection between the researcher and the phenomenon of study since this phenomenon is fluctuating and constructed, emerging from that specific connection. A form of method can thus be identified with a responsiveness to the emerging and transforming constitutive elements of the phenomenon of study, and this responsiveness relies on an aesthetic attentiveness and materialization. The research thus reflects an approach akin to constructivism. The values and justifications informing the aim of the study (to open the concept of negotiation by design) and the exercised method follow the idea of knowledge as a construct made by the design researcher.

Phenomenological method: densifying Anneberg Park

What is it about our physical surroundings which holds a presence? This question was raised by a professor at the Royal Danish Academy of Fine Arts during a student review I followed during my fieldwork at the school from October 2017 to June 2018. It became a key question at the review, which was held after one month of on-site registration, with drawings and rich descriptions of the private experience of the architecture. The review marked the end of the first of three phases dividing the semester.

This first phase, referred to as the *blik* (gaze), consisted of a phenomenological registration, measurement workshop, and historical and technical analysis of Anneberg Park, the project site. Anneberg Park is a mental institution by architect Kristoffer Varming, built between 1913 and 1921 and located on the island of Zealand, Denmark. The programme of the brief was to densify the Anneberg Park by making residential homes: row houses, social housing, and multiple-family homes. This new architecture was to communicate with the existing tradition without blindly following its pattern—an objective made viable by the knowledge acquired during the initial research phase, summed up in the brief: 'Through studies of the existing settlement's materials and use, we will develop an understanding of the logic, structure and organization of the settlement. The idea is to acquire an understanding of the modus operandi of the place, and thereby be able to extend the settlement in/with its specificity and distinctiveness, not as copying of style, but as a way of thinking and building; a way of assembling materials and spaces.'[34]

At the review, a student had just finished reading his phenomenological descriptive text aloud to the audience. The text formed part of the phenomenological registration of Anneberg Park, which would form the basis for the extension of the settlement. Besides the text, the phenomenological registration consisted of an imaging of the sensory qualities of Anneberg Park, including proportions, geometry, material qualities, light and shade, spatial atmospheres, colours, and an album with drawings and photos. Altogether, these on-site observations, bound to the phenomenon of study, were put together on three A2 sheets, catching a specific gaze. The gaze (*blik*) was meant as a guiding principle for the students for the rest of the project.[35]

It was clear that the focus of this research project was on the relation between the student and Anneberg Park, the subject and the object, and that the core of the exercise was to give the student the chance to extract phenomenological knowledge from that concrete object to use as a design principle. In this way, the teachers provided the students with more guidance than was the case with the board game study. This approach to teaching reflects an open and conscious strategy of the studio to provide students with some clearer guidelines. It is the idea that when a project has gone through the phenomenological exercises, then a certain understanding of the architectural qualities of the building site would have been achieved, along with the ability to communicate this understanding through assorted visual materials.

Unlike the previous case, the research approach of this studio started with an analysis of a physical object: a piece of architecture. In this way, the design decisions were not based entirely on subjective reasoning but were, to an extent, bound to the physical site and an exact as well as experience-based site analysis. Or to phrase it differently: design decisions built on a dialectical subject-object knowledge base.

Methodologically, at the core of the studio's approach is the 'lived experience': a sensitive, bodily understanding of the world, which we unconsciously use when we experience a work of architecture. Nicolai Bo Andersen takes Steen Eiler Rasmussen's experience-oriented approach to architecture as departure point for describing a '"methodological outline" for architectural investigation, description and design.'[36] This outline is further based on a phenomenology of practice as described by Max van Manen[37] and writing

34 Nicolai Bo Andersen et al., 'Transformation og restaurering 2, BYMÆSSIG FORTÆTNING', *Transformation/2017* (Copenhagen: Vester kopi, 2017).
35 Bo Andersen et al., 'Transformation og restaurering' (see note 34).
36 Steen Eiler Rasmussen, *Om at Opleve Arkitektur/How to Experience Architecture* (Copenhagen: Architegn, 1957).
37 Max Van Manen, 'Practicing Phenomenological Writing', *Phenomenology + Pedagogy* 2, no. 1 (1984), 36–69.

exercises developed by Finn Thorbjørn Hansen,[38] arguing for an architectural phenomenological description as the departure point for architectural design.[39] It was partly such descriptions that formed the basis for the architectural design projects encountered in Copenhagen—when a description was well written, it encapsulated and effectively communicated that sense of presence described by the professor during the review.

In this way, the design principle was the gaze (*blik*) presented at the student review, which was the result of the students' individual work employing the phenomenological methodological tools in relation to the specific phenomenon of study, Anneberg Park. The gaze should give the student a tangible sense of the specific awareness that was derived through the study of Anneberg Park and particularly the relation between the student and the site. The phenomenological description of the atmospheric qualities of that specific relation is what the student tries to translate in the design, and the text operates as a guiding companion, an anchor point, throughout the process of designing.

The phenomenological method describes the totality of the methodological activities described above developed with reference to a phenomenological theory of knowledge. Rigour in the phenomenological method is found in the student's ability to encapsulate the experience of the phenomenon of study and rearticulate this experience in visual material. This phenomenon, however, is not fully contingent and constructed as in the case of the constructivist method. The subjective phenomenological experience—the connection—is bound to a somewhat stable material object, whose constitutive features can be investigated in more exact ways. The desired knowledge is thus found somewhere between the subjective and the objective.

Positivist method: a new tower for Notre Dame

During my fieldwork at Delft University of Technology in the spring semester of 2019, I followed the teaching of a studio course for fourth- and fifth-year students. In the course, students had been working with the task of constructing a new tower for Notre Dame in Paris after the existing tower burned down on 15 April 2019. It was the day of the final reviews. One by one, the students guided the audience through their projects, explaining the central elements and how they came to the design proposal. I noted a remarkable level of precision in regard to technological viability, and thus demand for in-depth knowledge of building construction. Another observation was the absence of references to cultural and atmospheric qualities of the site as well as to art and architecture history and theory in the reasoning of the design.

These impressions of presence and absence of different types of architectural reference points came together in an exemplary episode, where an invited guest critic was questioning the proportionality of one of the design proposals. The student had rigorously guided the audience through the construction of the ornament (the tower), explaining its construction, materiality, movement flow, and functional urban qualities as a landmark. The student explained how a steel framework would give shape to the structure of the design, with the horizontal elements creating stability to the structure. However, the student mentioned little about the phenomenological qualities of the design or its qualities as an extension to a site-specific, religious, cultural, and historical narrative. The guest critic found that there was a disproportionality between the ornament (the steel construction) and a cross placed on top of the ornament. To the guest critic, the cross failed to connect to the design of the ornament in a way other than through its sheer religious

38 Finn Thorbjørn Hansen, 'Det personlige essay som en filosofisk praksis', *Skriftsserie for Barnevernets utviklingssenter i Nord-Norge* 3 (2007).
39 Nicolai Bo Andersen, 'Phenomenological Method: Towards an Approach to Architectural Investigation, Description and Design', *Formation: Architectural Education in a Nordic Perspective* (2018), 74–95, here 75.

symbolism, and the critic questioned if it was simply added because it had to be. Since this critique was based on an immediate, emotional response to the aesthetic qualities of the design, rather than analysis, the guest critic spoke in apologetic terms about his argumentation. In combination with the focus of the design on the material construction, this humility of using one's feelings and intuition as a source of knowledge for a critical response told me that I was encountering yet a different studio approach. With the constructivist method I experienced in Copenhagen, the focus of the design and its presentation would likely have been on the feelings that the design evokes and how the story relates to the historic, cultural, and religious narrative of the site, but only little attention would have been given to the viability and feasibility of the construction. Altogether, there was a strong focus on precision and attention to technological performance, and thus demand for knowledge of building construction, but there was less emphasis placed on the atmospheric qualities of the materiality and design in relation to the physical and historical context.

The approach encountered in Delft for the new tower of Notre Dame differs from the phenomenological method used for Anneberg Park and the constructivist method identified with the board game for Køge Harbour in terms of the nature of the problem field, the material and technical objects, and the use of references. The representation of design proposals seemed to be oriented more towards communicating the viability and feasibility of the construction than the material-atmospheric qualities. While the site-context of Notre Dame was indeed taken into consideration, it was not the main reference for the design, which also did not respond to an abstract concept like the board game did with the exploration of negotiation and chance in relation to Køge Harbour. Rather, the form features of the design pointed inward to the construction of the design object itself, and to its capacities and innovation in regard to building construction and technical performance. Underpinning the methodological choices of the studio, I argue, another philosophical position can be traced. Relying on research methods more akin to those of positivism, the discipline of building construction refers to more concrete and exact forms of knowledge, and investigations into the 'objective' world.[40] The representation seemed simultaneously closer (technologically) and farther (phenomenologically) from the material. The specific design principle for the tower of Notre Dame was the construction of the steel framework. The selection of methodological tools was underpinned by a more positivist philosophical position. The process of making the design principle required exact methods to extract exact knowledge about the phenomenon of study.

Multiple positions: assessing a regeneration of the Klybeck district

All design teaching is constructivist in the sense that, in studio education, learners are actively involved in a process of meaning and knowledge construction as opposed to passively receiving information. However, the defining factor for this differentiation of design teaching into varying approaches lies with the ontologies encountered in the various studios, the phenomena of study taken on, how the students are taught to 'come to know' about these phenomena, and by which means. In this last example, two of the described approaches came together during a final review at ETH Zurich. A student presented her project: a nondescript, large, floor-plated labyrinthine laboratory building repurposed as part of the regeneration of the new Klybeck district of Basel. The student had deconstructed and reconstructed the existing building by removing its heavy cores, instead adding a lightweight timber structure as counterpoint to the remaining concrete wings to provide the building's new circulation system. The design intervention required solving a major building construction issue.

---

40 Ponce Leon, 'Research, Practice' (see note 22).

The project's core qualities were its sustainable use, reuse, and phenomenological awareness of materials. These qualities were communicated through a series of precise technical drawings, which were debated during the review. While jury members praised the project's sustainable solution, innovative construction design, sensibility to material compatibility, and spatial flow, one jury from another studio argued that the translation of the phenomenological qualities actually achieved by the design did not come across as well in the drawings. They were exceptional as technical drawings but lacked some of the atmospheric qualities achieved by the spatio-material composition. This review evoked critiques of the study of Anneberg Park, in particular the strong focus on (hand) drawings and working with colour, materiality, and proportion.

In this way, two of the three approaches were represented during the course of one critique, exemplifying how a successful project would often work with multiple approaches simultaneously and excel in bringing them together. At the same time, it also showed how studios tend to operate predominantly along the lines of one of these approaches, with other approaches falling more into the background. The design principle for the Klybeck project was the replacement of an existing building's heavy cores with a lightweight timber structure, but what was the method and its philosophical underpinning? I argue that a positivist method laid the ground for the innovative intervention, with a structural analysis of the existing building and a testing of material capacity and compatibility being examples of the activities included in this approach. The process of constructing the design principle required exact methods to extract exact knowledge about the phenomenon under study. In addition, emphasis was placed on the atmospheric qualities accomplished by the spatio-material composition, requiring a phenomenological enquiry of the materials—individually and in assembly. The main focus, however, was on the innovation in regard to construction, the reuse of materials and the project's viability and feasibility, and the representation directed towards precise communication of this accomplishment.

Positions in contemporary studio teaching

Comparing the three methods outlined, I argue that (at least) three philosophical positions on research can be identified across the landscape of contemporary architectural design education in Europe. Figure ii reflects an ongoing synthesizing of field data with theory and provides a conceptual framework for further empirical enquiry into architectural design teaching as research. Figure ii builds upon figure i, with an additional category—the manageability of problems—added to incorporate Donald Schön's distinction between high grounds and low lands: 'In the varied topography of professional practice, there is a high, hard ground which overlooks a swamp. On the high ground, manageable problems lend themselves to the use of research-based theory and technique. In the swampy lowlands, problems are messy and confusing and incapable of technical solution.'[41]

ii Research positions in contemporary architectural design education. The number of circles ● represents the manageability of problems.

Philosophical position	Institutional orientation	
	Problem-solving (Application)	Problem-framing (Development)
Constructivism	●●●● University of Applied Arts	● Contemporary Art School
Phenomenology		
Positivism	●●●●●●● University of Applied Sciences	●●●● Technical University

41 Schön, *Reflective Practitioner* (see note 13), 42.

The more a problem field requires the researcher to connect with it, blurring the boundaries between researcher and field, and the more it focuses on problem-framing, the more difficult that problem is to manage. Problems that are not easily manageable are typically abstract rather than concrete, and cannot be approached through existing methods and strategies. Conversely, the more a problem field requires the researcher to separate from it, demarcating boundaries between researcher and field, and the more it focuses on problem-solving, the more manageable it is. Highly manageable problems are typically concrete rather than abstract and can be approached with methods and strategies that already exist.

The manageability of problems relates to the philosophical position of the research in the sense that constructivist research tends to take on problems that are less easily manageable than does positivist research. Developing a physical board game to materially translate and concretize an abstract problem field about negotiation and chance was more a type of conceptual design research than the innovation to replace the heavy core of an existing building with a lightweight timber structure. The timber structure, on the other hand, required precise research-based knowledge and calculation. Both design principles, however, required preliminary research and aimed at developing rather than applying existing research. Thus, the manageability of problems also relates to the institutional orientation in the way that applied research tends to take on problems which have already been framed but need to be solved. Such problems are highly manageable since they have already been largely defined and relate to existing theory, which is instead in need of application leading to other forms of knowing and ways of 'coming to know'. Conversely, in institutions oriented towards developing research, problems are not easily manageable since they are still in need of framing. All the presented cases in this way were examples of problem-framing research activities, part of institutional settings oriented towards developing research. This means that the manageability of the problems taken on in the different cases could be differentiated from each other as highly manageable or not easily manageable solely along the axis of philosophical position. The orientation of institutional setting, and the aim of the research as problem-framing or problem-solving, thus was not affected since there were no considerable comparative differences in this regard. A future study of design studios in universities for applied arts and sciences and their philosophical underpinnings, as well as comparisons between these and design studios in technical universities and art academies, would contribute further to the discourse.

Together, the three axes present a continuum of ideal-type positions in contemporary studio education spanning from the contemporary art school on one end of the continuum to the applied science university on the other end. As an ideal type, the contemporary art school takes on problems which are not easily manageable, as they are in need of framing, are often abstract, and the research at such an institution aims at developing new forms of practice, methods and perspectives. These problem-framing activities and their methods are often underpinned by a constructivist approach which emphasizes the phenomenon under analysis by connecting with it, letting the phenomenon guide the methodological choice. In contrast, on the other end of the continuum the applied science university takes on problems which are highly manageable, as they have already been framed and instead need solutions. These problems are often more concrete, and the research aims at knowledge resulting from the application of existing research methods and theories, often underpinned by a positivist approach. This argument, however, remains hypothetical, since my research neither includes cases of teaching in applied arts and science faculties nor intends to explain identities of institutions. In the same way, the suggested positions of institutions are relational and contingent rather than absolute and stable. I have placed the columns of ideal type institutions symmetrically to underline their meaning as relational positions rather than absolutes or precise reflections of specific institutional profiles. Thus, the relational position they represent as theoretical constructs is more important than their labelling.[42] Generalization and extrapolation of findings into these ideal types is meant to encourage discussion and future research into the subject matter by providing a starting point for such an endeavour, not as a comprehensive view of types of contemporary institutional identities.

Finally, I would like to add that the comparison and differentiation across philosophical positions in regard to manageability of problems is not a reflection of the cases described as more or less academic in their scope. The exemplified projects were rigorous but each in their own way. The project encountered in Zurich, meant to solve a limited and concrete problem of updating an existing building complex for a sustainable future, was rigorous in regard to its phenomenon of study due to its precise and technical innovation. It paved the way for additional design decisions. In comparison, the Køge Harbour project in Copenhagen found its rigour in its ability to formulate a problem that was not yet defined through architectural means. Both projects were innovative, but they both operated from different philosophical positions and with different aims.

Research-teaching cultures and their reproduction: suggestions for further enquiry

While research has been linked to teaching in the architectural design studio, a question of reproduction remains underexposed. A reproductive element behind the shaping of research-teaching cultures can be found with an often tacit influence of wider networks of knowledge on the methods taught in studios and on the problems taken on. Defining more precisely wider networks and how exactly they inform methods in the studios is beyond the scope of the present argument, which primarily intends to pave the way for future investigations into the subject matter.

Whilst the investigation touched upon negotiations of the design objects during student reviews, the sociology of the review itself was not further considered. Plentiful scholarship exists on the social dynamics of the design review and on the knowledge production in design studios, in isolation, but research into the co-dynamics of the two forces of (re)production is needed.

---

42 The institutions could be oriented differently on the axes of problem-solving/framing, philosophical position, and manageability of problems. For example, technical universities could be positioned closer to phenomenology since awareness and understanding of the atmospheric qualities of different materials and their compatibility are typically important aims at those institutions.

Part Four

Knowledge Production in the Design Studio

Albena Yaneva

The New Studio: A Mapping Controversies Experiment[1]

As an applied and skills-oriented discipline, architecture's traditional orientation has always been that of a professional education. No matter where architecture is taught—at traditional universities, technical universities, or universities of applied sciences—the design studio remains at the centre of knowledge production and exchange, playing a central role in shaping the fundamental characteristics of the discipline and its pedagogy. Design practice has evolved from apprenticeship through to the Beaux-Arts and then the Bauhaus traditions,[2] which has resulted in different types of studio teaching.[3]

The pedagogy of design studios and juries has been studied extensively from different perspectives.[4] Schön's theory

---

[1] Albena Yaneva is Professor of Architectural Theory at the Department of Architecture, University of Manchester.
[2] Mark Crinson and Jules Lubbock, *Three Hundred Years of Architectural Education in Britain* (Manchester: Manchester University Press, 1994).
[3] Ashraf M. Salama, *New Trends in Architectural Education: Designing the Design Studio* (Raleigh: Tailored Text and Unlimited Potential Publishing, 1995); Lance N. Green and Elivio Bonollo, 'Studio-Based Teaching: History and Advantages in the Teaching of Design', *World Transactions on Engineering and Technology Education* 2, no. 2 (2003), 269–72.
[4] Kathryn H. Anthony, *Design Juries on Trial: The Renaissance of the Design Studio* (New York: Van Nostrand Reinhold, 1991); Thomas A. Dutton, 'Design and Studio Pedagogy', *Journal of Architectural Education* 41, no. 1 (1987), 16–25; Donald A. Schön, *The Design Studio: An Exploration of Its Traditions and Potentials* (London: RIBA Publications, 1985); Garry Stevens, 'Struggle in the Studio: A Bourdivian Look at Architectural Pedagogy', *Journal of Architectural Education* 49, no. 2 (1995), 105–22; Helena Webster, 'A Study of Ritual, Acculturation and Reproduction in Architectural Education', *Arts and Humanities in Higher Education* 4, no. 3 (2005), 265–82.

of 'reflective practice'[5] revolutionized design anthropology by founding a new epistemology of practice and by considering the competence and artistry already embedded in skilful practice. This type of studio-based reflexivity can be found in many architectural schools today and is commonly privileged by the professional schools of many research universities. It has, however, been widely criticized for promoting an inadequate idea of design learning as a mostly passive process of observation and replication in which the teacher's main role is to correct the student's work rather than to help them develop or hone their skills.

Schön's well-known understanding of studio teaching involves reflective conversations and a constant reframing of problems posed by students and tutors and implications of design moves. Yet, he explicitly positions students' prior knowledge as invalid for the task at hand and thereby, according to his critics, perpetuates 'an abuse of power' that is unhelpful to the development of architecture as a profession.[6] This implies a narrow notion that learning takes place through formal interactions only and fails to recognize the other dimensions of learning in addition to the cognitive—the affective and corporeal learning experiences and the student's potential to be an active learner. The idea of the studio as solely occupied by students and teachers is also to be questioned.

Extending the critique to Schön's anthropology of design education, I analyse one studio experiment: the use of the controversy mapping method, its format and results, how it adds to the performative dimension of studio pedagogy, and how it advocates an alternative epistemic culture to 'reflection-in-action'. This experiment allows an exploration and analysis of the specific role of the studio in generating and translating knowledge at the intersection between humanities and the wider social and economic networks of design, as well as the realities of the profession.

Today's studio is based on transdisciplinarity[7] and requires a complex group learning environment that involves a larger number of actors. The process of learning to think like an architect implies a composite network where the lecturer is one of many participants in design pedagogy. Design teaching and learning involves different actors—digital tools, people, policies, representations, learning environments, material arrangements, and spatial devices. The studio is a complex spatial setting where different temporalities and spatial arrangements coalesce; it offers a dual context of learning about design and learning to design, endorsed and cultivated through teaching a specific attention to the performativity of design.[8] Designers today are also 'browsing practitioners'[9] who surf large amounts of data, and the studio is heavily influenced by computational methods.[10] In addition, students work in material environments that no longer involve sketches and drawings only but a larger amount of hybrid objects such as simulations, tests, material samples, experimental models, video and audio materials, statistics, archival documents. Instead of being a site of asymmetric reflective practice or power-based coaching, the design studio happens within a lager urban and cultural network and therefore cannot be studied in isolation. Studio pedagogy responds to the social and political challenges of the day.

5 Donald A. Schön, *The Reflective Practitioner: How Professionals Think in Action* (New York: Basic Books, 1983).
6 Laura L. Willenbrock, 'An Undergraduate Voice in Architectural Education', in Thomas A. Dutton, ed., *Voices in Architectural Education: Cultural Politics and Pedagogy* (New York: Bergin & Garvey, 1991), 97–120.
7 Isabelle Doucet and Nel Janssens, eds., *Transdisciplinary Knowledge Production in Architecture and Urbanism: Towards Hybrid Modes of Inquiry* (Vienna: Springer, 2011).
8 Inger Mewburn, 'Lost in Translation: Reconsidering Reflective Practice and Design Studio Pedagogy', *Arts and Humanities in Higher Education* 11, no. 4 (2012), 363–79.
9 Albena Yaneva, *Mapping Controversies in Architecture* (Farnham: Ashgate, 2012).
10 Malcolm McCullough, William J. Mitchell, and Patrick Purcell, eds., *The Electronic Design Studio: Architectural Education in the Computer Era* (Cambridge, MA: MIT Press, 1990).

In this contribution, I discuss the controversy mapping method as it has been practised in a master of architecture studio at the Manchester School of Architecture and argue that architects today need to engage more with similar pragmatist types of architectural enquiry that are situation-based, distributed ways of learning about architecture and its various entanglements, rather than one that would rely on a stable stock of systematic, scientific knowledge about architectural humanities.

Mapping controversies

The methodological and conceptual roots of the mapping controversies approach stem from the discipline of science and technology studies, developed from French sociologist and philosopher Bruno Latour's analysis of scientific and technological 'controversies.'[11] The word 'controversy' refers to every bit of science and technology which is not yet stabilized, closed, or 'black-boxed'. It neither means that there is a fierce dispute nor that it has been politicized; it is used as a general term to describe shared uncertainty. Controversy analysis is the educational application of Actor-Network Theory.[12] It consists in following, documenting, and mapping ongoing controversies.

Developing further disciplinary dialogues between design studies and Actor-Network Theory,[13] I have introduced controversy studies in different bachelor's-level humanities courses at the Manchester School of Architecture since 2009. For the experiment described in this chapter, I asked students pursuing a master's degree in architecture to use their advanced design skills to draw, map, and visualize not an object (typically a building or a site) but a controversy—that is, a complex ecology of connections of an architectural, cultural, economic, and political nature. They followed and mapped different controversies to focus on the dynamic debates surrounding particular buildings or construction projects ranging from the redevelopment of Manhattan's Ground Zero to the reform of 1930s modernist high-rise buildings in Sheffield, England. In line with Latour's definition of controversy, we took it not to refer particularly to media debates, scandals, rumours surrounding design plans, uncertain architectural knowledge, buildings-in-progress, tentative technologies, or building innovation but rather to the series of uncertainties that a design project, a building, an urban plan, or a construction process undergoes: a situation of disagreement among different actors over a design issue. It is rather a synonym of 'architecture in the making'.

Why deal with controversies rather than simply with buildings and shapes? Mapping controversies entails analysing controversies through research that enables us to describe the successive stages in the production of architectural knowledge and artefacts, buildings, and urban plans. In tracing how a controversy evolves, students learn about the nature of dissent. They identify the actors involved, follow the different events, and discover a complex timeline of the controversy. By mapping controversies, we also refer to a variety of new representational techniques and tools that permit us to describe the successive stages of controversies.

The Garden Bridge controversy

Here is a controversy example. It is 2019, and we are following the controversy surrounding the Garden Bridge project in London. The original design was proposed by Joanna Lumley and FAT Architects in 1997 but was rejected by the

---

11 Bruno Latour, *Science in Action: How to Follow Scientists and Engineers through Society* (Cambridge, MA: MIT Press, 1987).
12 Bruno Latour, *Reassembling the Social: An Introduction to Actor-Network-Theory* (Oxford: Oxford University Press, 1985).
13 Bruno Latour and Albena Yaneva, 'Give Me a Gun and I Will Make Buildings Move: An Ant's View of Architecture', in Reto Geiser, ed., *Explorations in Architecture: Teaching, Design, Research* (Basel: Birkhäuser, 2008), 80–9; Albena Yaneva, 'Making the Social Hold: Towards an Actor-Network-Theory of Design', *Design and Culture* 1, no. 3 (2009), 273–88.

London mayor at the time, Ken Livingstone. The most recent proposal was produced by Heatherwick Studio in 2013 as part of a design competition put forward by Transport for London. Adam, a M.Arch student, and his colleagues plunge into the press clippings and image galleries on the web to try to unravel all the traces this controversy has left in the digital sphere: archives, governmental papers, press clippings covering the community protests, images, and videos. Articles, images, and YouTube material inform us about the key actors, and we can literally hear their voices of protest: 'Officials at St Paul's Cathedral Complaining That the Bridge Will Spoil the View of Sir Christopher Wren's Famous Dome', 'Protesters Trying to Save Public Space on the South Bank and over the River Thames'. We continue to list all those groups who voice concerns about the proposal as being democratically and environmentally damaging.

The students immerse themselves in the complex data sets that allow them to reflect on not only the design of Garden Bridge but all those issues design is related to: How will the bridge affect the surroundings? How will it affect landscapes? How will the new design affect the residents? How much public money will be spent on it? Will the campaigns against Garden Bridge change the design plans? As the students collect data on the controversy and try to analyse and visualize it, they actively engage in the pragmatist enquiry known as mapping controversies.

The steps of mapping

How does this type of enquiry lead us to a different epistemology of practice in design education? How does it complement both the systematic way of knowing and 'reflection-in-action' that rejects a linear methodical way of knowing? As opposed to reflective studio-based design learning, mapping controversies implies a way of learning about design that is simultaneously an out-of-the-studio mode of questioning the multifarious connections of architecture, society, economics, culture, and politics.

To witness the learning effect, follow the students for a moment. In their attempt to map a controversy, they spend many hours browsing the Internet. First, they start by following the course of the controversy: the actors (individuals, groups or institutions), their arguments, the different positions and how they change over time, the spaces in which they develop, the many ways of closing and reopening the debates, and the extent of public involvement and participation in the process. Second, they document the controversy, collect a variety of materials, and compile a research dossier of press clippings, images, and interviews with architects, clients, investors, public bodies, concerned citizens, and users. They add materials and literature extracts related to other buildings of a similar type, look for information from governmental papers and archives, and examine architectural plans, drawings, and diagrams. In a third, and more challenging step, they map, analyse, and visualize their findings to present the chronological development of the disputes surrounding the airport expansion design plans. They visualize the dynamics, timeline, chronology of the controversies, weight of the different actors' positions, how they disperse or converge, and how a personal position might change the whole configuration of arguments and the spacing and timing of these arguments. They also sometimes make or use videos or podcasts. The software used to embed actors into a representational space ranges from basic web tools such as web page editors, Flash, and Java to 3D visual software and VOSviewer in accordance with the content. Overall, the design students create novel modes of visually incorporating controversy studies suited to a digital format. The creative use of visuals helps them to trace the dynamics of the controversy and its changing argumentative spaces.

The students have no definitions to learn and no strict recipes to follow; they simply describe what they see with the variety of tools available, meaning that they must be attentive to the details to find a uniquely adequate account of a given situation. This is an experiment for two reasons. First, because the students should restrain themselves from explaining the design through a single theory or viewpoint—for instance, the political or the ecological perspective that would give a particular shape to the design. Second, they should try to observe the controversy not only through a singular design viewpoint or through the narrow lens of the sketch. Instead, Adam and his colleagues had to consider the design project from as many viewpoints as possible. Attempting to ignore the design critics and theorists that could provide quick and easy explanatory schemes, the students listen to what the actors say and forget (for a while) all assumptions of what this controversy might be about.

Using new techniques of representation, the students do not simply tell a story about a possible or impossible new design. They also tackle the classic question of representing the subjects of design, whose composition is always variable. The mapping refers to the variety of tools that permit us to describe the consecutive steps in the production of architectural knowledge, focusing on visual representations of the stakeholders, linking their various interests, and tracing their development through time. The same tools used by students in the studio to document and represent static objects are used here to trace their dynamics and become immersed in design ecologies. Students can employ many digital technologies, and I encourage them to choose freely from both what we provide and also what they may find on their own.

Thus, following these steps helps describe and analyse the controversy. The aim is not to unveil some general structure of social and political factors concealed behind the phenomena. The only purpose is to provide the most detailed description of the phenomena as seen by their protagonists. As Latour says, 'If your description needs an explanation, it's not a good description'.[14] The visuals used by architects in the studio do not simply represent but rather deploy—this is the distinction between description and deployment. In the first step (following the controversy) and the second step of the enquiry (documenting the controversy) the students observe and describe what they see and find, thus putting aside any social theory, any meta-reflexive frameworks that would explain particular courses of actions or the specific nature of actors. Then, in the third step of mapping, they develop further their design skills when studying a controversy on the move. The results are presented in interactive portfolios in the form of descriptive accounts of design controversies.

Back in the studio, we witness that in tracing the actors' trajectories, drawing their diagrams of relations and the timeline of the controversy while collecting the data, the students interact with a much vaster and heterogeneous assembly of actors: the London Mayor Sadiq Khan and his predecessor Boris Johnson, Joanna Lumley, Thomas Heatherwick and his studio, Arup, Transport for London, public money, sponsors such as Apple Store and SKY, officials at St Paul's Cathedral, protesting communities, environmental impacts, democratic concerns, activist groups, Westminster Council, and Garden Bridge Trust. All these actors become part of the complex ecology of the proposed design.

The mapping analytics

Let us now zoom into some specific visuals from the mapping portfolio of the Garden Bridge controversy. This project had a vast amount of media coverage (around one thousand articles written over a five-year period from sources like *The Times, Evening Standard*, *The Guardian*, *The Financial Times*, *The Independent*, *The Telegraph*, and *The Architects' Journal*) which allowed the students to perform large mapping studies. After introducing the nature of the disagreement

---

14 Bruno Latour, 'On Using ANT for Studying Information Systems: A (Somewhat) Socratic Dialogue', in Chrisanthi Avgerou, Claudio Ciborra, and Frank F. Land, eds., *The Social Study of Information and Communication Study* (Oxford: Oxford University Press, 2004), 62–76, here 67.

and the history of the controversy, Adam carefully put together a timeline that represents the key events during the project. The timeline does not simply present a chronology of events; it illustrates that this project was unique due to its amount of media coverage by playing a diagram below the timeline that shows the increase of media reports over time in line with the key events happening within the same frames with a peak in 2016 and 2017. He collected this data using the Dow Jones[15] news database website Factiva's article search builder and setting the parameters to UK news sources for the search term 'Garden Bridge'. He used the database to extract specific data for each map so he could draw clear comparisons between certain aspects of the controversy. The total number of articles for each year was extracted and put into an Excel file to create the graph and match to the key events' timeline to show the relationship between the two.

Adam identified and mapped an actor diagram and a diagram that connected the key actors' positions to videos or media sources. Through this technique, we can trace the main positions of key actors like Lumley, Heatherwick, Johnson, Khan, Arup, Transport for London, sponsors, St Paul's Cathedral officials, and protesters. To further understand these actors, Adam compared data from the timeline, the press, and the actors' diagram to compile a frequency graph to show the frequency of the actors' involvement in the controversy over time. Adam extracted data from Factiva every three months, downloading text files to analyse each time period. Using the data and the search term 'Garden Bridge', key terms for the individual actors were extracted using VOSviewer. The total number of mentions were extracted, carefully avoiding duplicates (such as Boris Johnson being referred to as 'Boris', 'Mr Johnson', and 'Mayor'). The frequency of the data was then put into Excel to extract the data curves.

Through the actor frequency graph, we witness that, contrary to the students' expectations, Heatherwick as a designer was not the key actor in the public limelight, despite his consistent presence in the press and a constant level of involvement. Arup, although heavily involved in the technical development, was mentioned far less. Khan's and Johnson's involvement as the mayors during the project is also interesting—soon after the project ended, Khan's involvement dwindled but Johnson's increased massively.

Adam further filtered the database search results by each specific news source and downloaded a set of data for each of them. Due to the varying number of results, he allowed for up to 300 terms to be included. This enables an accurate cross-comparison of data that is altered according to the difference in size of the news outlets. The maps reveal different media outlets' concerns—while all of them focus on budgets and politics, *The Architects' Journal*, for example, focuses on the architectural and engineering features of the project.

Further on, Adam analysed the Dame Margaret Hodge report. Through carefully produced maps, he concluded that this report was the reason for cancelling the project due to the high costs. The process revealed surprising findings: the designer's name is not linked to the costs, as there seems to be a disconnection between design and feasibility; the gap between estimated costs at the start (60 million pounds) and later estimates (200 million pounds) is huge; the name of Richard de Cani, which was not visible in the other maps, appears clearly here in relation to his work for Arup and Transport for London.

Mapping the controversy further, each transcript was downloaded and run through VOSviewer to produce individual maps based on documents used for the report (interviews with different protagonists). Adam found out that only two of the key actors did not see the rising costs of the project as a concern. Money was not mentioned by Heatherwick or

15 https://professional.dowjones.com/factiva (accessed 5 March 2021).

RIBA president Jane Duncan, whose focus remained on the aesthetically pleasing design of Garden Bridge in the heart of London. All other actors stated concerns about procurement and budgets.

Finally, filtering data downloaded exclusively from articles that referenced the Garden Bridge published after the project had officially been scrapped allowed Adam to generate a map of the aftermath in VOSviewer. It provided an overview: 38 million pounds of public money was spent on an unrealized project; while the blame was easily placed on politicians, little was done to question the design, procurement, and tender processes or to ensure a realistic planning. Overall, the students found that an unrealistic and overambitious design combined with an unfair procurement method based on a biased competition is not a good investment of public money in iconic design.

The new studio: integrating controversy studies

Through this mapping controversies project, the students did not learn what design is; they rather learnt about what design does—what kind of effects it can trigger and how it can affect citizens, divide communities, and provoke disagreements. They immersed themselves into the many consequences of design practice and gained an awareness of its various implications. If they were to design a new bridge, especially after the controversy of this one, would they still stay in the studio, absorbed in a meditative dialogue with the sketch, staring at a model and 'engaging in a dialogue with materials and shapes', trying to solve the paradoxes of design? No. They would rather plunge into the design world outside the studio and face its complex ontology.

What kind of enquiry is this, and how does it differ from the studio type of reflection-in-action? It is neither a purely meta-reflexive enquiry on design nor one that situates it into reflexive frameworks (that is, a critical theory–inspired view of architecture). As compared to the studio reflection-in-action that deals with the uncertainty of design, taken in the specific materiality of cognition, mapping is rather a self-exemplifying type of enquiry that deals with the consequences of the manoeuvres of all actors involved in situations of uncertainty and their implications, changing positions, and opinions. As Adam and his colleagues searched among the piles of articles and navigated databases and image galleries on the Internet, they witnessed a web of actors' stances involved in the controversy. This exercise is not about designing a building and trying to 'fit it into a slot' but rather about weighing the impacts a proposed building could have, evaluating the consequences of design and its implications. Mapping does not advance a subsequent reframing of the problem or offer sketching and re-sketching of different options and possible scenarios; it rather follows extending webs and multiplies their proliferation. Adam and his colleagues tried to comprehend the consequences of design and the web of shifting positions within the controversy.

In studio teaching, learning about architecture by mapping controversies can cultivate a specific attention to the performativity of design and can ultimately result in better design. In the studio today, designers consider various digital datasets when designing; they no longer engage in solitary coach-and-student problem-solving with the help of a sketch. Drawing is instead complemented by an intense data search of information, design precedents, image retrieval, actors' statements, archival materials, government papers, and information about the architects in charge. Mobilizing these new digital sources in design would imply a different mode of communication with materials and shapes, a different type of cognitive practice.

If design happens by surfing and drawing at the same time, how can this type of enquiry generate a new type of design practice? What epistemology of practice is implied in this new type of studio? The introduction of the mapping controversies approach in studios demonstrates the impact of digital technologies on studio learning and how digital tools influence the ways knowledge is generated, communicated, and used. The cartography of controversies provides a toolkit to cope with the different hybridizations of knowledge as a dispute often cuts across disciplinary boundaries. Mapping design controversies in studios pushes the investigation of architecture students far beyond the limits of humanities and towards technology and even natural sciences. It provides an opportunity for students to showcase independent and valid knowledge; often they become experts of the specific controversy they have mapped more than any tutor could be. Rather than being an asymmetrical power game, studio learning becomes symmetrical in its temporal and epistemic rhythms of studio praxis.

The students gain valuable insights into the meaning of design through these enquiries. They learn that, when seen through a series of contested projects and users' demands, a building resembles much more a complex ecology than it does a static object. According to Schön, designers deal with uncertainty and with complex, incoherent, and messy situations and convert them to a determined form; they 'construct and impose a coherence of their own'.[16] In our mapping controversies case, the designer is one who recognizes and accounts for the complexity of design by observing a dispute before making sense of it through the production of descriptions and visualizations that account for the rhythm, intensity, and scope of the disagreement; the dispersion of the actors' positions; the trajectory of their arguments; the spacing and timing; and the different ways of ending the controversy. When we observe controversies, we focus on the liquid side of social relations[17] as new actors and concerns become visible. The description of controversies contributes to the solidification of these relations, reducing the complexity.

The experiment of mapping controversies makes us perceive design as part of the entire web of moves that are traced by the actions of design, including landscapes, trees, climate, affected nature, pollution, London landmarks, skyline coherence, contested regulations, public money, mayoral politics, tender processes, legacy, and community concerns. Visuals (interactive diagrams, timelines, actor diagrams) reveal the complex, networked nature of architecture and conflicting demands on urban projects. Designing is indeed much more complex than simply trying to put a building on a site and adjust its scale to solve building problems.

Surfing designers like Adam nevertheless dream about 'putting a building on a site'. Mapping controversies make them realize that design controversies involve all kinds of actors: activists' groups, single architects, mayors, communities, landmarks, transport organizations, and public budgets. They all need a space to meet and debate different issues and important technical choices. In addition, the people involved and their representatives are heterogeneous: experts, politicians, clients, architects, technicians, and concerned people of the community. Their concerns are equally diverse, from politics to ethics, mechanical engineering, procurement, and aesthetics. These actors are always connected in a network. Thus, mapping controversies provides a realistic view of the social and economic complexity of the practice of designers and prepares them better for these realities. Students learn about tender and procurement processes, the role of the different public bodies involved, and the importance of acknowledging the local urban dynamics and the concerns of local communities, as well as the professional regulations at a national level.

Aiming to understand controversies in architecture, this experiment also brings theory and practice together by reconnecting and strengthening the synergies between them. It prevents students from falling into the trap of reductionism—of reducing and explaining the protest to

16 Donald A. Schön, *Educating the Reflective Practitioner: Toward a New Design for Teaching and Learning in the Professions* (San Francisco: Jossey-Bass, 1987), 42.
17 Tommaso Venturini, 'Diving in Magma: How to Explore Controversies with Actor-Network Theory', *Public Understanding of Science* 19, no. 3 (2010), 258–73.

Garden Bridge, with political, cultural, or social factors. These are easy frameworks of explanation. Instead, following controversies allows designers to witness the social and the architectural in a state not yet stabilized and to follow the actors through agreement and disagreement, how they shape alliances, how they scale and rescale the spaces where they move, and how they create spatial disjunctions. Here is where you find the social; here is where you can fully unpack the complex realities of design. Questioning the failed Garden Bridge proposal led designers to tackle issues of politics, urban design, climate change, iconicity, ecology, and community life. All these issues deserve more attention. The mapping controversies approach provides a new epistemic repertoire for studio teaching and better prepares students for the new political and economic realities of design practice today. It paves new pedagogical avenues that can guide architectural practitioners in further explorations of design. Moreover, this pragmatist methodology can ignite new possibilities for practitioners to be present in a world that is constantly changing.

Jan Silberberger

Referencing in Architectural Design[1]

Judging from the broad ethnographic study which Helmersen and I conducted (see the introduction to this volume), it seems safe to say that every architect with a higher education must be familiar with the practice of drawing on the works of others—either to obtain clues for further developing or rethinking a project, to guide pending decisions, or to substantiate decisions taken. As Jadwiga Krupinska explains, when architects in the professional as well as academic sphere mention names of peers (historical as well as contemporary), this is to be understood 'as a specific way of summarizing complex situations and ways to create and think.'[2] In this way, names of different architects (and/or buildings) represent and imply 'characteristic methods for solving certain problems'.[3]

Strangely though, there is an apparent lack of scholarship with respect to 'referencing' in architectural design. In fact, there is only literature, mostly from the 1980s and 1990s, about so-called precedent studies.[4] The problem with precedent studies (and much of the corresponding literature) is that they mostly analyse buildings devoid of their 'context'. Not only do they often neglect the societal values, aesthetic preferences, and the state of the art of technology prevalent at the time the studied building had been constructed, they also typically refrain from analysing buildings as solution approaches to specific problems. This disregard for the conditions of the analysed buildings frequently

---

1 Jan Silberberger, ETH Zurich.
2 Jadwiga Krupinska, *What an Architecture Student Should Know* (New York: Routledge, 2014), 83.
3 Krupinska, *What an Architecture Student*, 83 (see note 2).
4 See, e.g., Roger H. Clark and Michael Pause, *Precedents in Architecture* (New York: Van Nostrand Reinhold, 1996); Simon Unwin, *Analysing Architecture* (London: Routledge, 1997).

reduces precedent studies to largely formal exercises concerned with issues such as identifying geometrical patterns within building structures.

In contrast, the chapter at hand aims to shed light on the practice of referencing in architectural design by presenting and discussing two pronounced and equally meaningful examples. Drawing on empirical data gathered when observing intermediate and final reviews at the Chair of Architectural Design, Rebuilding, and Conservation (Professor Andreas Hild) at the Technical University of Munich as well as at the Chair of Architecture and Construction (Professor Adam Caruso) at ETH Zurich, this chapter will provide a thick description of two approaches towards working with references as traceable processes of knowledge transfer and creation.

The two design tasks

Both Hild's and Caruso's studio explicitly demanded students make use of references for developing their projects, and both studios were concerned with conversion. While Hild's was about finding a suitable building as a reference to be analysed for supporting decision-making regarding rebuilding an abandoned bank, Caruso's was about interpreting the work of selected artists for reimagining a neglected streetscape.

Labelled 'Bank(h)aus',[5] the brief Hild's studio issued for the 2018–2019 winter semester addressed the conversion of an abandoned bank branch in Munich's inner city. Constructed in the late 1950s as a post office, it fills part of a city block and basically comprises two five-storey elements: a main building oriented towards Sattlerplatz (a small, slightly neglected city square) and a U-shaped annex which forms an inner courtyard. In contrast to the annex, the main building features a distinct base level with significantly greater ceiling heights, natural stone cladding, and windows offset to the inside, with the rest of the building plastered.

The assignment consisted of developing an idea regarding a new way of using this slightly unspectacular building[6] and a corresponding design proposal. Furthermore, students were instructed to find a way of adequately dealing with the structure and expression of the existing building. In parallel to developing ideas for reusing and remodelling the bank, students were directed to identify suitable buildings as references to support and guide their design process further. In the lecture series that accompanied the studio course, ways of using these references were explained by drawing comparisons to appropriation art. In a first step, students were directed to employ their references with little to no transformation applied to them, basically superimposing them on the bank building. Only in a second step were, these superimpositions to be tweaked, thereby experimenting with the references' capacities for adaption.

Caruso's studio dealt with the issue of conversion in a broader (societal) sense. Titled 'What Is Worthless', the brief for the 2020 spring semester asked students to reimagine 'the unloved [early 1980s] buildings that line [Zurich's] Thurgauerstrasse, once prestigious corporate headquarters, today standing half occupied, waiting for redevelopment.'[7] The brief provided a concise account of the 1970s as 'a time when small, alternative communities took advantage of the frequently selfish freedoms of the sixties to develop something more coherent and substantial, a second phase of modernism that was no longer reliant on post-war positivism and the

---

5 This is a pun playing on the words *Bankhaus*, or a bank building, and *Bank aus*, which roughly means 'the end of the bank' and refers to the increasing tendency of banks shutting down more and more of their subsidiaries as a result of shifting a considerable part of their service activities to the Internet.

6 The brief indicates that especially the annex and the upper storeys are more closely related to the 'everyday architecture' produced in the course of the reconstruction of Munich after the Second World War than to the more finely differentiated, reservedly elegant post offices of the Munich Postbauschule in the 1920s and 1930s.

7 'What Is Worthless', Studio Adam Caruso, https://www.caruso.arch.ethz.ch/programme/fs-2020/documents?asset=643 (accessed 20 July 2020).

state, but had not yet succumbed to neo-liberal consumerism.'[8] The studio wanted students to 'engage with the spirit of the second phase of modernism, and deploy some of its instruments to ... encourag[e] the conditions of openness, mutability and inclusion that were possible in the ruins of the 70s, and are essential if we are going to make a sustainable and democratic city today.'[9]

As a basis, Caruso's students were provided with an extensive reader (discussed in biweekly reading circles the whole semester) that featured a variety of texts ranging from an excerpt from Karl Marx to an interview with the artist Pierre Huyghe, to reflections on artistic and architectural practice (such as by Martha Rosler and Helen Thomas). Equipped with that reader, students were assigned the work of an artist as reference.[10] Procedurally, the course was divided into three parts. In the first part, students were required to analyse the artist's work with the aim of identifying underlying methodological principles, thereby making use of the reader. The second part entailed applying the identified methodological principles for analysing a selected site in Zurich by means of an intervention in the scale of 1:1. Finally, the third part was aimed at using this latter study as a springboard for architectural interventions (to be represented in plans and models at scales from 1:20 to 1:500) into the ensemble of office buildings lining Thurgauerstrasse.

Methodology

In the following sections, I present a concentrated, self-contained reconstruction of the observed proceedings with regard to each course. Based on field notes and recollections from memory, these reconstructions merge observations of a variety of students' projects into two fictitious cases. Far from claiming that these fabrications reproduce the observed proceedings in a neutral manner, I consider them as an attempt at generalizing (as they abstract from data referring to specific, singular students' projects) and at the same time at densifying (as they draw on selected observations that refer to a variety of students' projects and put them into a direct relationship within a single, specifically fabricated design project).

Based on the assumption that knowledge (and its creation) in architectural design is inherently linked to its use for and within the development of specific design proposals, I describe it in relation to the specific object parameters and design rationales in which it is manifested and expressed. Architects seldom discuss purely on the basis of general terms but rather relate to concrete design features and specific properties. They often literally point to these properties displayed on an architectural plan or model while speaking. Hence, an adequate account of referencing in architectural design as a form of knowledge transfer and creation has to not only include the statements made by designers but also ensure that these statements are intimately linked to particular properties of a design object—since without that link they become devoid of purpose.

The approach to create fictitious cases is based on two considerations. The first is length: Using statements which refer to specific properties of six different design proposals would require accurate descriptions of the latter, which would easily exceed the scope of a book chapter. The second is to use these fictitious cases as a thick description—that is, as an interpretation of observations and an attempt to comprehend the perspectives of ethnographic subjects in relation to their own world.[11] Such presentation of ethnographic data is not about 'making things up and disguising them as facts'.[12] Rather, the two fictitious cases that I constructed are

---

8 Studio Adam Caruso, 'What Is Worthless' (see note 7).
9 Studio Adam Caruso, 'What Is Worthless' (see note 7).
10 The list of artists included Sophie Calle, Hanne Darboven, Andrea Fraser, Huyghe, Gordon Matta-Clark, Daido Moriyama, Rosler, Cindy Sherman, and Taryn Simon.
11 Clifford Geertz, *The Interpretation of Cultures* (London: Hutchinson, 1975).
12 Michael Angrosino, *Doing Ethnographic and Observational Research* (London: SAGE, 2007), 81.

to be seen as a translation of observations into a project that hopefully also speaks to the people whose work was observed for the research.[13] Therefore, the fictitious cases constitute an attempt to situate my study in its investigated setting, deliberately placed between the studied actors.[14]

As regards the description of the proceedings observed at Caruso's studio, two further clarifications should be made. Firstly, the artist David Claerbout, whose work I assign to the two fictitious students, was not one of the artists in the actual assignment. I chose Claerbout since I know his work well, and it fits the studio's selection of artists in terms of the issues it addresses and the approach it is based on. Secondly, the studio course was affected by the coronavirus pandemic. Roughly four weeks into the semester, immediately after the first intermediate crit, the studio had to shift to remote teaching and adjusted the brief. Instead of developing an intervention for Thurgauerstrasse, students worked further with the site assigned to them for the first phase.[15] The fictitious project I created, however, sticks with the initial brief, primarily since I am familiar with Thurgauerstrasse and found it easier to describe my observations by devising a project for a site that does not coincide with that of a particular student.

Bank(h)aus: appropriating architectural references

Let us follow our two fictitious students, A and B, through their semester at Hild's studio. Let us imagine they developed the idea of converting the Munich bank into a boutique hotel. In line with Munich's efforts at inner-city densification, A and B propose to extend the bank by adding two extra storeys. Scribbling on printouts that show the bank branch and part of its surroundings, A and B produce first ideas. At their first desk crit they present three design sketches. The first shows a simple two-storeyed box, which takes up the bank's length and width, the second a tent-like structure slightly reminiscent of Munich's Olympic Stadium, the third an organic, biomorphic shape, each of these sitting on top of the former bank.

A and B browse the Internet for adequate references. Eventually, they come across the Standard in London: a luxury hotel, opened in 2019, also the result of a conversion. Finished in 1974 (and therefore just about fifteen years younger than the bank), the building was used as a town hall until 2014. As part of the conversion two storeys were added to the former town hall. Hild had made it clear in his lectures that references do not necessarily have to resemble the intended design project. Yet, A and B decide to continue with this rather congruent reference. To check whether it could work, they use image-processing software to combine photos of the bank building and the Standard's rooftop extension, without putting any effort into smoothing the edges of the clashing photo material. Although some of these combinations look convincing, most of them reveal serious sources of conflict. The simple, rectangular bank building with its completely plain facade, for instance, precludes the expressive, slightly flamboyant rounded corners of the reference.

In an early intermediate crit, pointing to one of A and B's cut-and-paste montages, Hild tells them that reference and bank do not connect. 'So far', he states, 'this is not more than a quote, copy and paste.' To further develop their design, he instructs A and B to turn to the underlying principles that define the character of the reference. 'Use the sources of conflict that the montage highlights', he tells them, 'and analyse how the reference works in that respect. This is not about how things look; it's about asking how things are done.' Hild then explains that 'the findings of this analysis will necessarily deform the montage. ... This deformation', he continues, 'is something you have to appreciate! This is the moment of appropriation; this is when the reference

13 Anna Banks and Stephen P. Banks, eds., *Fiction and Social Research: By Ice or Fire* (Walnut Creek, CA: AltaMira, 1998).
14 Bruno Latour, *Reassembling the Social: An Introduction to Actor-Network-Theory* (Oxford: Oxford University Press, 2005).
15 Studio Adam Caruso, 'What Is Worthless' (see note 7).

becomes your project. The modifications and adjustments, the adaptations that you make must reflect the knowledge that you have obtained. They have to be deliberate operations, lawful inscriptions of information.'

Examining their reference, A and B notice that the Standard's rooftop extension looks somewhat like a crown: clearly distinguishable as a subsequent addition but at the same time not sharply opposed to the structure of the former town hall. They realize that the extension is set back, that its building outline adopts the rounded corners of the former town hall, and that there is sort of a separating layer between the extension and the plinth building. A and B conceive this as a '(distinguishable) continuation of the base building'— their first underlying principle. Based on that first principle, A and B define a second one as '(distinguishable) continuation of the facade' arguing that the Standard's extension takes up the honeycombed windows as well as the window proportion of the plinth building and that the vertical structure of the extension's facade relates to the formative elements of the base building's facade. A and B then turn towards the construction material used in the reference and detect a continuation there as well. Despite the obvious difference between extension (steel and glass) and plinth building (reinforced concrete), the extension relates to the time when the town hall was constructed. It has a subtle early 1970s look and feel. Hence, A and B define a third principle as a 'shift in building material as continuation'. Furthermore, they discern that the extension exhibits greater ceiling heights than the former town hall, which makes a fourth underlying principle: 'increase in ceiling heights'. Based on this analysis, A and B frame their target as follows: they want to extend the bank by a clearly distinguishable structure that subtly takes up the basic formative elements by perpetuating them.

They determine that the form of the extension should be unpretentious: a simple box. In addition, following the reference, they decide that it should be set back and that there should be a separating layer. Then, A and B apply the 'increase in ceiling heights' principle. Again following the reference, they decide to have floor-to-ceiling windows on the top floor and almost floor-to-ceiling windows on the floor below. They ponder that, to achieve a certain degree of continuity for window proportion and facade structure, they will either have to change the bank's windows (but this would mean a significant change of its facade) or modify the reference implant with respect to window proportion and positioning. Regarding the distinctive depth of the facade proposed by the reference, A and B see two options: either keep it (following the reference) or choose a completely plain facade (following the 1950s bank building). Regarding the 'shift in building material as continuation' principle, they feel that they could stick with the reference's glass and steel structure. Appreciating its lightness, A and B think about making it even more delicate, even finer. As a second option, instead of glass and steel, they consider using the typical brick and concrete mix that is reminiscent of the post-war era. They reason that combining brick and concrete with a plain facade and the window proportions of the bank would grant a high degree of continuation: besides having higher ceilings, a separating layer, and the setback, the aspired contrast could be obtained by showing the bricks and concrete in the extension (while they remain plastered in the plinth building). Combining a glass and steel structure with a deep facade (as suggested by the montage) would instead give maximum contrast. A and B argue that if they decide for the latter, they should probably retain the bank's window proportions and facade structure to achieve the necessary degree of continuation.

If we recap the proceedings, we can state that students within Hild's studio start off by literally displacing a reference building; that is, a fully determined combination of fully formulated design parameters. Apparently, in the case of conversions, building tasks are typically highly constrained. Several design parameters of the building in question—such as its supporting structure or the location of staircases (as well as all parameters affected by preservation order, if applicable)—must be considered as immutable, therefore adding to the usual set of contextual constraints (as defined, for example, in the zoning code or the building law). The constraints which originate from the building to be converted inevitably create a conflict when implanting the reference. Besides obvious adjustment requirements regarding span widths, overall geometry, and size, they generate ambiguous, undirected values for a variety of further design variables (for example, for those concerning the facade structure as in the case described above). Such ambiguities become apparent when the implant's predefined design parameters are imported by means of montages. The result of a basic cut-and-paste operation, the students' montages reveal the problems in merging the reference with the building at hand and provide entry points for a focused examination of the reference. It can be argued that such montages 'have the value of a test' while at the same time being 'prophetic of the direction … to take'.[16] They trigger questions regarding a variety of decisive design aspects: How to connect the extension to the existing building? What about its building line? What about its facade? What about ceiling heights? And what kind of material to use?

In order to address these issues—that is, in order to 'deform' reference implants in a well-informed manner—students are advised to search for underlying principles defining the character of the reference. Derived from an analysis of the reference's visible properties, these underlying principles are more abstract and invisible in nature. Determining whether, for instance, to perpetuate a facade (or to create a contrast), such underlying principles do not define single, isolated design parameters (such as the size of windows or the degree to which they are offset) but operate on the level of determining possible value combinations for interconnected design parameters. When it is argued that a building's facade is to be perpetuated, this does not mean that every single design variable coincides; rather, their combination must produce the envisaged continuation. Hence, these underlying principles do not determine values of single design parameters but effectively shape the set of possible approaches. They do not just relate to the level of appearance of form ('how things look'), but to the dimension of composition of form ('how things are done'). Thus, the method of appropriating architectural references as promoted by Hild's teaching studio requires an investigation that relates visible surfaces to the constitutive traits of their composition.

Systematically deployed as additional constraints, the identified principles of composition allow for defining a distinctively restricted set of possible alternatives. The identified principle of a shift in building material as continuation, for instance, calls for using construction material that reflects the look and feel of the bank's date of origin, thereby narrowing down the set of possible values for the design variable 'building material' while the principle of a 'distinguishable continuation of building structure' determines the design variables 'form' (as 'box'), 'building outline' (as 'set back'), and 'separating layer' (as 'positive'). By progressively applying the four identified underlying principles, possibilities can be reduced in a deliberate and traceable manner as the result of a sequence of logical operations. Descriptive knowledge (the identified underlying principles) is steadily inscribed into the reference implant, thereby successively adapting it to the present circumstances. Instead of using references as loose inspiration, the observed conduct relies on utilizing references as sets of instructions. As the description of A and B's conduct has shown, references are selected in relation to the interpretation of the conditions of the problem at hand and then used to deduce guidelines for consistently and convincingly narrowing down the problem's solution space.

16 Dawn Ades, Photomontage (New York: Pantheon Books, 1976), 8.

'What Is Worthless': deploying artists' methodologies

Let us directly jump into Caruso's studio and follow our second fictitious pair of students, X and Y, through their semester project. Let us assume that they had been assigned the work of the Belgian artist David Claerbout, namely his 2016 video piece entitled *The Pure Necessity*, a fifty-minute-long animated film that reworks the 1967 Disney classic *The Jungle Book*. For this piece Claerbout hired animators to redraw *The Jungle Book*, stripping (many of) its layers of anthropocentric projection. In Claerbout's version, the animals, instead of 'dancing, singing, and trumpet-playing … behave … in a manner befitting their species. Balloo, Bagheera and Kaa … are now back to being bear, panther and python.'[17]

In the first procedural step, X and Y analyse Claerbout's video to identify underlying methodological principles. After watching the video and reading up on Claerbout's work on the Internet, X and Y consider 'The Pure Necessity' an antithesis to the sentimental Disney musical comedy. Whereas Disney's goal was to entertain the masses, Claerbout's version, to them, is the opposite of entertaining. They use the reader provided by Caruso's studio to interpret Claerbout's work. Taking up an idea from the interview with Huyghe, who speaks about French conceptual artist and sculptor Daniel Buren and his ways of 'freeing' 'space from its given scenario, and from its conventional uses',[18] X and Y interpret Claerbout's approach as to 'free' the cartoon characters from the anthropomorphisms projected onto them.

Meanwhile, X and Y have been assigned the Toni Areal (a former dairy factory occupied by Zurich University of the Arts since 2014) as the site for their intervention in the scale of 1:1. Translating their interpretation of Claerbout's methodology into the analysis of the Toni Areal and the development of a corresponding intervention, X and Y play through various ways of 'dispensing the building of the use that is currently projected on it.' Contemplating the issue of the former dairy factory, X and Y remember having recently read about dairy farmers struggling for fair milk pricing. Browsing the Internet, they find pictures of farmers dumping milk on their fields. In a flash of inspiration they decide to install a square of sixteen blue barrels, each filled with two hundred litres of milk, in the foyer of the Zurich University of the Arts. They contact the European Milk Board and the responsible person from the university and present their idea. As they get permission to show their installation for one day, the European Milk Board puts them in touch with a local dairy farmer, who agrees to deliver nine barrels filled with milk directly into the foyer. X and Y film the installation for presentation at an intermediate crit.

Presenting their work, X and Y argue: 'The question is, why did Claerbout redraw these cartoons? He could have filmed real bears using one of these cameras that people put in the woods to film shy wildlife. Cartoons are per se anthropomorphic projections—and still, Claerbout uses this technique. It is this contradiction we are interested in. We wanted to challenge the entrenched ways of running an art school—by means of an art project, which aims at turning the school into a site for the struggle of dairy farmers.' A critic responds: 'I appreciate your intention to activate the building as a site of contestation and negotiation. However, I think your intervention might be a bit too illustrative. For sure, the Toni Areal used to be a dairy factory, and farmers used to bring their milk there, but I'm a bit sceptical regarding this concept of "going back". This, mind you, also goes for Claerbout's piece. Wouldn't it be more in line with your thinking to raise awareness of the current governance of art schools instead of milk pricing?' A second critic adds: 'You mentioned the interview with Huyghe in which he speaks about these unfinished houses in the Mediterranean, which

---

17 *The Pure Necessity*, David Claerbout, https://davidclaerbout.com/the-pure-necessity-2016 (accessed 20 July 2020).
18 George Baker, 'An Interview with Pierre Huyghe', *October* 110 (2004), 80–106.

most people perceive as a nuisance. Huyghe instead hires a professional architectural photographer to document this type of architecture as a form of potentiality and possibility. I consider your intervention as related to this reformulation. You try to destabilize the Toni Areal and to push it into a transitory state. That's a desirable approach. I agree with my colleague though that evoking the days when it had been a dairy factory is a bit unidimensional.'

Working on the third procedural step—that is, on their architectural intervention for Thurgauerstrasse—X and Y take the second critic's hint and reconsider the Huyghe interview. Since John Cage is mentioned several times there, X and Y browse the Internet for his work. They find a quotation instructing: 'If something is boring after two minutes, try it for four. If still boring, then eight. Then sixteen. Then thirty-two. Eventually one discovers that it is not boring at all.' X and Y directly apply this instruction to Claerbout's piece, which they watch repeatedly. After several repetitions they decide that they want to work affirmatively with Thurgauerstrasse's dullness. X and Y claim that adopting Claerbout's method of remaking an outdated mainstream cartoon into a piece, which, in the eyes of contemporary capitalist society, is even far less entertaining, calls for not destroying the dullness of the equally outdated early 1980s mainstream buildings lining Thurgauerstrasse by acts of intrusive ingenuity. They develop the hypothesis that the perception of Thurgauerstrasse intended by its planners has already been stripped from the site during the last thirty years, as they ponder that 'society has done to the site what Claerbout has done to *The Jungle Book*.' Taking up the critique they received at the intermediate review, and following Huyghe, they understand Thurgauerstrasse now as a 'platform of potentiality'. Referring to the studio's brief, X and Y reason that, to sustain this 'state of suppleness' and allow for other, unexpected, new ways of actualization, Thurgauerstrasse needs to be as unattractive to capital as possible—so that it remains insignificant with regard to capitalist utilization. X and Y repeatedly walk and cycle up and down Thurgauerstrasse, which runs from the southwest to the northeast. On one of these walks, they develop the idea to construct a wall to block the buildings southeast of the street from view. They consider different materials and finally go for the cheapest possible raw, prefabricated concrete elements (4 × 1.8 metres). These elements will be mounted at an angle of thirty degrees to leave 0.8-metre clearances for people to walk through, but prevent transport users from getting an unobstructed view of the buildings.

At the final review, X and Y present their project, arguing that the state of the buildings lining Thurgauerstrasse can be considered as being close to 'pure potentiality'. They explain: 'Hence, we turned away from the buildings as such and created this permeable wall directly in front of them. For someone who drives by in a car, it comes across as a slightly oversized noise protection barrier, while for a pedestrian it has this playful character and creates an almost serene atmosphere.' The critics in unison value their argumentation and rationale, yet some criticize X and Y's intervention for being preservationist rather than imaginative. A guest critic says: 'I appreciate your reasoning. But your project does not really create a new perspective on the buildings as such. You declare them as platforms awaiting forms of activation, which are not driven by capital. But your project does not show us anything about such forms of activation. It just hides the buildings from view, which I consider as too one-dimensional'. However, another critic adds: 'The project deliberately refuses to make suggestions for the activation of the buildings, which I think is highly consistent. After all, Claerbout makes no actual proposals regarding reimagining our relation with fauna, nor does Huyghe with respect to actualizing the potential buildings in the Mediterranean.'

If we recap Caruso's studio, a striking feature is that students were assigned to a specific reference while they were granted room for interpretation. As the detailed quotations from the brief show, students were expected to address and reframe a societal problem in all its broadness and complexity. Regarding deploying references, Caruso's studio encouraged lateral thinking and intuition while simultaneously challenging students to find plausible interpretations of what they had been doing. As we have seen, the three carefully conceptualized procedural steps supported students in their complex unfolding of references. The works of the artists assigned provided models for opening other, new perspectives and reformulating given conventions. The reader in turn provided important cues for analysing and interpreting the artists' ways of achieving such reframing. The second procedural step served as a test for the identified methodological principles. The sites selected for this test correspond to Thurgauerstrasse, as all of them share key characteristics with the latter. The Toni Areal assigned to X and Y, for example, originates roughly from the same period (it had been finished in 1977). Furthermore, it had been abandoned in 2000, then made available for cultural use, and finally converted into the University of the Arts—which is something that could very well also happen to the buildings lining Thurgauerstrasse. These similarities increase the probability that an intervention in one of the test sites generates workable hunches for the reimagination of Thurgauerstrasse.

It is for these two preceding procedural steps that X and Y can successively tackle a task as complex as developing a new, unexpected understanding of Thurgauerstrasse. The coherent relationship between the predefined procedure and the object of study provides a sound basis for well-founded discussions and reflections despite the studio's openness regarding possible outcomes. In this way, students can let their design processes spin off into unexpected directions as they are supported and guided to realign even those processes which are prone to being lost in arbitrariness (X and Y's 'milk' installation) in a comprehensible manner. The well-informed interpretation of the artist's way of proceeding and its consistent application to the case at hand lead to the desired reformulation of Thurgauerstrasse. The discussion during the final review is a further indication for the high degree of coherency between procedure and object of study: in contrast to the guest critic (whose expectation contravenes the studio's spirit), the second critic acknowledges that if the procedure, consistently executed, generates findings which suggest reformulating the brief—and adjusting the object of study—then this is what must be done.

Conclusion

Far from understanding referenced buildings or art pieces respectively as merely loose inspiration, the two procedures discussed in this chapter constitute methodical attempts at deploying references as sources of knowledge. In both, Hild's and Caruso's studio, references were systematically analysed regarding underlying methodological principles, which could then be transferred to the problem at hand. While Hild's studio was primarily concerned with problem-solving, and hence, oriented gathering insights for developing an optimal solution to a well-defined problem, Caruso's was rather interested in problem-framing, and hence, about developing design proposals to get a different, new understanding of a problem. The method of importing reference buildings as fully formed, early solution proposals taught at Hild's studio aimed at rapidly increasing the understanding of the problem and its solution space. The systematic examination of the reference building then led to a set of constraints that could be applied for plausibly deforming the reference implant into an adequate solution. Caruso's studio in turn deployed references as a basis for explorations into the unknown as well as for the systematic reflection of the latter. The thorough analysis of the methodologies of selected artists engendered lateral thinking and simultaneously provided a sound foundation for its interpretation.

For both studios, it is the consistent procedure and its coherent relation to the object of study which facilitates plausible and profound discussions about decisions taken and decisions to be made. Against the background of the two modes of referencing, an understanding of designing that focuses only on intuition, subjectivity, and singularity, thereby neglecting methodical procedure and the transferability of insights would be blatantly incomplete. Instead, a perspective is needed that does not neglect traceability, knowledge transfer, and attempts at generalization—a perspective that combines rationality and objectivity well-balanced with subjective judgements and intuition. The two examples illustrated above show that it is possible.

Part Five

Review Practice in the Studio

Adam Jasper, Amy Perkins, and Jeremy Waterfield

The Crit: Constructive and Personal[1]

The crit, as it is regularly conducted in architecture schools, is usually taken to be a historically stable ritual. While questions are sometimes raised about its efficacy, and by extension, if the crit is entirely up-to-date, the purported origins of the crit are rarely interrogated. This is partly because the alibi is well known: the origin of the contemporary crit is to be found in the École des Beaux-Arts tradition of architectural training,[2] to some extent updated and softened by the influence of the Bauhaus *Vorkurs* (foundation course).

This narrative is not false, but it is partial. The crit also has a second wellspring, a counter-tradition that can be traced back to a peer-based, salon style of architectural criticism that bears more than coincidental resemblances to French revolutionary clubs—the *Privatgesellschaften* of the Prussian architectural tradition. The emphasis on the École des Beaux-Arts obscures this alternative tradition of the crit. However, this alternative tradition offers a legitimizing rationale for the extension of experimentation within architecture studios and for our analysis of different contemporary crit practices.

As in most contemporary architecture schools today, the core of the École was an atelier system, with students gathered in studios run by influential patrons—we may as well call them professors. The training was competitive: students were continually pitted against each other for hotly contested prizes. The Beaux-Arts jury was a council of experts, usually made up of rival professors, who met behind closed doors to award these prizes and issued their judgement (and their reasoning) in writing. The ultimate prize, the Grand Prix de Rome, entitled the winner to multiple years of residency at the Villa Medici. The resonance of the Beaux-Arts model in pedagogy remains palpable, even as the nominal content of studios has changed.

The lineage of this tradition can be traced. By the 1890s, British schools were also consciously modelling themselves on the Beaux-Arts curriculum and format, with educators having created links both to France and the United States, where this system was already in place.[3] American professors who had studied at the École brought its teaching techniques to the United States—not least, prominent architect Paul Philippe Cret, who ultimately became a professor at the University of Pennsylvania. Cret's own concern regarding teaching was that the hyper-competitive nature of

---

1 Adam Jasper is a postdoctoral researcher at the Institute for the History and Theory of Architecture (gta) at the Department of Architecture, ETH Zurich. Amy Perkins, architect, is a lecturer and a scientific assistant at the Department of Architecture, ETH Zurich. Jeremy Waterfield studied history at St Andrews and University College London and is currently studying at the Department of Architecture, ETH Zurich.

2 The École des Beaux-Arts originated in the patronage of Cardinal Mazarin and Louis XIV. It was the dominant institution of French architectural education from the Bourbon Restoration of 1817 until the decentralization of the architecture schools in 1903 and its final abolition following the protests of 1968, though many of its main tenets continued to be employed. See Richard Chafee, 'The Teaching of Architecture at the École des Beaux-Arts', in Arthur Drexler, ed., *The Architecture of the École des Beaux-Arts* (Cambridge, MA: MIT Press, 1977), 61–109, here 77, 109; Jean-Paul Carlian, 'The École des Beaux-Arts: Modes and Manners', *Journal of Architecture Education* 33, no. 2 (1979), 7–17. The global persistence of the Beaux-Arts approach is attested to by multiple authors. To cite only one example, formal architectural education in Iran was almost entirely based on a pastiche of excerpts from Beaux-Arts texts until the mid-1960s: Reza Naghdbishi, Shahindokht Barghjelveh, Seyed Gholamreza Islami, and Hamed Kamelnia, 'The Qualitative Analysis on Contemporary Approaches toward Architectural Training in Iran', *International Journal of Architecture and Urban Development* 5, no. 3 (2015), 63–72, here 65.

3 Jules Lubbock and Mark Crinson, *Architecture, Art or Profession? Three Hundred Years of Architectural Education in Britain* (Manchester: Manchester University Press, 1994), 78, 82.

Beaux-Arts education 'soon gave birth in each atelier to a little group of "racehorses" trained especially to "run the Grand Prix". These students, having completed the regular work of the school and armed with a certain prestige, spread the view among the younger men that winning competitions was more important than disinterested study.'[4] Despite this criticism, both America and the United Kingdom regularly held a series of prestigious prize-giving competitions.

There are, of course, substantial differences between the contemporary crit and the École des Beaux-Arts jury. For one thing, students were not admitted to Beaux-Arts jury deliberations. The presence of students in contemporary crits goes back, in US schools, to the period directly after the Second World War. It was taken at the time to be a considerable reform, one partly experienced under the influence of émigré members of the Bauhaus school.[5]

However, as Joan Ockman puts it, 'the development of architecture education in the United States and Canada was considerably less straightforward than "Beaux-Arts to Bauhaus" would suggest.'[6] Within central Europe in particular, the practice of peer critique can be traced far before the Bauhaus, back to the salon—either conducted in the architectural atelier itself or in private student clubs. For example, Friedrich Gilly and Johann Heinrich Gentz's Privatgesellschaft junger Architekten, founded in 1799 as an alternative to the Berlin Akademie der Bildenden Künste, can be taken to show that the crit is not only as old as the modern École des Beaux-Arts; it predates it. The organization of such clubs was modelled on French revolutionary cells, but they were also embodiments of Friedrich von Schiller's much-lauded idea of the aesthetic education. In such groups, only the collectively determined judgement of freely associating peers had any weight—and even then, it was not so much the judgement as the discourse preceding it that was the focus of attention.

Even considering that lived institutional practices are vastly less consistent than the literature can convey, there is a significant stake in this historical debate. In our interviews reflecting on the crit, a research project prompted by general dissent within the architecture school regarding teaching practices, there was nonetheless a widespread acceptance that the crit had a linear and progressive history. Teaching staff assumed that crits used to be stricter, more formal, and conducted in even more authoritarian settings than they are now, and that they have been progressively liberalized to include more participants and to allow for more student engagement. On the one hand, this assumption supported the reassuring sense that we are continuously improving our teaching. On the other hand, it created an implicit argument against some teaching experiments: that they are excessive, that they are ahead of their time, that students are not ready, or that the suggested experiment deviates too far from accepted (Beaux-Arts) practice.[7] If, however, the contemporary crit has dual and contradictory origins, within both the academy and the radically anti-authoritarian peer exchange of the

---

4 Paul Philippe Cret, 'The École des Beaux-Arts and Architectural Education', *Journal of the American Society of Architectural Historians* 1, no. 2 (1941), 3–15, here 13.

5 This history of the crit in the United States is thoroughly examined in Kathryn Anthony, *Design Juries on Trial: The Renaissance of the Design Studio* (New York: Van Nostrand Reinhold, 1991).

6 Joan Ockman, 'Introduction: The Turn of Education', in Joan Ockmam and Rebecca Williamson, eds., *Architecture School: Three Centuries of Educating Architects in North America* (Washington, D.C.: MIT Press, 2012), 10–11.

7 Another claim, made from a different direction, is that the purpose of the crit is to prepare students for the rigours of participating in professional competitions. But this claim appears to be a rationalization. In professional practice, architects are supported in teams of designers and consultants and simply win or lose; they do not have to 'defend' their work live in front of a jury. Furthermore, in presentations, the client usually has an interest in finding solutions rather than issuing comparative judgements. As a result, professional presentations are usually framed in the constructive terms of cooperative work.

salon, then both the notional faith in progress and the sense that progress might happen 'too fast' become questionable.

There is, however, a deeper objection to invoking the image of the salon that should be addressed here, one that lurks within the word's nostalgic connotations of a cosy interior. The romantic concept of a salon accords all too well with the way that professors already discuss their roles. The image of the peer group, arguing freely in the service of collective wisdom, corresponds to the idealized self-image (if not the reality) of collegial relationships in academic settings. The image is, however, rendered toothless in practice because it only applies to the professors themselves. Their rivalry in crit sessions, as they debate the merits of each other's studios and each other's students, occludes the silence of the students themselves, who operate under a completely different set of rules. The students are set against each other in what they have learned (from discussions of precarity to the discipline of the marketplace) in a contest of survival, but within the most liberal crits the discussions are treated as if a pure contest of ideas. The image of intellectual freedom and equality remains, but the franchise has been reduced to those with the confidence to speak, underwritten less by expertise than by invulnerability. For teachers who perceive their practice as progressive, the danger is that they see only the interior of their own salon.

Positioning research

Our own position as observers is shaped by the curious position of being trained within the Anglo-Saxon system while currently working in a central European context at ETH Zurich. Our understanding of institutions and their histories is both informed and distorted by contextual shifts. As the institution in which we work attracts students and faculty from around the world, instruction is often in English, leading to both revealing and deceptive similarities with teaching practice in our previous institutions. Studies of the history of architectural education in general, and the crit in particular, in English—more than we can address here—include Donald Schön's approach to the process of creative work in design education more generally[8] and studio traditions.[9] Scholars like Jacqueline Cossentino have updated and applied Schön's work, seeking to draw out principles which can be applied to a wider curriculum.[10] Kathryn Anthony presents a survey of students' experience of design juries, including control groups in adjacent disciplines and surveys of other educators in order to understand the applicability of the findings.[11] The scientification that characterizes Anthony's methods—her use of quantification and controls—not only served to broaden the scope of her results beyond the seemingly typical university where her study took place but also facilitated the standardization of teaching practice. The techniques of observation and control coalesce to both reveal and help produce the broad homogeneity of assessment practices within accredited courses in the United States. Gustav Lymer's 2010 study from Sweden further draws attention to how internationally standardized the crit is[12] and how close crit practices in Sweden are to our own observations. He makes a valuable distinction between instruction based on a set of shared norms for the professionalized critique of a project and instruction that acknowledges the role that personal intention plays in the creative process. Lymer also pays prescient

---

8 Donald Schön, *The Reflective Practitioner* (New York: Basic Books, 1983).
9 Donald Schön, *The Design Studio: An Exploration of Its Traditions and Potentials* (London: RIBA,1985).
10 Jacqueline Cossentino, 'Importing Artistry: Further Lessons from the Design Studio', *Reflective Practice* 3, no.1 (2002), 39–52.
11 Kathryn Anthony, 'Private Reactions to Public Criticism: Students, Faculty, and Practicing Architects State Their Views on Design Juries in Architectural Education', *Journal of Architectural Education* 40, no. 3 (1987), 2–11.
12 Gustav Lymer, *The Work of Critique in Architectural Education*, Gothenburg Studies in Educational Sciences vol. 298 (Gothenburg: Acta Universitatis Gothoburgensis, 2010).

attention to the distinction between analogue and digital modes of presentation, a distinction still relevant in our own study. Other interesting approaches to crit practices bring in psychoanalysis[13] and institutional psychotherapy[14] to dissect the interactions of architectural education and the crit.

Most promising for our investigation of the crit is the general methodology of action research. The term 'action research' is attributed to the organizational psychologist Kurt Lewin in the 1940s, in relation to empowering health practitioners in the face of the bureaucratic domination of hospitals.[15] From the beginning, action research was understood to be research that culminated in social action, not merely epistemological insights. Olav Eikeland notes that action research is now often considered in terms of interventions, practitioner research, and collaborative research.[16] Eikeland elaborates on a distinction between 'technique' and what many in the literature call 'praxis': a more rigorous expression of all the connotations around the word 'practice', a transition from automatic performance to self-conscious knowledge on the part of the practitioner, and the process of work that leads to expertise. We suggest that action research is not only compatible with architecture as it is practised and as it perceives itself as a profession historically, but that it is 'native' to it. The epistemic function of the crit is that it breaks open the black box of the studio. Action research, in turn, allows us to break open the black box of the crit.

What's good?

As Jürgen Habermas argued, the problems of truth are not just problems of epistemology; they are problems of anthropology.[17] Translated into our own research problem, how do we study the crit without sliding into false objectivity, without 'scientism'?

Although our responses are shaped by the literature above, our methodology and our intentions were guided by two further factors. The first was the parity movement, a political shift within the ETH Department of Architecture against an entrenched culture of sexism. Even as enrolments moved towards an equal number of female and male students, and studio teaching was increasingly delivered by women, the overwhelming majority of senior academic positions remained occupied by men. The parity movement agitated for the implementation of non-negotiable rules of equal representation of the genders—in public presentations, in studio crits, and in hiring committees. The movement interrupted an academic culture that had generated deep frustration amongst the students and teaching staff but that had been effectively invisible to senior faculty. Although they were rarely directly referred to in class, the parity discussions led to a heightened sensitivity around the propriety of criticism and respect.

The second factor, so obvious at the time of writing that it barely needs to be referred to, was the outbreak of the novel coronavirus, which resulted in the cancellation of live midterm and final crits and their transferal to online video platforms. Crit observations of a half-dozen different professorial chairs were supplemented by interviews with multiple

```
13 Jeffrey Karl Ochsner, 'Behind the Mask:
A Psychoanalytic Perspective on Interaction in the Design
Studio', Journal of Architectural Education 53, no. 4
(2000), 194–206.
14 Félix Guattari, Psychoanalysis and Transversality
(Los Angeles: Semiotext(e), 2015), 14. The basic outline of
institutional psychotherapy appears at the same time as
action research, in the period following the Second World
War. Its central place of development was the La Borde
clinic in rural France, where Félix Guattari was a
practising psychiatrist.
15 See, for example, Kurt Lewin, 'Action Research and
Minority Problems', Journal of Social Issues 2, no. 4
(1946), 34–46.
16 Olav Eikeland, 'Action Research: Applied Research,
Intervention Research, Collaborative Research, Practitioner
Research, or Praxis Research?', International Journal of
Action Research 8, no. 1 (2012), 9–44, here 12.
17 Jürgen Habermas, Knowledge and Human Interests, trans.
Jeremy Shapiro (Boston: Beacon Press, 1971), 304.
```

professors in which they expressed their own perceptions of the crit.

Our observations of and interviews about the crit revealed discomfort regarding the hierarchy of all involved, basis and criteria for evaluation, and practices of critique in the crit itself. Several professors expressed discomfort and criticism or ambivalence towards the crit practice in general. In the interviews, one professor expressed unease with the crit's conventions, noted that the standard crit from their student days had followed the blunt model of 'present, wait, be shot at'. Another professor who had taught at a North American Ivy League university ten years previously described the classic crit scenario as 'twelve critics, all lined up in a row, and a crying student'. For this professor, the model had not aged well and, in the somewhat tense political climate of the department, had been subject to numerous ameliorations, none of which could be described as systematic. As another professor remarked, 'We know what we don't want to do'—but also did not know what was wanted.

One major difference from studio to studio was a disparity in implicit or explicit judgement criteria. One of the characteristics of studios is that students are encouraged to identify themselves with their work, so, as one professor argued, it is then very hard to distinguish between a criticism of work and criticism of its author. As he remarked, 'if your work is just an investigation, you are much more free'. We witnessed this gesture of identification repeatedly in recordings: One student, who laced their project with artistic and fashion references but presented a meticulously rendered digital project was told that without 'doing first and thinking later' he would never be able to emulate the artists that he admired. This observation has been corroborated by others. Lymer and Bill Hillier draw attention to the intention of designers and how frequently the question of intention is invoked in architectural settings.[18] The claim of 'we can see what you intended, but …' or even beginning a question with 'what did you intend with ___?' are often precursors for the most devastating critiques. Attributing intention to a designer acknowledges the gap between any given design and the intention behind it and asserts the fundamental importance of intention in the creative process. But in the crit context, it also serves the rhetorical function of imputing a specific goal upon the designer and committing them to the implicit criteria for success or failure that come with that goal.

Frequent judgement criteria were clustered under comments regarding 'internal logical consistency'. Internal logical consistency could refer to the legibility of a project's stated intentions: it was expected that floor plans, sections, and visualizations were all immediately relatable to each other, and each image would convey a clear hierarchy of information. Furthermore, criticism was often levelled at the idea that the student had 'not gone far enough', which usually meant that the project was either insufficiently radical or insufficiently detailed. The best projects, it was observed, were perceived as having a clear internal logic that could be traced from the master plan down to the architectural detail without obvious inconsistency or loss of 'resolution'. At the same time, students were sometimes accused of having gone too far, of having become too rigid in their deductions from master plan to detail or too precise in their delineation of such details. These criticisms were often expressed as 'formalism'. The instructional justification for these charges was interesting. The implication was that the 'formalist' project had become solipsistically inflexible to the contingencies of its realization. An allied but distinct criticism was that the over-detailed project inhibited the potential for experimentation with materials. It is worth noting that terms like 'resolution' (usually good) and 'formalism' (usually bad) had attained somewhat idiosyncratic meanings in this context but that this did not prevent their being immediately understood by the students in the crit.

18 Bill Hillier, *Space Is the Machine* (Cambridge: Cambridge University Press, 1996); cited in Lymer, *The Work of Critique* (see note 12), 52.

It was noteworthy how many criticisms of projects were presented in veiled or euphemistic form. Professors often uneasily project the subjective nature of judgements back upon the students by referring to a detail of the project and demanding that the students assert their own criteria with questions like, 'why did you put this here?' or, 'is this really what you wanted/intended?' One repeatedly observed circumlocution for a critical comment was the phrase, 'I'm saying this as a provocation.' Comments prefaced in this way were often doubly insulated by being directed at another juror. Such questions are often constructed in a way that places the onus on the student to articulate their own criteria for a project. A salient feature of a project would be identified, and the student would be asked where it came from and why they chose it. In such scenarios, even a seemingly poor decision can offer the student the opportunity to show their capacity for architectural argumentation. Students mostly responded to such personal criticism with passive acceptance. A single strategy that was repeatedly observed, which enabled the student both to submit and to deflect, was that they would often say in response to a point of criticism, 'I had thought of that, but …', before referring to decisions visible in the project.

Additional tensions were occasionally visible between guests, professors, and studio assistants. In one review some of the assistants could be seen on Zoom rolling their eyes and laughing when a juror repeatedly condescendingly invited a younger female architect to comment on a project first in a poorly calibrated attempt at chivalry. The same guest betrayed inattentiveness and short attention span, publicly stating his boredom and speaking only to the other guests as if students were oblivious, perhaps thereby triggering the assistants' subversive body language. The assistants' strategies were directed towards the professor who they felt had invited an inappropriate juror, as well as to the students, to whom they were signalling that the guest should not be taken seriously.

Almost without exception, students did not speak during other students' crits. Only twice in one of the recordings we observed did a student step in—the same student both times—and make statements or ask questions in defence of a project that was being harshly reviewed. In both cases the student sought to bring in alternative criteria to support a project. In the first instance, the student claimed that they had gained an intimate knowledge of the site through regular visits during the semester. On the basis of this knowledge, they claimed that many of the aspects criticized of the presenting group's project were instead valid and that criticisms of judgement should in fact be merely questions of representation. This display of bravery ended a sequence of harsh criticisms. The professor confirmed that he did not know the site well, although both professor and guests clearly remained unconvinced. In the second instance, a group was criticized for not having a clear enough hierarchy in the floor plan, and the student intervened to ask—somewhat tendentiously—whether they had perhaps been thinking about Persian carpets or mandalas, which are based on different aesthetic traditions. The exceptional nature of this intervention by a student indicated something quite significant. As one of our interviewees pointed out, 'it's an unwritten law that our assistants actually contribute very little in the crits'. By extension, the students contribute even less. The removal of the spatial constraints of the crit did not make this 'unwritten law' less apparent but rather more, as the sudden insecurity of distinction made communication and resistance to judgements even harder to articulate than before.

Three studios we observed had briefs that made direct relationships to climate change, thus explicitly specifying judgement criteria for the projects. This meant that those crits avoided any controversy that the dominant criteria involved questions of grey energy use (the energy expended in the production of materials) and sustainability. One studio even had a tool for calculating the carbon footprint of each student project, and the resulting 'league table' was referred to frequently. Quantitative science was embraced as a relief from more ambiguous topics. Interestingly, classic architectural problems (and even engineering ones, such as structural integrity) were effectively de-prioritized. Noteworthy was that criticisms directed to political or ethical dimensions of architectural projects in the (climate change) studio elicited an immediate defence of the student by the professor or developed into an argument between guests—as if criteria for what consisted of admissible and inadmissible evidence had been developed and were used in the defence of an accused like in a courtroom. More general comments directed towards politics or ethical questions were treated as implicitly critical of the construction of the studio as a whole. In the face of such questions, professors tended to react as if they were personally or professionally required to explain their stance.

Hierarchies in the online crit

The change to online crits because of the coronavirus pandemic was initially perceived by many as a catastrophe but revealed advantages. Chief among them was that the crits were routinely recorded. We gained access to some forty hours of recordings of crits plus notes from participation in some twenty hours of crits. The recordings enabled the careful examination of gestures, comments, and responses. All references to crits and direct quotes in this article are taken from these recordings.

There is no doubt that the movement to Zoom disrupted some of the standard practices of the crit, but as all the researchers had observed crits over the past two years, we allowed our experience to compensate for any distortion caused by the medium. Within the crits themselves, the shift in medium was mentioned multiple times, but usually with the observation that not much had changed and that the crits proceeded very much as they always had. Multiple comments congratulating all the members of the studio were made for how well the crits were prepared and how 'normal' they were. It was also noted that the online format allowed for a larger than usual number of outside observers.

The standard spatial arrangement of the crit is well known, and often criticized for its hierarchical format. As one of interviewees remarked: 'We always do this presentation at the wall ... standing students, sitting jury, and it's also a technical problem, because acoustically it's impossible. If you sit four rows behind you don't really follow. And I'm not so sure what the students can follow because they're nervous.' This is a striking contrast between the conventional crit and the Zoom crit: both phatic and spatial elements of the conversation are completely missing. Faces appear in a grid that is arranged by order of when people enter the virtual room. Students cannot privately greet each other nor acknowledge each other's presence. Furthermore, jury members, unless they have been assembled beforehand, are effectively teleported into the collective space of the crit. This particular feature of the Zoom crit is altering the conventions of mutual acknowledgement, introduction, and social distancing (in the pre-2020 sense of the term) that are a typical part of socially hierarchical exchange. One effect of it was a tendency, observed more than once, to spend more time than usual reciting the biographies of jury members, their professional experience, accreditations, and achievements: as if, in the absence of spatial features asserting their status, their importance had to be rendered explicitly.

Regardless of traditional crits or those over Zoom, in situations in which the jury is framed as people who know, and students as people who do not know, criteria are subject to redefinition based upon the authority of the speaker. The more important the jury member, the more likely their implicit criteria would be taken up by the next speaker. It was interesting to note that when a high-status jury member commented after a lower-status jury member they might discretely assert their position not by contradicting the previous speaker but simply by ignoring the implicit criteria of their comments. The senior guest would merely pause and then direct attention to an altogether different aspect of a drawing.

We identified several phenomena from the recordings that indicate the reflexive complexity of the crit. Well aware of the controversy amongst students, teaching staff often played the role of 'defending' the students against overtly negative criticism by jury members. Another of our interviewees made this point very early on in our discussion: 'my primary role is to defend the student'. This amounts to a shift in the courtroom metaphor noted above: the student would present the case, the professor would defend it, and the jury would politely feign posing critical questions. As researchers, we do not object to this experimentation with roles but did wonder that so little could be done to change the dominant imaginary scenario that still dictated the general flow of proceedings.

One concern with the contemporary push to a less confrontational atmosphere in the crit is that less confrontation does not necessarily imply less hierarchy. If negative assessments become too euphemistic or too indirectly worded, although they may be understood by some parties in the room, they become much harder to address or discuss openly. As one interviewee pointed out, the old regime had been 'extremely personal', with the professor throwing out entire projects and insisting that the student restart. As our interviewee observed, 'it would be impossible to teach like that today', yet the same interviewee added that 'he was a fantastic teacher'. The interviewee went on to remark (repeating the trope of identifying the student with the work) 'we wouldn't dare to be as personal anymore. It wouldn't be possible anymore, and to be honest … I think it's a loss, because architecture, it is personal. What you do, you are not a technician, you don't just learn something and apply something, it comes really from the heart and from your gut'. It should be possible to navigate between the surface learning that is created by an environment of anxiety, on the one hand, and the superficiality or unnecessary ambiguity that is created by only positive comments. As another professor observed, there is also a frustration induced by the lack of feedback: a student needs clues to understand the criteria for evaluation. As he remarked, architecture competitions are a kind of black box. If your entry does not win, you are not told why. This, he noted, is not polite; it is merely confusing.

Conclusions

Some of the professors we interviewed proposed suggestions for how crits might be improved. One tactic for breaking the conventions of presentation would be to ask students to present each other's projects. The Students would need to improvise based on the presented material and would be asked to defend the work of their peers. After such an attempt, the students responsible for the project would be able to respond with the presentation that they had intended to give. This is an approach that has its own precedents. As an interviewee noted: 'Hans Pölzig did a system in which the students had to present their colleagues' projects, not their own. Which I think can also be interesting, where you don't have this psychological pressure of it being me, but you really can objectively talk about architectural qualities and problems. And you as an author of a project, you can learn how somebody else sees it coming from outside. Which can maybe help you because it breaks up this too-close distance to your work.'[19] The gap between the response of a well-intentioned audience and the author's statement might reveal the gap between the intention of the work and its effect more explicitly than critique could. Another strategy would be to ask students to present the problems in their

---

19 This tactic can also be compared to the art school teaching of the video artist and professor Stan Douglas, who notoriously inverted the format of the art school crit by asking students to respond to the work of their peers, only afterwards requesting the student to read a prewritten summary of their work.

projects as questions to the critics, to present the least confident solutions, or to ask the questions that they found most intractable. Another more fanciful suggestion was for students not to present their projects as solutions to problems but to treat their projects as if they were already built and to offer 'guided tours' through the imagined structures.

Often, the honest feedback on the programme of the studio is only heard after the crit itself. Post-crit drinks, which have become a ritual in many studios, are 'where you finally get to hear what the students really think', one interviewee mentioned. Could this feedback be brought into the crit itself, with the students being encouraged not only to 'answer the problem of the studio' but to present projects which offered a counter-proposal to the studio's approach? Each studio palpably formed a microcosm of meanings, euphemisms, and private references that overlapped with (but could not be equated to) any other studio nor reduced to a subset of the language of professional architecture. Although educators we spoke to did state that they saw the studio as a shared endeavour, the perception among students is largely that its programme related very clearly to the interests of the professors. Can we ask of professors that, like students, they refrain from identifying with their studios and instead see them as objects of investigation?

In the introduction, we argued that the practice of the crit derives as much from the avant-garde salon as from the Beaux-Arts tradition. The avant-garde potential of the crit is therefore not a new discovery but can be traced back to its origins. At the same time, nostalgia for the salon is no method. The image of the salon continues to be operative, but in practice only applies to the professors and crit guests—that is, those who speak. In the language of institutional psychotherapy, we can identify the professors and crit guests as functioning as an independent group, even as the students continue (sometimes invisibly) to function as a dependent group. From an action research perspective, the de facto student performance of dependency during the crit amounts to an epistemic loss for the teaching staff as well. Teaching cannot function as collaborative research when the collaboration is reduced to a homogenization of aesthetic styles between projects. There are good reasons for seeing the current organization of the crit as by no means inevitable or organic but rather as a kind of historical hybrid, a chimera of stitched-together conventions subject to a series of contingent historical changes. This is not entirely bad news. What could have been taught differently in the past can also be taught differently in the future.

Jan Silberberger

Reimagining the Crit [1,2]

The design studio constitutes a highly advanced training environment: a form of education characterized by collective action in which learning, teaching, making, and reflecting all merge into one practice.[3] The studio form of teaching allows for adequately dealing with the uncertainties, ambiguities, and the non-linearity that govern our complex world. A central aspect of studio teaching concerns the fact that students are very closely mentored, which contrasts mentoring practices in other academic fields. As Joan Ockman writes, 'The intense interpersonal relationship between the student and instructor ... remains at the heart of a form of education that has revolved around the design studio since the Beaux-Arts epoch (and, at an earlier moment, around the close social and professional bonds between master and apprentice)'.[4]

At the same time, critiques (crits), a key form of interaction between teachers and students, and especially the larger public crits, are highly criticized. Not only are they often reduced to static instances of a one-way knowledge transfer,[5] these public reviews are also typically governed by a 'climate of fear, defensiveness, anxiety, and stress',[6] so much so that 'from the students' perspective the crit is probably the most gruelling and potentially humiliating experience of their education'.[7] Despite the crit format's 'strength in providing feedback instantaneously', it simultaneously runs the risk of becoming 'overly negative—sarcastic even',[8] leaving students 'distraught, humiliated'.[9] Crits are all too often 'experienced by students as a frightening event'[10] inducing even in extreme cases 'vomiting, fainting through fear'[11] whereby 'students, for the major part of their presentation, are literally frozen with fear'.[12] The list could easily be extended.

Apart from the often-terrifying ritual of the crit, design studios are usually referred to as 'sheltered' spaces. Teachers, assistants, as well as many students with whom I spoke described the studio as a space that allows for experimentation because it is protected from the outside world's ready-made assessment criteria and demand for exploitable, marketable results. If 'sheltered' means an environment that facilitates profound, thorough, independent, and impartial research into questions and problems, it may be regarded as the central quality of academia.[13] The 'Atlas of Radical Pedagogies'[14]

1 Jan Silberberger, ETH Zurich.
2 For an earlier version of this paper see Jan Silberberger, 'Public Crits in Architectural Design Education: Some Critical Reflections', *Charrette* 6, no. 2 (2020), 95–105.
3 Donald A. Schön, *The Reflective Practitioner: How Professionals Think in Action* (London: Temple Smith, 1983); Johan De Walsche, 'Genus, Locus, Nexus: An Inquiry into the Nature of Research in Architectural Design Education' (PhD diss., University of Antwerp, 2018).
4 Joan Ockman, *Architecture School: Three Centuries of Educating Architects in North America* (Cambridge, MA: MIT Press, 2012), 29.
5 Dana Cuff, *Architecture: The Story of Practice* (Cambridge, MA: MIT Press, 1992).
6 Richard Tucker and David Beynon, 'Crit Panel', in Hedda H. Askland, Michael Ostwald, and Anthony Williams, eds., *Assessing Creativity: Supporting Learning in Architecture and Design* (Sydney: Office for Learning and Teaching, 2012), 133–56, here 145.
7 Cuff, *Story of Practice*, 126 (see note 5).
8 Charlie Smith, 'Understanding Students' Views of the Crit Assessment', *Journal for Education in the Built Environment* 6, no. 1 (2011), 44–67, here 56.
9 Kathryn H. Anthony, *Design Juries on Trial: The Renaissance of the Design Studio* (New York: Van Nostrand Reinhold, 1991), 4.
10 Helena Webster, 'The Architectural Review: A Study of Ritual, Acculturation and Reproduction in Architectural Education', *Arts & Humanities in Higher Education* 4, no. 3 (2005), 265–82, here 265.
11 Tucker and Beynon, 'Crit Panel' (see note 6), 147.
12 Bernadette Blair, 'At the End of a Huge Crit in the Summer It Was "Crap"—I'd Worked Really Hard but All She Said Was "Fine" and I Was Gutted', *Art, Design & Communication in Higher Education* 5, no. 2 (2006), 83–95, here 89.
13 Paula Stephan, *How Economics Shapes Science* (Cambridge, MA: Harvard University Press, 2012).
14 Beatriz Colomina, 'Radical Pedagogies', https://radical-pedagogies.com/ (accessed 20 July 2020).

maps out how, in the wake of the 1968 student protests, design education came under attack for the withdrawal of studios from society. Students argued that studio education should get out of the ivory tower, deal with real-world problems, and seek interaction with the public. Instead of withdrawing from public life, students demanded design studios to strive for ways of engaging with public discourse and interfering with burning issues—from a perspective not required to submit to commercial demands or exploitability.

On the other side, if 'sheltered space' denotes an environment 'protected from the pressure of accountability', these spaces run the risk of creating toxic power structures. When professors adopt an understanding of architectural design essentially related to taste—'one of the cherished myths of modernity'[15]—not only the process of designing but also the assessment of design proposals is governed by subjective judgements and personal, tacit knowledge. This stance would lead architecture education to be simply a process of acculturation whereby students reproduce and imitate their teachers to become inaugurated. Teaching that promotes individual expression (instead of, for example, traceability and comprehensibility) and relies mainly on personal, tacit knowledge (instead of, for example, a coherent methodology) is thus prone to create a highly teacher-centred environment of extreme dependencies.

In mapping the struggles for radical democratization and self-determination, the 'Atlas of Radical Pedagogies' does not specifically address public crits. This crucial ritual of studio education undoubtedly underwent fundamental changes over the course of the student protests. Yet, as the atlas makes clear, most of the changes that resulted from the student protests were short-lived experiments. Soon after their hard-earned assertion and successful implementation, many of their decisive elements had been reversed and the inherited structures restored.

In personal communications, a professor mentioned that at midterm crits at ETH Zurich even in the late 2000s, 'assistants were not allowed to say anything other than "Do you want some coffee?"' There have been positive changes in the meantime—and things really seem to be moving forward as I write this chapter—but many (if not almost all) of the crits that I have observed have still been characterized by a striking passivity required of (and performed by) students. This aspect of passivity as a significant shortcoming that prevents the format of the crit from unleashing its full potential as a review and training procedure is the focus of the chapter at hand.

I gathered data from selected studios at four architecture schools in Europe: ETH Zurich, Technical University of Munich, University of Stuttgart, and AA London. Although the sample is not statistically representative, it covers a broad and expressive range regarding approaches studios promote, tasks they assign, and objectives they pursue. I played a variety of roles in the crits I observed, from solely silent observer to an active member of the jury panel directly involved in criticizing students' projects.

The passive role assigned to and adopted by students in public crits presented itself as a recurring pattern common to almost all cases I studied. Due to this striking recurrence, I focus on developing a theoretical reasoning for the necessity to reframe the public crits.

The general pattern of the public crit

Most of the public crits that I observed followed the same operational sequence. After students' well-prepared presentations of their work, they receive the professors' and guest critics' well-phrased verdict. In their presentations, students guide the critics proficiently through the material (plans, renderings, models, photos, sketches, movies, texts) they produced—not unlike a tech company representative

---

15 Michael Sorkin, 'Democracy Degree Zero', in Österreichische Gesellschaft für Architektur, ed., *Wettbewerb! Competition!* (Vienna: ÖGFA, 2005), 105–16, here 108.

presenting a new product at a sales conference. Most of these presentations describe what can be seen, but little is said about why something has been done. Furthermore, students often conceal the flaws and problematic aspects of their designs as well as the difficulties they themselves see in mending them—especially in final reviews (which are oral examinations) but also, less obviously, in intermediate crits. After such sleek presentations, it is up to the critics to detect and address problematic aspects of the design proposal. Their verdict often has the nature of an assessment of an entry in an architectural competition. It might get 'overly negative'[16] at times but is usually a balanced mixture of criticism and appreciation. Critics make use of architectural history and theory to reinforce and substantiate their statements, suggest references (buildings, texts, works of art, movies) to consider, propose alternative solutions, or raise practical concerns with issues like statics or construction.

This intermixed character of the assessment, the variety of aspects and criteria, and the sheer amount of information thrown at students—often in no particular order—poses an enormous challenge for them. Since the points of criticism are often not prioritized, which can be related to the 'syncretic nature of architectural education' combining 'technics and aesthetics, sciences and humanities',[17] students have difficulty in gathering and making use of feedback—especially considering that students are often nervous, exhausted, overworked, and sometimes outright frightened during public crits. While this emotional and physical state provides a partial explanation, I still found it striking that students almost never asked a question. For full days of crits, students never spoke up or tried to contribute to the discussion, let alone challenge a critic's argument. If they said something presenting their work, it was only to defend their project. The following conceptual framework for understanding design processes helps lay out how this defensiveness, passiveness, and non-participation prevents the current crit format from unleashing its full potential as a procedure of training and learning.

Conceptualizing the design process

I draw on ideas developed by Horst Rittel, an early pioneer of the design methods movement. While Rittel considered his description of the design process a scientific, functional model or even a guideline that architects and (urban) designers could directly apply and make use of in order to rationalize and improve their procedures,[18] I propose to understand it rather as a philosophical concept in the sense of Gilles Deleuze and Félix Guattari.[19] According to Rittel, design processes are characterized by an arrangement of three sub-processes: firstly, the understanding of the environment in which the design to be developed is supposed to intervene; secondly, the production of a spectrum of solution proposals; and thirdly, the assessment of each solution proposal. Rittel stresses that each of these three models represents a distinct process, yet, at the same time, these three processes are mutually dependent. Understanding the intervention site for the intended design informs the breadth of the spectrum of possible solutions and each solution's assessment—which can again inform the understanding of the problem. Rittel emphasizes that designing is an iterative, multidirectional process and that feedback loops constitute an integral part. For Rittel, designing is characterized by an iterative interplay between opening and closing the variety of solution proposals. Stressing that designing is to be understood as developing an 'image' or 'idea' relative to the problem and its solution, Rittel proposes that the resonance between the three distinct, heterogeneous sub-processes of developing

---

16 Smith, 'Understanding Students' Views'(see note 8), 56.
17 Ockman, *Architecture School* (see note 4), 10.
18 Horst Rittel, 'Der Planungsprozess als iterativer Vorgang von Varietätserzeugung und Varietätseinschränkung', in Institut für Grundlagen der modernen Architektur, ed., *Arbeitsberichte zur Planungsmethodik 4: Entwurfsmethoden in der Bauplanung* (Stuttgart: Karl Kramer Verlag, 1970), 17–31.
19 Gilles Deleuze and Félix Guattari, *What Is Philosophy?* (New York: Columbia University Press, 1994).

interpretations of the context, design proposals, and their assessment shape and reshape the activity of designing.

Deleuze and Guattari define concepts as having 'components that may, in turn, be grasped as concepts', which renders components as inseparable within themselves, 'distinct, heterogenous, and yet not separable'.[20] Combining this perspective with Rittel's construct of ideas, I emphasize the close relationship and seamless transition between the three distinct yet inseparable procedures of interpretation of context, development of solution proposals, and performance assessment of the latter. I would argue that understanding designing as combining these three distinct yet mutually dependent procedures conforms well to the realities perceived by most design architects.

Following the inseparability of problem-framing from development of solution proposals and their assessment, and the distinctiveness of the three procedures, three entry points into the design process emerge. The first enters the design process via problem-framing, focusing on interpreting the problem conditions and thereby predisposing a solution space and assessment criteria. This approach is typically chosen in experimental studios. The second enters through developing design proposals, searching for a satisfying problem solution which is (at least in the first instance) relatively stable and relatively well defined. This second approach is widespread and used in most studios. The third entry point to the design process analyses existing solution proposals to gain a deeper insight into the problem. This approach is not explicitly considered by most architects, but when faced with a building task many nevertheless search for buildings that responded to comparable problems and assess their performance to better understand the problem at hand. Hence, this third approach is practised frequently. Of course, in the process of designing, the distinction between the three components or sub-processes becomes indiscernible. Nevertheless, it can be stated that the different entry points push forward different (initial) conducts.

Regarding the third approach, the ability to judge design proposals is not only important for own creations (as designers constantly assess interim findings when designing) but also for drawing on references—that is, for effectively using the existing knowledge base, which for the research field of architecture is largely folded into buildings. This ability to judge solution proposals is trained, mentored, and assessed in the studio. It is, however, addressed indirectly—that is, as a cause variable that becomes manifest in the objects and artefacts students produce—and is oftentimes not specifically discussed as a distinct skill. Given the important role of judgement in architectural design, I ask: could the public crit not be understood as an ideal setup for training people how to judge designs? That is, could it not be a setting where students are mentored regarding their abilities to produce and judge design proposals?

Reassessing the crit

Making the crit a more valuable learning experience would require reframing it in terms of how single projects are discussed and how students, assistants, and professors are organized and perceive their roles. Professors and assistants at all architecture schools I observed constantly stressed the importance of the studio as a collective training area, reminding their students to work in the shared studio space instead of at home. In practice, sharing a studio does not just mean that students are exposed to the development of differing solution proposals but also that they receive feedback from their fellow students, are asked for advice, and are asked to judge their peers' work. In this way, as several of the professors and assistants I spoke to stated, 'students might learn as much from each other as they learn from us'. Thus, in the shared studio, students exercise their capabilities to judge solution proposals not just with respect to their

---

20 Deleuze and Guattari, *What Is Philosophy?* (see note 19), 19–20.

own projects but also with respect to those of their peers. Yet, this form of training is not specifically mentored. Rather, when it comes to practising the skill of assessing design proposals developed by others—which, according to the concept developed in the previous section should be understood as an integral component of designing—students are left on their own.

This is where I reimagine the crit as a collective training ground for practising to judge solution proposals. 'As a student, I learned quite a lot from watching professors and guest critics judging the projects of my fellow students', one professor that I interviewed stated, adding that this training in judgement did not involve her own input but was limited to 'listening carefully'. This demonstration mode of teaching also plays a role in desk crits, where students, as several professors pointed out, 'also learn by watching the instructor sketching possible solution proposals'; that is, 'by watching a knowledgeable architect literally demonstrating the act of designing'. Yet, even though it is impossible to quantify the impact of this latter mode of design teaching, architecture schools throughout history—whether they follow a polytechnical model or a Beaux-Arts tradition—have based student education on the axiom that learning to design can most effectively be done by practising the act of designing. While Rittel's paper can be read as a constant reminder that learning to develop design proposals cannot be separated from learning either in interpreting the problem's basic conditions or in learning to judge the performance of solution proposals, it simultaneously helps pull apart these three inseparable procedures on a conceptual level. Executing such separation leads me to ask: if designing is trained by doing the act of designing, could crits be an ideal environment for students to learn how to judge solution proposals by judging proposals themselves? This would require profound intervention into prevailing crit practices on two levels. First, more effective ways of discussing and reviewing the single student projects would have to be created. Second, students would need to be integrated into the assessment of their peers' projects.

During fieldwork, I encountered several promising endeavours for these interventions. For enhancing the review practice of single design projects, two examples that may seem small could have far-reaching effects. The first was of a professor who radically reduced the 'sales pitch' character of presentations by explicitly asking students to prepare two or three questions for crits. This forced students to address and lay bare the critical aspects of their design proposals and the problems they encountered when developing them. This generated a completely different type of conversation than was common in other crits. Raising questions means formulating claims and defining and representing interests. This small intervention greatly increased the crit's effectiveness as a mode of peer review. The second example separated the author from the presenter. Instead of presenting their own projects, students were assigned to present the work of a fellow student, thereby eliminating the extreme degree of emotional involvement that often characterizes crits and creating a distance that fostered more open debate. In this way, a project presented was not confused with its author's personality but was rather considered an 'objectified' piece of work to be assessed.

As far as redefining crit assessment as collective events, one intervention deserves mention: it altered the spatial setting and included students in the jury panel. Replacing the typical movable walls with a large round table and assigning students as discussants (whereby each student was asked to comment on the work of one of their peers as part of the jury) provoked many of the involved persons (students, assistants, as well as teachers) to abandon the typical performances of highly formal, frontal presentations and instead participate in the crit as a highly compressed instance of collaboration.

It is evident that crit practice has become a concern at architecture schools in recent years—understandably so, for the fear, stress, and defensiveness crits too often cause among students. Consequentially, in recent years a substantial body of literature has emerged that proposes concrete ideas for improving crits that are ready for exploration and refinement.[21] Given the necessity and urgency for change, it should not be forgotten that the crit (and the whole studio approach), compared to review processes in other academic fields, is nevertheless highly sophisticated. Architecture students consistently present precisely crafted, well-prepared work as of their first semester and receive precise and thorough feedback from a variety of reviewers. Students in other disciplines often only experience this type of interaction with their work at the doctoral level, if even there. Hence, despite its flaws, the crit format could offer great potential for learning.

My questions remain thus: Could crits enable students to practise their abilities to judge design proposals? Would crits that do not solely rely on professors and assistants to demonstrate how to assess projects but empower students to display their judgement abilities (and be coached in doing so) not expand the studio approach? And would such practices not improve the mood and learning effects of reviewing to an extent that they could provide a benchmark for other academic fields?

---

21 Rachel Sara and Rosie Parnell, 'Fear and Learning in the Architectural Crit', field 5, no. 1 (2013), 101–25, esp. 117–18; 'Megacrits', The Architecture Foundation, https://www.architecturefoundation.org.uk/megacrit/ (accessed 20 July 2020).

Part Six
Practitioners' Views

Oriented towards Transparency and Comprehensibility[1]

○ Jan Silberberger: My assumption would be that a significant part of that which shapes design processes remains tacit. One does not make that explicit; one is unaware of it.

● **Dietmar Eberle:** For me, designing is a process that I am totally aware of.

○ … And yet, even professors who might not be fully aware of all the decisions that are made during a design process are forced to provide a rationale for their decisions when teaching.

● **DE** Yes, and this is where we often have major problems. Much of what happens within the teaching of architectural design is simply not comprehensible for students. How should they know what happens within the mind of their teacher? It is oftentimes unclear what the goal of a studio course is, the questions it addresses are, or the conditions and assumptions on which it operates—the criteria according to which it assesses design projects.

○ On the contrary, your teaching at the ETH, which you have summarized in your publication *9 × 9*, constitutes a highly rational, logical sequence of exercises.

● **DE** The teaching I have done has always been oriented towards transparency, comprehensibility, and, yes, rationality. In this sense, I would argue that it comes rather close to meeting scientific standards.

○ During field research, I repeatedly noticed how critics mixed assessment criteria in a rather non-hierarchical manner. There were situations where one critic said something relating to fire protection immediately followed by a fellow juror who addressed issues of urban design, and then someone who addressed a specific material used for the facade.

● **DE** You have to understand this as a form of politeness. You pick an issue that gives you something to talk about. That would be a positive reading of this behaviour. A negative one is just this: the arrogance of know-it-alls. You can find both situations. But an architectural project can be discussed from a wide variety of angles, a much wider variety than in most other disciplines. The problem is that there is often no consciousness with regard to prioritizing these different angles. We are running into a problem at many architecture schools at the moment since we have more and more people teaching design who have no understanding of such prioritization, as they have no clue how design works in practice. They are a bit aloof with regard to their selection of relevant issues, which seems to depend solely on their individual educational career. They have never objectified the hierarchies they propose, as they have never tested and verified their meaning in relation to built objects. This is the reason why, during my time at the ETH, I have always emphasized the importance of having people teach design who have proven their ability by means of realized buildings. If you simply apply the criteria of a traditional academic career to the discipline of architecture, a doctoral thesis of mediocre quality becomes more important than one single realized building object where the teacher was obliged to relate their thinking to the consequences as they become manifest in reality. And that is a problem in my opinion.

○ One of the major contributions of *9 × 9* is that it proposes a clear hierarchization of learning content.

● **DE** The structure of *9 × 9* is based on two criteria: Firstly, and that is something most people do not understand, it mirrors the logical stages of the building process. The exercises mirror exactly what happens during the realization of a building project. Secondly, these different stages can be assigned totally different life expectancies in the end. That is what I mean with this somehow abstracted statement of '200, 100, 50, 20, 10'. It refers to the fact that the individual decisions made within these different stages simply have

1 Dietmar Eberle, principal of be – Baumschlager Eberle Architekten, Lustenau, was formerly Professor of Architecture and Design at ETH Zurich.

completely different life spans: 200 years, 100 years, 50, 20, 10 years. If we think about sustainability and the role of architecture, the question of life expectancy plays a key role, since it is primarily the aspect of life expectancy that determines a building's ecological footprint in terms of grey energy. And still today, this is where the biggest error is made: demands, which usually last only for one generation, 25 years, are set in concrete or bricks. Most people still do not understand that what they base their decisions upon, namely function and spatial specifications, most probably will be outdated a generation from now. That is kind of the problem with the whole idea of modern architecture, which inherently focuses on the fulfilment of certain spatial specifications, of functionality in particular, without realizing that this functionality undergoes rapid change—or even, that the idea of a certain functionality undergoes rapid change. And that is exactly why we observe the demolition of large parts of the building stock from the 1950s, 1960s, 1970s, and 1980s—not because they are technically broken but because their functionality cannot be modified. That is the big problem; it is the demolition of something that has become useless. That the idea of a long-lasting usability defines the process of decision-making in architecture is what *9 × 9* is about. Therefore it is in fact simple, though the fact that all this can be verified with numbers and data is, of course, wonderful.

○ How would you understand functionality or the practical value of a building?

● **DE** I usually explain this somewhat generally. In the twentieth century, whenever we discussed user satisfaction in relation to buildings, the decisive question was how satisfied the people who used the interiors of buildings had been. In the twenty-first century, the most important user is the one who passes by. It is in the mind of the passer-by where an image of the future is formed, which grants the building durability and a long life expectancy. I would argue that the users of interiors should be granted the opportunity to create an atmosphere according to their own liking. If someone chooses to commission a highly distinguished interior designer, then so be it. Most people, however, decorate their interiors in a very subjective manner, which reflects their personal trajectories, their experiences, the values they share. We, as architects, are responsible for the contribution the building makes to the public realm, which relates to the building's life expectancy. When we talk about sustainable buildings, this contribution is what we should address. If passers-by do not like a building, history will sort it out.

○ Nevertheless, many briefs at architecture schools still feature detailed lists of spatial specifications.

● **DE** On the one hand, that is just what people have learned and still consider valid. On the other hand, many architects act as servants of developers. I think one of the most important tasks of those who develop architectural designs is to unfold the potential of a building. Let me tell you something: I have quite some experience with realizing large-scale buildings. And guess what? There has not been one single instance where the list of spatial specifications defined at the beginning lived to see the day of the building's grand opening. And that is why I always tell people, sure, you want this kind of use, but that's rather a question of structural design. How high are the span widths and ceiling heights? That is what disposes potential forms of use. In the 1990s, we still had this nice little discipline in architecture, the 'programming of buildings', and I say that is idiotic, since in real life, economic and societal developments constantly inscribe themselves into the building, defining its 'biography'. For instance, I have this case at hand: an investor buys a Kempinski hotel with 100,000 square metres and wants to turn it into an office building. This hotel is for sure less than twenty years old and at a prime location. And now the question arises, do we have to tear it down completely, or can it be reused? One has to analyse if and to what extent the original structure has the capacity to assume different types of use. Had one thought of this beforehand, one would have no trouble converting the hotel. But now this means a huge investment—and that unfortunately is highly typical.

○ The precisely framed series of procedural steps and corresponding exercises proposed in *9 × 9* also suggest something like a stopping rule. Maybe one could relate that to a statement made by design theorist Horst Rittel in the late 1960s. He argued: 'It is a matter of judgment and basic conviction where to stop proliferating complexity and intellectual penetration, to settle the problem at hand. No methodology can substitute for this judgment.' Taking a look at the ways architecture schools deal with this problem of deciding when the process of research, experimentation, and testing needs to be abandoned, I see no real awareness of this issue—there is solely a sort of pragmatism: to stop two or three weeks before submission. Until then, students are supposed to go on trying different ways, even if they have arrived at a satisfactory interim result, because, who knows, they could miss out on an even better solution. Though this might be true, as it sounds plausible—and really every mentor demands it—I ask myself if there may not be a better, more deliberate handling of this issue.

● **DE** The problem is that there is a certain ignorance with regard to 'what is actually important and how important is it?' And that is what leads to these confusions where people do not differentiate between what is decisive, what is the very nature of a building, and what is not. The procedural steps in *9 × 9* are based on a specific set of values, a certain societal concept of meaning and importance. If you execute the first two steps of the work process accurately, not that much can go wrong afterwards. Of course, one has to check constantly each step's consequences on the next. So that is what is important to me within this method of *9 × 9*, that students gain an understanding for the building they have to design, that they learn to differentiate important issues from unimportant ones. And what is important in my opinion are the long-lasting components, as the short-lived ones will be replaced at some point anyway. When it comes to buildings, people need to understand one thing: society and history and the users appropriate buildings in a way that is impossible to predict beforehand. At the ETH Wohnforum, we (together with Susan Gysi) have done research, and we found that apartments are rarely used in the way they had been planned. At the risk of repeating myself, the subsequent agents, the users, inscribe a story of their own upon the building. The more the building allows for that, the better! This might sound cynical: our responsibility as architects is the public realm. The staircase is the last public space in a building; after that, no matter if it is a door to a flat or an office space, the private realm begins. And everybody shall do as they please in their private realm! If you ask me, in 90 per cent of the cases, if you cannot decide on importance, you will not be able to say: that will do. Of course, open questions will always remain, but you will not be able to tell if you have answered the ones that matter.

○ During fieldwork Kim Helmersen and I hardly saw any crits in which students took part in the discussions. I always wonder why they are not encouraged to participate more actively in the assessment of their peers' projects.

● **DE** You have to understand that students are often completely exhausted during these crits. To expect them to engage in a big debate is an illusion. Anyway, I think it is obvious that what is being said during crits leaves its mark in the minds of the students. This is why it is very important that crits take place in the presence of all students and not just within the small group concerned. I have done crits in such a way that five students presented one after the other, and then we discussed the specific projects within a comparative analysis. In this way, a form of generalizability emerges. I have usually made sure that the guest critics we invited did not hold the same views as myself, so that our discussions generated a discourse that could be of interest to the students. And I always ask students to conclude their presentations with a question so that we know what touches them. These typical crits where you have a student presenting and then you talk a bit about the work are awfully one-dimensional, sometimes outright embarrassing.

○ Do you sometimes learn from students' projects? That is, when interacting with their solution proposals do you sometimes find new insights into the problem at hand?

● **DE** Not directly. What I learn from students is about their values, feelings, emotions, and aspirations. And why is that important? Because in ten to fifteen years these students will be in positions, as architects or civil servants, where the architectural discourse is determined. It has always been fascinating to see how architectural debates in the city of Zurich have reflected exactly what we taught a decade earlier. Insofar, what we teach is rather a service to society than an individual one. See, the learning curve for most people flattens rapidly after their studies, which is why they simply keep repeating what they learned during their studies. So this is how our teaching influences the societal discourse ten to fifteen years ahead.

○ In *9 × 9* you describe a building as a set of intertwined technical systems—built environment, structure, building envelope, types of use, and interior material—each with its own lifespan. Would you understand this systematization in relation to efforts of systematizing design processes as put forward by the design methods movement during the 1960s?

● **DE** No. *9 × 9* is a reflection of my own practice and what I have experienced in my teaching. That's its impetus.

○ There is this paper by Rittel from 1970, in which he applies the so-called morphological box (as developed by Fritz Zwicky) to planning problems. This also constitutes an attempt to conceive buildings as sets of interrelated components, as combinations of values assigned to the various interrelated components.

● **DE** The problem with that is that it is completely devoid of any prioritization. All parameters are on the same level, all decisions are equally important. That's hazardous. There is a clear hierarchy between the technical systems. The procedural steps in *9 × 9* stipulate that you first try to understand each system in a rather isolated manner, starting with the most important one—the built environment—then successively go down the hierarchical order, before you recognize the intersections between the different systems. A second aspect that is problematic with the morphological box is that there is no ideal towards which you would like to work. If you don't have an idea of a goal, then these combinations of design parameters become arbitrary, a technicist game. This is classic modernism. There is this total absence of an idea of recoverability, of identity, of culture, aesthetic appearance, and atmosphere. That's why it is slightly outdated.

○ The procedure you propose and describe in 9×9 is so clear and comprehensible that I wonder whether everyone could learn to design. Would you say that, analogous to sports, this training method in combination with work ethic would get every student far enough to be able to produce a rather decent building—so that a lack of talent can be compensated for?

● **DE** Let me put it this way: Maybe half a per cent of students are highly talented. They'll make their way, anyway. They don't even need you. You give them support and guide them, which is a privilege. On the other hand, about 40 per cent of students lack the core competency for architectural design: creative potential.

○ What do you mean by that?

● **DE** Imagine you want to become a pianist. What do you have to do for that? You have to do two things. On the one hand, you have to train and train and train. But technique training alone does not make you a good pianist. In parallel, you have to study literature to learn about the background of what you are playing, to understand what you are playing. But then, the crucial problem is to transfer the knowledge that you have accumulated into your fingers. While playing, there's no way of telling people 'This is important because …'—people have to feel that. The same goes for architecture. You have to increase your knowledge with regard to theory, history, and society, and in parallel you have to train to translate your ideas into form. This process of translation is highly complex, and this is where 40 per cent of students ultimately fail. The majority of students, however, have the capacity to train this ability to turn thoughts and perceptions into form. This is an ability of its own, which needs an incredible amount of training—and you need systematic training methods.

○ Almost every teaching studio started off with a process of enquiry, a process of knowledge gathering and then, in a second step, aimed at translating this knowledge into designs that are not just mere illustrations of the former.

● **DE** Obviously! If you intervene in an existing built environment, you have to know the societal conditions that shaped the buildings. You have to know what happened in politics, in the economy, in the arts. You have to understand the material conditions in order to be able to understand the expression of a building. Architecture is always an expression of societal values. When I walk through a city, I can tell the year of construction for almost every building—and if I'm wrong by five years, that is a lot. Without knowing about societal developments, you cannot see what is there. But with this understanding, you suddenly see why a particular architect did something in the way she or he did.

○ So if architects use buildings as references, they have to decode the building against the background of its societal conditions but also in the sense that they have to reverse the creative process in order to identify or speculate about the architect's values, thinking, and principles of designing?

● **DE** I think references are important, first and foremost, as an orientation, as an aid to get a better understanding of yourself. They are for sure not to be recreated. But they tell you something about yourself—in fact, that is their secret. From references, you can learn about the broadness of the vocabulary of means of expression. And they may tell you about your goals. But I always say that architecture has to be a document of its times. So, I do not think much of indulging in structural conventions, design conventions, of, let's say, the nineteenth century. The societal context that produced them is so different to our contemporary one and you cannot separate the built result from its context, which by all means restricts the possibilities of referencing. Again, architecture, for me, is the most important public document of the societal values of its times. I think the big question for architecture at the moment is relatively simple: What is the specific societal context which we would ultimately like to have expressed in our built environment?

Objectivity and Rationality without Neglecting the Subjective[1]

○ Jan Silberberger: How would you describe the relation between design practice in your office and design practice in your teaching studio?

● **Elli Mosayebi:** There are fundamental differences. In the office, problems and tasks come from outside, usually from clients. Now and then we design without having been commissioned, but that is rarely the case. At ETH Zurich, we develop everything from within; there is no client, and there is no demand for a particular issue. Nevertheless, I would argue that professional practice is extremely important for teaching since it points out relevant issues that deserve academic enquiry. Obviously, you handle certain topics differently in the office than in the teaching studio.

○ Do you usually work according to the same methodological principles?

● **EM** I think, in the teaching studio, the focus is in fact on method—it is about making a series of steps that we as teachers define. In the office it is not as didactic, of course. But even there: when we take part in a competition, we read the programme and analyse what questions it addresses and how we would frame what is indicated or what we read into it. Then we start to research, driven by an intuitive reading of the brief, of the site and such. In the teaching studio, however, we formulate an abstract task for which the students also do research—especially in the first three weeks—in order to be able to provide more specific answers. For instance, one semester we dealt with the question of how energy can become architectural form. We did not have any preconceived views. We simply wanted to find out how certain energy systems work at all, what potential they offer, and what that could mean in a spatial sense. So that was a form of systematic research in a way that we had never done before in our office.

○ Within our fieldwork we oftentimes observed studios that more or less imitate real-life projects, which leads to an abundance of topics and aspects to consider. Should studios conceive of themselves as sites of precisely framed exercises instead?

● **EM** Our semester is divided into four phases. We have three interim crits as sort of milestones, and then there is the final review. The first phase is about data gathering, the second phase is about developing a design, the third phase is about revision and during the fourth phase students need to get to the heart of their projects. During the last three semesters we have been trying to cooperate with experts from other fields, integrating them into our studio. For instance, we had Arno Schlüter from the chair of architecture and building systems and Josef Schwartz from the chair of structural design, and this semester we have Guillaume Habert from the chair of sustainable construction. They also bring topics from their realms to the table, topics that may be not familiar to us but which we would like to address. There is also an artist, Shirana Shahbazi, with whom we collaborate in parallel. This also points to the broadness of the field. We have to translate findings which are not necessarily produced by us into our projects—this is a scientific investigation. At the same time there is a more intuitive enquiry: What could be the more abstract ideas to which the task points? How should we approach and handle the problem given? There are many things that you cannot explain rationally but that naturally point to the next steps. Yet, what we want to push with our second modernity approach is: I want to guide the students so their work becomes more objective and also improve their skills with regard to defending their designs argumentatively. That is why we put emphasis on including experts in our studio and deal with the knowledge that is constantly produced at the ETH. I think one should

[1] Elli Mosayebi, co-principal of Edelaar Mosayebi Inderbitzin Architekten, Zurich, is Professor for Architecture and Design at ETH Zurich.

engage with such research and keep asking what it means for architecture—without giving up on oneself.

○ Have you been developing the concept of the second modernity first and foremost within and in relation to your own teaching?

● **EM** The second modernity is essentially a reaction to a certain contemporary practice that bothers me a bit. Within my own studies, it went like this: we were given an extremely precise building task, and the studio was simply about solving this task. So everything was about intra-architectural topics, and that was okay—one learned a lot. Then, when I started to teach here at ETH Zurich, I noticed sort of a new postmodernism where many chairs dealt with the evolution of history and referenced historic buildings in a slightly superficial manner. They took Plenik, Mies, or Schinkel and made use of them for a project in the middle of Zurich which was supposed to make a valid contribution to contemporary society. For sure, this way of referencing yields a prolific output since, as one could say, the input is directly and linearly converted to an output. At the same time, though, it is a bit foolish, as the questions of why this is done and if it is appropriate are never raised. When I was a student, we of course also looked at references, but never that strategically. We looked to the left and to the right, but this was more to get an idea, to enrich one's vocabulary, never about a detailed analysis of an antetype. But this new postmodernism was a bit troubling to me. So the second modernity is a reaction to what had been going on at ETH but also to what happened in the city of Zurich, where buildings have been constructed that copied Milanese architecture, which is also a bit strange to me. And that led to us wanting to frame our studio differently: to know why we do what we do. It became this idea, if we could dare to bring back the question of objectivity and rationality. Modernism is an extremely contested concept and to appropriate it in an affirmative manner is a provocation in itself. Anyway, we thought it valuable in relation to the question of how architecture can escape this current dead. It is not at all about cutting off modernism. On the contrary, it is about opening up to get a bit further.

○ I have the impression that architecture as an academic discipline has started to move in this direction.

● **EM** I would say that, at ETH Zurich, since the four new professors started, this has become less of a problem. It has been guys like Šik and Märkli who have perpetuated this new postmodernism.

○ Just to clarify, using historic buildings as references as such is not necessarily a problem, is it? I mean, you could adapt underlying principles to contemporary tasks.

● **EM** Yes, but that means translating structural properties, not simply taking over pictorial elements. What I have been criticizing is the lack of transformation and criticality. If you refer to certain characteristics, you have to ask what would that mean in our contemporary context.

○ I wonder if the second modernity also constitutes an attempt to jump back and forth between the swamp—being entangled with and immersed in the project—and the commander's hill, from which one views a project from a critical distance?

● **EM** At a certain stage, all of us become so obsessed with a project that, in the end, our personality is literally built into the project. So, it is difficult to achieve and maintain this kind of critical distance until the end. I think the second modernity is more about creating different, new starting conditions, which, hopefully, exert influence throughout the process.

○ You are one of the very few professors for architectural design at the ETH who hold a doctoral degree. Your thesis deals with the work of Milan-based architect and urban designer Luigi Caccia Dominioni. I would assume that instead of doing a text-based architecture historiography, given your background, you could as well have done a study that relies more on design-based modes of enquiry. Did you ever think about doing a so-called PhD by Design?

● **EM** I think fifteen years ago, I used to be really sceptical of this mode of doctoral studies; meanwhile I consider it a reasonable possibility. I believe that much of what is referred to as 'design' ways of thinking is in fact not that far away from how ways of thinking are practised in hard science disciplines. But I didn't really think about that back then. I was simply interested in this particular architecture—yet, at the same time, I didn't just want to write a dissertation. I wanted to be financed by the Swiss National Science Foundation; that is, have my proposal go through double-blind peer review to ensure its scientific relevance.

○ Do your doctoral studies and their findings somehow find their way into your design practice?

● **EM** They have laid various tracks, I would say. This whole trajectory of performative architecture that we are currently working on can be traced back, even to specific text sections. It might be seen as a way of furthering the investigation into Caccia's method of setting things into motion. Whereas Caccia relied on means of expression, plasticity, and materialization, we now, as a matter of fact, experiment with houses that can literally be transformed by their users.

○ When architecture schools appoint professors for architectural design, it is often argued that a realized building can be seen as an equivalent to a publication in other scientific disciplines. On the one hand, this view is quite plausible. On the other hand, wouldn't it imply that these buildings have to be presented in a way that enables peers to discuss them in an unobstructed manner, both in relation to the findings they produce as well as to the decisions that were made throughout the design and building process?

● **EM** Sure, but moreover, this is an issue of knowledge production. There are buildings that do not produce any knowledge. Others, of course, do. But buildings are not 'single authored': it's never just the architect, and often the client is quite dominant. So this comparison does not work entirely. Still, if you build something that generates knowledge, that can be described in terms of a question or problem, a method, and findings, one could, for sure, see it as an equivalent. I think, though, that in most if not all cases this needs an accompanying written account.

○ You provide your students with a thesaurus and with a reader. How would you describe the relationship between these readings and the design process?

● **EM** There are texts that we consider important; by Bruno Latour, David Harvey, Donna Haraway, and so on. But I constantly urge students to conduct material trials; you know, make an object, reflect on it, remake it, think again—systematically. This is where we are extremely productive. You know, if you just read, you can think for a hundred years. And if you read a text, then make an analysis, and then think about how this has to inform your design proposal, this is way too rigid—and way too slow.

○ Throughout our fieldwork, Kim Helmersen and I often observed the phenomenon architects refer to as charrette: students working till the very last moment, up to the point of complete exhaustion. I think it was at the 2019 ETH Parity Talks that this issue was debated as a questionable, rather outdated model. I understand that design proposals might always be further improved, but is there really no better stopping rule than the deadline?

● **EM** I think our chair, and I myself, we are rather known for pushing and challenging students, also with regard to output. I admit it. Maybe this comes from professional practice—you know, this idea that you can never get far enough. But if something is well thought through, I don't think it's a problem if it is not finished. What is crucial is that you know where you want to go. So it's not about being finished, but about showing the potential of your design. … In the end, students have to find ways, means of expression that carry and give form to their ideas.

○ Isn't it problematic, though, that students are often extremely tired during reviews? We sometimes had the impression that a large majority of students tuned out.

● **EM** I would disagree. That is different for every student. I remember when I was a student, I was really attentive to these reviews. I found it highly interesting what my fellow students had done and how this was discussed.

○ Still, we observed these crits as strangely undynamic, with students being rather passive, defensive, covering problems up, hardly ever asking questions, not being involved in the discussion of their peers' projects. I was constantly asking myself whether they would not gain so much more by contributing to the discussions.

● **EM** First of all, that has to do with the format of presentation. You try to present the state of your project as well as possible. For me, it would be absolutely fine if students directly addressed problems that they have faced, but that is, in fact, very rare. There is the format of the desk crit, where exactly this is done. But in public crits, it's true that students do not actively take part in the discussions—which is something we should think about. I remember that as a student I did not say anything during such crits. However, you can take a lot from them, even without participating actively in the conversation. But I see how this can come across as a bit old school.

○ It has often been argued that imitation plays an important role for students, both to learn about architecture and to become architects.

● **EM** You cannot evade that as a student …

○ … as you probably do not have enough knowledge to oppose or set something against what you are presented.

● **EM** I am aware of the fact that I influence students. I am among the few professors who visit the studio on a weekly basis. When we do desk crits, I sometimes take a pencil and start to sketch, pondering how I would proceed. Sometimes, to judge possible solutions, I really have to draw; I cannot just do that in my head. As a student, I think I learned the most when a professor showed me via drawing how he—all professors were men back then at ETH Zurich—would approach the task. I still remember a desk crit where a professor sketched a bathroom. So I think this way of knowledge transfer, watching someone draw and thereby coming to understand their thinking: that is actually a very nice way. Maybe one can accuse me of influencing students too much; I get that feedback sometimes, but it might be a misunderstanding. You know, there are students who perfectly know what they want, right from the start. For those students, I just provide support. And with those who have difficulties, I start to develop ideas so that they, too, get a project that brings them further. You also learn from adopting ideas; they don't necessarily have to be your own. But if I feel that a student group is a bit stubborn, does not really want to hear my opinion, that is fine, too. People are different.

○ I think the problem with imitation is that students are highly dependent on their professors, since much of the teaching remains on a level of taste—which, if we take Bourdieu, is primarily an issue of class (and education).

● **EM** At the beginning of their studies, students learn a lot by imitation, and I think this is where students with a sophisticated family background, definitely have an advantage. They are familiar with many of the references, whereas students from working class families really have to catch up. If you look at ETH Zurich, the student body is extremely homogeneous—everybody has money; yet at TU Darmstadt, where I taught before, that was really different. There you have students with a bourgeois origin and those whose families immigrated from Anatolia. But those students mostly caught up. In the end, architecture is about asking why you like something.

○ There is the often-cited example of the brilliant architect who is a really bad teacher. Turning this upside down, can a bad architect be a good teacher?

● **EM** I don't think so. I believe that you need to be able to contribute to the state of the art, the state of research of the discipline, to be a good teacher for architectural design.

○ This reminds me of the comparison between a realized building and a scientific paper. Maybe it really works?

● **EM** Obviously, in architecture there is also a state of research, and if you're doing a project you should take that into account. Let's say you want to do a high-rise in wood. Of course, you sift through the state of research, compile some key references that represent solution proposals. And obviously, you analyse these solutions in order to identify specific guiding principles. The problem is that these references are often understood as prescriptions, which are directly imported without any alterations.

○ You might say the same about scientific publications. One can cite Foucault, throw in some quotes by Deleuze, and copy a bit of Latour without any effect, without contributing anything—just to show off academic credentials.

● **EM** That is what is dreary in architecture as well as in any other discipline. And this doesn't get you any further. We should really leave this behind.

I'm Not a Rationalist, but I Like Logic[1]

○ Jan Silberberger: In our research project my colleague Kim Helmersen and I are looking into the teaching of architectural design, particularly into intermediate crits, in order to trace and describe how methods of design are discussed, negotiated, and taught within a variety of studios.

● **Momoyo Kaijima:** Having read your book proposal, it seems to me that you are critical with regard to these methodologies. At least, you seem to be a little doubtful.

○ Not really. Our position is that teaching studios operate much more systematically than it is commonly assumed.

● **MK** What do you mean by systematic?

○ Most studios that we have observed exhibited a rather methodical way of conducting what you could term experiments. There is a formulation of a problem, a set of distinct approaches to tackle that problem, various trials alongside their analysis. While much of these trials may be carried out intuitively, or pre-reflexively, there is usually an effort to interpret and analyse them in descriptive terms.

● **MK** I understand. I was just asking to clarify. I am not a rationalist, not necessarily a systematic person—but I like logic. I like logical thinking to bring the results of research into practice—logic as the driving force to interlock research and practice. I wouldn't refer to that as systematic though. 'Systematic' sounds too rigid, not agile enough.

○ 'Systematic' as a term might be misleading.

● **MK** It is more about logical ways of using knowledge, about being comprehensible, plausible.

○ Your chair at ETH Zurich is titled 'Architectural Behaviorology'. It is obvious that this title directly links to research-driven, scientific fields such as cognitive science,

---

[1] Momoyo Kaijima, co-principal of Atelier Bow-Wow, Tokyo, is Professor of Architectural Behaviorology at ETH Zurich.

anthropology, ecology in a broad sense, and also philosophy and phenomenology. Do you understand your studio as a site where scientific research is done?

● **MK** I am not sure whether I would call it scientific—even though we use semiology, which is obviously an established research field. Back at the Tokyo Institute of Technology, where I studied under Professor [Kazunari] Sakamoto, together with Yoshiharu [Tsukamoto], we studied spatial composition in modern building—I think that was when we first tested semiology, in the 1980s. Back then, Sakamoto was interested in ways of reading architectural form and typology. Studying form and meaning, he also designed a survey to investigate how people perceive and experience these forms, what they think about form, which differences they see in various typologies. Already in his doctoral thesis, Sakamoto was interested in studies about language and how words or language would relate to form and thinking. He then took these studies to read spatial composition. On this basis, we used semiology to trace relationships between elements (that is, individual rooms, collectively shared rooms, public spaces) and meaning. As when you deal with a text: you read the compositional elements as symbols and study how they create meaning.

○ Again, I am not sure whether 'systematic' is the right word, but you clearly make an effort to make this process of reading a building or the built environment traceable, comprehensible, and communicable.

● **MK** We were taught by Sakamoto that architecture is primarily a social undertaking, a social project. This is the background for our use of semiology. When Yoshiharu and I speak of symbolic meaning, we mean the symbolic meaning of architecture for and within society. This also means scrutinizing how form affects people and how that impact might differ from the intended meaning. Sakamoto once said that he may have reacted too severely against formalism, so Yoshiharu and I tried to combine formalistic knowledge and existing architectural typologies with Sakamoto's attitude.

○ How would you describe the relation between your teaching studio, your office and research?

● **MK** They are basically the same. But of course we can always go in and out. We are sort of insiders of slightly different, but closely related, spheres. If we do research about contexts, about the subjective experience of space or the organization of space, our research touches political issues, and we reach out and try to open up the process by creating entry points for people to actively take part in politics and in architecture projects. A project for us is a frame for discourse, a platform for discussing different understandings of meaning. In our teaching, we also try to bring in stakeholders that then act as collaborators and tutors, thereby opening up and enriching the studio and the practice. So practice always leads to new research, but new research leads to new issues that are themes in new projects. In this way, we intervene in society, and at the same time societal issues drive our research and the projects we do.

○ I would assume that your students know examples of your work and, in particular, the approach which you call 'architectural ethnography'. It seems that your students also carry out sort of ethnographic studies. Do you specifically teach them how to do that? Do you, for instance, hand them selected ethnographic accounts to read?

● **MK** I select a site, and I tell them that this environment can be read quite differently. I introduce them to locals and community members and explain that it might be worth talking to these people, asking them about their ideas, their understanding of the place, and discussing drafts and proposals with them. You could say that I arrange or set up these ethnographic encounters, but at a certain point I just tell my students to go for it. I have taught for exactly twenty years now, and I am really happy to see that many of my former students have established strong relationships with local communities, dedicating themselves to the improvement of these areas.

○ I recently read a conversation between you and the anthropologist Tim Ingold, who attempted to connect architecture, anthropology, arts, and archaeology in a seminar which he taught at the University of Aberdeen. In this conversation, the boundaries between these four disciplines became rather blurry—in fact, the blur was very plausible and convincing—but I still wonder how you would describe the differences between what you call 'architectural ethnography' and ethnography or anthropology in general?

● **MK** I really enjoyed talking to Tim. I share many of his interests. We are both interested in space and people's behaviour and how this is connected. I also like the concept of closely relating the four A's [architecture, anthropology, arts, archaeology]; that is, his transdisciplinary approach. Architecture, as I understand it, could be like a hub, a platform to connect information and integrate it into a result that can be effectively shared, a design. An anthropologist does not do that. As architects, we listen to people, but then we have to translate our accounts, interpretations; and findings into a different form, and this transition from different media to architectural form, that is a very big skill, that is the important role of architectural design. Most anthropologists unfortunately have no design skills. Tim is very conscious of that fact.

○ A further difference between ethnographic accounts, which are usually text based, and the drawings that architectural ethnographies produce and rely on is that the latter directly combine observation and description. The artist David Hockney once claimed that painting provides far better means for creating an adequate idea of how we perceive our surroundings than photography. After experimenting for almost twenty years with photography, he argued that we should try to forget the understanding that we perceive our environment as if we were cameras. Would you say that drawing, in a similar way, constitutes a well-developed means when it comes to portraying a certain space, and also when it comes to speculating about potential different ways of using this space?

● **MK** Yes. I think drawing is a method that involves the body, the movement of the body. Drawing is procedural.

Nowadays we are flooded with information. With a computer, you get loads of visual images very easily. But all this information alone is not enough. It is not usable, in a way. We cannot directly apply it in design processes. That is, we cannot directly use it in practice. It seems as if it is not inherent, not part of our bodies, not part of our experience. You see, we have books and we talk, and that is very important for our understanding, but understanding also requires bodily forms of knowledge. Knowledge somehow has to be incorporated into our body, into our blood.

○ The method of public drawing, which you also use on a regular basis—which involves a group of people drawing together to produce one collective drawing on a huge piece of paper—constitutes an exemplary way of involving a multiplicity of stakeholders to develop, assess, and discuss the findings.

● **MK** First of all, public drawing should be a platform for creating a deeper understanding of people's behaviour and the space—a deeper understanding of the overall condition of that space, you could say. These public drawings are done by pencil so that they can easily be erased and redrawn. Public drawing means not to fix and finish everything; rather, it is about being tentative. Furthermore, the piece of paper is big enough that, if you look closely, you can see a single person, whereas if you step back, you have the opportunity to grasp the studied space on a larger scale. By means of public drawing, we collect and gather information in one single piece. A large paper is truly helpful to visualize, grasp, and experiment with the totality of that information. With the computer, a lot of such information remains divided. We can try to bring it together in our brains, but unfortunately we cannot see inside our brains—that is why physical paper as a platform is so important.

○ At the beginning of this interview, you said that you like logic. Do you require your students to be logical with regard to the ways they explain their design and how they speak about it?

● **MK** I always ask them to make sharp notes for explanation. If we consider architecture as part of society, we have to acknowledge that people also need words to understand the meaning of architecture. Sometimes people have the skill to read architecture and the imagination to see how this or that space would be, but I think we as architects need to think about this in terms of literacy, and we need to speak about projects not in technical terms but in common language.

○ Your book *Made in Tokyo* presents an immense number of case studies. Generally, I assume that knowledge in architecture depends to a large extent on detailed case studies. If your students carry out an architectural ethnography and develop a design in relation to a specific problem, do you sometimes also learn from their work?

● **MK** Of course. I always try to find a new site with regard to the tasks I assign in the teaching studio—sometimes a city or a municipality approaches me for doing a project there together with my students. Obviously, a semester is too short, so the lens, so to speak, should be sharper with respect to the observations, but even within one semester, if we read a certain built environment, or learn to read it, we gather knowledge. This curiosity, the excitement to discover something, is very important for my teaching. We started to experiment with semiology in urban and suburban settings, but since 2011 with our contribution to the reconstruction of fishing villages in the prefecture of Miyagi [Japan], we have become increasingly oriented towards rural regions and conditions. This means including new, different elements, such as cedar forests or agricultural forests, and investigating their relation to the local conditions of life. So this semester [spring 2020] at ETH Zurich—this is my third year in Switzerland now—we are looking into the valley of Goms in Wallis. We called the course 'Cattle Behaviorology', with the aim that students design commons focused on cattle breeding. Some of my students even have a family background there, so they are very motivated to develop ideas regarding possible future scenarios for the valley. I would see our work there, the ethnographies we are conducting there, and the projects we develop as instances of collective learning, not as a one-way knowledge transfer.

○ As a final question I would like to ask you about the relationship between intuition, meaning pre-reflexive conduct, and rational explanation in your work. Even though you are an experienced architect, I could imagine that, when drawing, there might be situations where you do something which you intuitively know is right, yet you cannot tell why. If that happens, do you then urge yourself to reflect on this instance in order to be able to put it into words?

● **MK** Yoshiharu and I are very conscious about the things we are doing—even about the things we do a bit illogically. Yes, we really force ourselves to make sense of such instances. Everything should become clear and sharp. The clearer it gets, the more convincing and meaningful it becomes—to everybody. We do not work according to a formalistic way; we always need a reason.

Adam Caruso

Teaching from the Head Rather Than from the Belly[1]

○ Jan Silberberger: You studied architecture at McGill University in Montreal, which I see as a rather technical school. Your work, however, does not appear as overly technical to me; rather, it primarily focuses on engaging with the specificities and the history of the site.

● **Adam Caruso:** Yes, McGill was quite technical, though I wouldn't say that it was technical in a very interesting way. Whatever I learned in school had to do with other students, who were interested in the more cultural, historic, and societal aspects of architecture. Also in my teaching I always distanced myself from being overly technical. I am a practitioner, which at ETH Zurich is not so rare; but in other places where I've taught, like in North London or even at Harvard, it is a lot more exotic that somebody who has a real practice is also teaching. And I think that, just by being a practitioner, I probably encounter enough reality and do not need to dwell on it. I've always thought that the way you learn about how to really be a practising architect is to work for a good practice. And the way you learn about many, many other things having to do with architecture starts at school, but then you have to continue. Art history, for instance, has had a huge impact on how I engage with architecture and how I teach architecture and how I practise. So that for sure has a big influence as a subject area.

○ In recent years, there seems to be a paradigm shift in the teaching of architectural design towards traceability and accountability.

● **AC** It would have been interesting if you had looked at ETH Zurich four years ago, because it was so different. Look at how Miroslav Šik or even Peter Märkli taught and how they did their crits—it was really another age that almost doesn't exist in the school anymore. The new generation, of which I may be the oldest member—Brandlhuber, De

Vylder, Fonteyne—what we teach and how we teach is very different, but what connects all of those studios is that they have a very structured, very tight methodology. But at the same time, we are all prepared to be flexible with that methodology; we are all interested in developing the methodology. So it's not like a fixed thing, but we all believe that in order to impart knowledge and in order for students to be productive you need to be quite clear in how to make a structure for their semester. I think being a good teacher means that you not only have something to teach but you also have a methodology to impart that knowledge. In the history of architectural teaching, a lot of people have not done that. It's like they left that to their charisma. Peter Märkli, for instance, was a great teacher, but I think probably one of the reasons he retired early is that he wasn't getting so much feedback from the teaching after ten years because he relied entirely on his belly to teach. Of course you learned a lot being his student, and he is a very important architect, too. But I think teaching from your belly gets boring after a while. So that is one of my motivations for changing quite a lot quite often. My primary reason for teaching is to learn things.

○ Having looked into a variety of studios at a variety of schools, I wonder whether to understand architecture as a unified academic discipline or rather as a multitude of different research cultures?

● **AC** I think that is another interesting change recently at ETH Zurich. Ten years ago, I think many of the studios had evidently more to do with each other. But I don't know how friendly the different people and faculty were. There were a lot of feuds, at least when I started. There were certain people for whom the only way they could communicate was to shout at each other. And professors' conferences were not so productive; a lot of people just stayed away. What is really

---

[1] Adam Caruso, co-principal of Caruso St John Architects, London, is Professor of Architecture and Construction at ETH Zurich.

interesting is, with this new generation, there is much more respect for each other, and not just implicitly. I think it is something which is expressed. Professors' conferences are much more constructive, I would say. Maybe architecture has become unavoidably so complex that we recognize that we need other models to even understand what we are doing. I find that very interesting. So my answer to your question is that I believe it is a single discipline. I think what has happened is that the complexity and the fact that you need to think about things in different ways has become so obvious that it is unavoidable for architecture schools to become much more diverse. And I think the diversity is really a reflection of the complexity of the discipline and of the culture of the discipline; even my practice is deeply affected by that. We have to have many strategies and also various kind of emotional states in order to deal with the things that are thrown upon us in practice.

○ Maybe nowadays people are far better at identifying and explaining these differences, whereas ten years ago it was basically a battle of tastes?

● **AC** I think many of these people used to think or teach 'from their belly'. And even the term! People really would say that! For example, I taught for a year with Zumthor, and he would talk about it: 'from my belly'. He was a great teacher, mind you, and I'm not sure that he always taught from his belly. But that is just laughable nowadays, that you would teach from your belly! There is much more recognition that we are in an academic situation and we have to be capable of articulating what we are doing and why we are doing it. The other thing is, and this is like chicken and egg, the students are much more demanding, more political. I remember thinking, 'we've got to do this, we have to leave that thinking and teaching from the belly behind', but at the same time I was wondering if the students might collapse, if they might all just go have a nervous breakdown. There used to be a lot more places to hide in the school. And so, in that sink-or-swim scenario, the majority of students have really taken up the challenge, and they are demanding much more of us, which is why the teachers are not only more interested in articulating their position vis-a-vis the other studios but are also becoming more able to do so. If students nowadays have Brandlhuber, 'Made In', and Emerson in second year and then me, they're bringing quite a diverse set of ideas and skills to the table.

○ I imagine this also means that, especially during crits, students challenge professors to provide comprehensible, plausible judgements and feedback.

● **AC** Yes, sure. Another big change is that in the classic ETH scenario at midterm crits, assistants were not allowed to say anything other than, 'Do you want some coffee?' Now we are really pushing like hell for the assistants to be more vocal, for them to have more autonomy. In my studio we agreed that we won't have tutorial groups. We usually see the students twice a week, and they see different assistants; they don't see the same assistants all the time. Generally, the assistants teach in pairs, and these pairs change, so you really are getting a lot of input, but in the end you have to decide.

○ I also have the impression that, fortunately and hopefully, a lot is about to change in that respect. Some crits in the old days must have been excruciating.

● **AC** Crits were much more formal back then. And there were some professors where, at the final crits, the order would go from the worst student to the best student. Can you imagine?

○ You provide students with an extensive reader. I suppose that you do not discuss this literature in a purely academic manner but rather recognize the pieces as more general influences that are meaningful in more than one sense and encourage students also in the sense of a library of sentiments and impulses.

● **AC** Have you been to the reading circles we organize? You must go. Two weeks ago I went to one where they did Donna Haraway. Four students became these hybrids of native people and insects, and they were the first, the second, the third, and the fourth generation, and they talked about the world around them and they talked about the kind of biological and cultural impetus behind their existence—it was completely fantastic! When I used to teach in London, figures like Haraway were very big at the Bartlett, and I had friends who taught how to design these cyborgs, and I thought, 'That's such bullshit!' Donna Haraway is of course much more complex and meaningful than that. The students somehow had connected with the text; they had never heard of Donna Haraway before. The idea is that the texts are instruments. So it is certainly not about a kind of pseudo-intellectualism, so that we are giving you a little bit of extra cream on top. We really choose the texts so that they can be instruments in the development of the studio project. And for the best students, they are, generally. The last three semesters have been less architectural because the students had been looking at issues of gender, more explicitly political aspects, and this semester obviously included texts about gentrification and the role of the artist in society.

○ The list for this semester comprises, for instance, Martha Rosler, Samuel Beckett, Donna Haraway, and Karl Marx.

● **AC** Again, the idea is that you can do a close reading of something and it is useful. And it is also a way of connecting the studio to the gta [the Institute for the History and Theory of Architecture at ETH Zurich]. I have collaborated with people from the gta on various occasions, and it is amazing that you can do that, because in many schools of architecture, the history and theory is so separated from the studio that you could never imagine doing that.

○ How would you describe the relation between your teaching studio, your office, and research?

● **AC** The studio and the practice used to be indivisible, but that is a bit of a crisis I have at the moment. The references I gave at the studio were the buildings we had been looking at in the office. And after ten years of practising, you rely a lot on the people in your office to bring new energy to the core ideas of the practice, so there are always young people in the office who are bringing up new references—like the whole Milan scene, for example. Having studied in Canada, and Peter [St John] having studied at the AA, we didn't know anything about it; it was really by coming to ETH Zurich and having a few people in our office in London that we got into that. So, the studio and the office were indivisible. But clearly, the last couple of years I have been teaching less about formal issues in architecture. The teaching has become more in parallel, trying to open up things that I believe are really missing in mainstream practice. It is connected to my experience of practice, but it is a reaction to the things that I find problematic in practice. So it is much less obvious how those things can be applied to the office. That used to be obvious. So that is a bit of a crisis. I have a feeling at the moment that the thinking and the work in the studio is ahead of the practice, and that is problematic. As for the research, the four books that Helen Thomas and I did, they were a bit connected to that previous relationship between office and practice. They were books done in an academic context, they have the rigour of academia, but they are really for professionals. But now we are in the process of doing a Swiss National Science Foundation application for a research project that is about gender and the curriculum, which is very much connected to what the studio has been looking at. I am not so content in practice anymore, because practising now in comparison to ten years ago is really hard: we have good projects and great clients and all of that, and nonetheless the impetus of money is present in a way that is unprecedented.

❍ Many studios nowadays, yours among them, are explicitly trying to encourage and provoke collaboration among students. In contrast, a decade ago the large majority of studios appeared to be simulating traditional architecture competitions, with students working separately on the exact same task. I wonder if this tendency towards more cooperation also reflects a change in perspective regarding professional practice?

● **AC** In my case that is something that has developed in the studio. I am so sick of competitions, and we are all trying to do fewer now. When you start to practise you dream about competitions, but thirty years ago, there were many fewer competitions. Now everything is a competition, and you realize it is really a part of late capitalism—it is literally competition! And so the idea of having an analogue of that in the studio and the diploma is the same. Six, seven years ago you couldn't talk about changing the diploma because it had this format and it was carved in stone. And now everybody hates the diploma, and we are going to change it. It should be an instrument to explore things—and the idea to see seventy-five examples of the same project is so boring it is killing. I like to think about the studio as a single research project where people feel really comfortable to share things and it doesn't feel like you're giving away a secret, so that everybody is learning and growing the project together. I don't know what it results in and I know that people in the school, like Freek [Persyn], for instance, push it even more—and I think it suits his subject because his subject is more about the city and the communal and the social—but it's in the air.

○ Currently you explicitly do not use buildings as references anymore in your teaching studio. For which reasons?

● **AC** It was last year when we did this semester on gender and we still had buildings as references. We gave the students a drawing, which was about the interior. So each of the students got a drawing, but the huge change was that some of the drawings were by architects who I didn't like. Previously, the references were always a positive paradigm that would tell something in relation to the theme of the semester. So we were looking at texts about gender, also trying to do references which had a gender balance, which is something we try to do. You know, professors say that too: 'We want the best people, we're gender-blind!' But that's bullshit. You want excellence that has been defined in the context of a male profession. So one has to find other ways of framing excellence—and I guess I've been trying to do that. And if you only take the kind of classic buildings that I like, they're almost all by male architects. So I need other ways of framing the discourse and the discipline.

○ In your studio you experiment with translating methodological principles of artists. During this semester your students started by analysing the work of, for example, Cindy Sherman, with the aim of identifying the underlying principles according to which she studies identity, role models, corporeality, and sexuality—and then applying these principles of enquiry to a building or a site. Would you see this procedure in close relation to the way of working with buildings as references?

● **AC** Yes, when we did references that were buildings, we proceeded in the same manner. You know, when I was a student, we used to do precedent studies, where we would get a precedent and we would do this shitty study and then somehow it would inform the project that we did. I hate that. To me, when you look at a reference, you look as deeply as possible—and what comes out of it, it might take you three looks before you understand what the connection is. It's about being able to understand the ideas behind the reference, so that you can make synthetic work. I'm not interested in making work which is just somehow copying—although sometimes you can also copy things, especially if that's part of the content of the reference.

○ I would assume that certain artists' methodologies are easier to translate because they are more clear-cut than others' are.

● **AC** It's never who you think is going to be the easier one! For the best students, it doesn't matter what you give them; they make something amazing out of it. I've used artists a lot in my teaching, and we use them a lot in the practice. Taryn Simon, for instance, is an interesting artist, but I don't necessarily think she's as interesting as Martha Rosler or Pierre Huyghe or someone like that, but her work is really good as a teaching instrument—there's a very clear methodology, and there's different ways you can apply it. But last semester, the two best projects had Sophie Calle as their reference. So again, I don't think it is ever the reference; these were simply the best students.

○ I imagine that when working with references, you often intuitively respond to what they are telling you.

● **AC** The way we used, or still sometimes use references in the office, was completely intuitive. It's something that Peter or I have seen, and then we describe it to the other—and the description might not be that much like the original thing, but that's what becomes, what has a life. You can use it and misuse it; it doesn't really make any difference—and in the end, if it's important, you try to understand how it is important. Obviously, in the studio, it's more didactic, so it has to be clearer. But the intention is that you really understand the reference in a sufficiently deep way so you can then work intuitively and associatively—it's not meant to be linear. Tony Fretton often said, and it's something that I really value, that intuitive intelligence, which is a form of intelligence that architects and artists and scientists rely on heavily, is so undervalued in our contemporary culture which tries to reduce everything to management systems that can be quantified.

○ Do you push your students to reflect on the decisions they took intuitively, so that they strive for a more rational reasoning?

● **AC** At crits—and students are usually really good at that—we say: 'You don't need to describe what you've done. We can see that and we can ask you questions. We want you to present why you've done it. We want you to present the ideas behind it.' And I also think there's a problem in Switzerland of people not asking questions and students not speaking, and that's something that's also changing in the school because there are more and more studios demanding that the students are articulate.

○ Having observed your studio, I sometimes had the feeling that the objects produced and discussed could have originated from a studio at an art school.

● **AC** I think art school is quite different from architecture school. As an art student you are expected to work as an artist, and you're making work which is 1:1. You're in the process of making a body of work, as torturous as that can be. Architecture school has a more didactic structure. Students are not making their work; they're making a kind of an analogue of architecture work. Maybe what we are doing this semester—we are not really doing buildings; we are making a critique around different issues—maybe that's actually closer to making architectural work than doing buildings is.

○ I'm always stunned when seeing the abundance of objects that architecture students produce within one semester. I completely understand that architecture is based on the principle that knowledge is to a large extent inscribed into such objects, but I still wonder whether students might, at times, just present thoughts, ideas of things that they have in their minds.

● **AC** That's something I refuse to do. We will only talk about what's there. I'm not interested in talking about what could be there, and I'm also not interested in seeing sketches, because I don't trust my own sketches, and I certainly don't trust the sketches of students. To me they are meaningless. They have to make work that in some way is a piece of work that's finished, and then we can look at it together. It doesn't take that long to make something.

You Have to Know When to Stop[1]

○ Jan Silberberger: How would you describe the relation between your teaching studio, your office, and research?

● **Anne Lacaton:** I think it is all connected. I am the same person when I am teaching or when I am doing projects in the office or when I am doing research in the school. It means that I have the same approach, I defend the same ideas, the same positions, but it's clear that the situations are different. It is a permanent adaptation to the different situations. It's clear that making a project in the office is absolutely different from teaching a group of students. But I am not thinking differently. I think with the same approach.

○ So there are projects that you do in the office that relate in a comparable manner to research as projects in the studio do?

● AL I don't think that research and practice is something separated and different. In doing projects we are doing research. The project, as sort of a finding, can in turn be analysed and assessed—by us as well as by peers. I think it does not make sense to separate between those who are practical and those who are thinking. For me, this is all totally mixed. And I think in the school it's absolutely the same: research and projects are intimately connected. The difference between research and the design of a project is that when researching you open up, you gather knowledge from a variety of fields; and when designing, you have to make something—not a synthesis—but something that comes out of this research. That doesn't mean that this is a reduction. It's a process of extracting something and making decisions with regard to a specific subject.

○ I remember that you presented your work at a scientific conference on 'open building' at ETH Zurich in 2015. Do you regularly speak at scientific conferences, or was that an exception?

● **AL** I remember this conference, but I don't remember it as very different to others. As an architect, when I am invited to a conference, I usually feel that I don't have the ability to make a theoretical contribution. I try to join through the explanation of our projects and our design process. Designing a project involves thinking. And, for example, this issue of open building is clearly very important for us. Most of our projects, actually nearly the totality, is based on this concept. For me, our projects are also an opportunity to enter the field of research and theory.

○ So when you went to that conference, you did not specifically read the literature on open building, for example by John Habraken?

● **AL** Open building is exactly our way of understanding architecture. It is a concept that has been extremely important for us from the very beginning. But our knowledge, the ideas we have, and our research is always directly related to the design of a project. It is clear, though, that the work of Habraken is part of our reference framework. Yet, our approach was never to develop that as a theory but to use the specific qualities of open building for our own practice.

○ Most of the projects that you do with your office connect to the issue of participation. And also the concept that user needs develop and shift over time (which results in buildings having to be adaptable if we want them to have a long duration) is related to research that is typically done within fields such as sociology or human geography. Do you read such publications?

● **AL** I think we have a very clear position regarding the role of architecture within society. We are not really close to the field of sociology that is, we are not extensively looking into that kind of scholarship. We always ask ourselves: What kind of architecture do we want to produce? This is always linked to the issue of freedom. It is important not to

1 Anne Lacaton, co-principal of Lacaton & Vassal Architectes, Paris, was formerly Professor of Architecture and Design at ETH Zurich.

confuse participation, which is a very specific process during the design phase aimed at involving people with their skills, knowledge, and information into the project, with appropriation. Appropriation is a process which happens after the design phase. This is what interests us most. How can architecture produce spaces for appropriation?

○ I was always wondering why debates on participation do not include this aspect of appropriation. Participation is usually about fixing user needs into a competition brief or into a project respectively. Often people have difficulties in telling precisely what they want; that's one thing. But then, their needs and wishes may change anyway after a couple of years.

● **AL** It's much more about the ability of a project or a space to give the freedom to everyone to live as they want. You can have a very accurate process of participation without providing this ability for appropriation. That is why it is very important to differentiate between this understanding of participation and the kind of appropriation we strive for. A participatory process is something which is absolutely important. It is important, especially when doing housing, to consider that inhabitants have skills and knowledge and that these are introduced into the design of the project. But for me, the design process is not about defining extremely precisely how these people will live later on. For me, architecture is not something on demand, precisely addressing some specific needs. Architecture is much more about how we can open the process and the space so that there is no need, finally, to be so accurate about everybody's specific needs—because everyone can find their place.

○ That has always been the most fascinating aspect, for me, in your design approach. You recognize architecture as truly processual instead of thinking in terms of static artefacts. That is, you don't think in precisely fixed flat layouts but in a more abstract manner about capacities or affordances that a building should provide for its users. I have the impression that you see a building as a space of possibilities and designing as a means to develop specific degrees of freedom. This is very distinct, also in terms of a design methodology.

● **AL** What is also important is that we hand over part of the design process to the users. This is the appropriation part. I don't see, for example, why I would know so much better than everyone how to finish a kitchen or how to organize a winter garden. So, of course we have something in mind, but the experience we have now with spaces, and especially with spaces for housing, which directly concerns everyone, is that, ultimately, the inhabitants are always more inventive than everything that you, as a designer, can have in your mind. As an architect you have to be extremely careful to feel the moment at which you have to stop designing—when you pass over a threshold narrowing a building's possibility space in an undesirable manner.

○ From a methodological perspective this is very interesting. When thinking and designing in terms of degrees of freedom, you have to be far more careful and precise than if you just developed a fully fixed floor plan, which would just look precise.

● **AL** If we come back to the discussion on open building, it is exactly in this way that we understand the word 'open'. We don't mean it in the sense that you can move the electricity or the water freely within a building. It's about creating affordances that enable all inhabitants to find their way of living and their way of organizing their spaces by themselves.

○ In your office as well as your teaching studio, you value architecture that many architects often refuse to recognize, such as the social housing estate in Saint-Nazaire. And your goal to significantly enhance these buildings in a cheap, affordable manner is rather outstanding. In architecture, it is my impression, much is (still) related to 'good taste'. With Bourdieu, one could argue that architecture often serves as an element of social distinction. I have the impression that your approach is in total opposition to that.

● **AL** I think it is clear that, as citizens, we cannot ignore that society is still divided into classes. We can say that we are not really on the way of reducing these distinctions. But as an architect, when designing a space, I don't see why that space should be different for people from different classes. As architects we are often faced with spaces which are, in a way, representative of classes. This is particularly evident for housing. But for me it is a big mistake to introduce these categorizations into the conception and understanding of architecture. Of course, we are inside a field where such distinctions exist, and sometimes we are asked to do social housing, but we don't make any differences in designing spaces for social housing or any kind of other housing. Regarding the issue of taste, I would say that architecture is something completely different than taste. Whenever we are visiting dwellings—new constructions or transformations that we did—we are fascinated by the variety of taste of the inhabitants and the creativity of people. I say that in a very positive way.

○ You say that there is a rich variety of tastes, whereas many people would argue that taste is directly related to class and predisposed by education.

● **AL** If this is case, where is the problem? I mean, if you don't design for target groups but allow for the appropriation of buildings by their inhabitants and according to their own preferences?

○ Throughout the studios that Kim Helmersen and I looked into, we observed a multitude of design approaches and objects of study. Referring to the anthropologist Karin Knorr Cetina, who developed the concept of 'epistemic culture' to address the diversity of the natural sciences—with regard to methods, types of reasoning, ways to establish evidence, and relationships between theory and empiricism—I am inclined to speak about the observed studios as representing a rich diversity of distinct cultures. But I am not sure whether I should focus on their similarities or on their differences.

● **AL** I would say the multitude is finally what appears to be most important. It's clear that what all studios have in common is the orientation towards architecture. You can observe striking differences, but throughout Europe we have a rather similar way of educating architecture students. What makes it different is the personal approach, what we do with our education. We obviously cannot say that architecture is a unified culture, but that is clearly not only the case with architecture. If you look at medicine, for example, there is also a huge diversity with controversial, even antagonistic opinions. Architecture is so closely connected to such a variety of fields. It's impossible to unify it.

○ So if you were invited as a guest critic to a studio at an art school, you would have no difficulties in contributing to the discussion?

● AL I don't see why. I think I would have difficulties in teaching at a place where someone would impose upon me to do this or that. But that was never the case. I have been invited to many different schools, in Europe and in the United States, and of course these schools were highly different regarding the approaches and the topics that students had in their minds. Their interests and their way of questioning were really different. But when I'm teaching, I'm not only there to bring something. I'm also there to observe and to learn. Of course, there are places where I feel less familiar, but I always found an interest to do it. It was always also challenging and scrutinizing my own practice. I never saw a problem. If I'm at an art school, it is evident that a big part of the architecture that we are doing is related to art. If I'm teaching at a technical university (which is supposed to be more technical, although, actually, this is often not the case), I have no problem to talk about construction. And if I'm at a place more oriented towards sociology, it is clear that I'm not a specialist, but from my position as an architect I can also think about sociological issues. I don't want to say that my skills are so vast that I can do everything, but within the frame of design teaching or working as an architect I think that designing a project leads to becoming aware and understanding many fields.

○ When we arranged for the interview and we spoke about your teaching, you told me that you do not want students to become copies of you. On the other hand, it is often argued that teaching works best if professors show, explain, and discuss the modes of operation, the underlying assumptions, the mistakes and successes that shape their practice. So, as a teacher, you expose a lot of your personal values towards architecture.

● **AL** Of course I rely on the projects that we are doing, but for me it is important to teach students design processes. Gathering, sorting, and analysing knowledge about the context and conditions of projects in order to develop a position. Obviously, I like students to listen to me, but it is important that they find their own way. I like when we share ideas, but as an architect, there is often no difference between the ideas or opinions you have as a person and as a professional. For example, personally I am really touched by bad housing—everywhere. And as an architect I cannot forget that. So, I expose my ideas, in relation to the projects we did, but there are different types of architecture that can be based on the same idea or general understanding. I don't want students to copy me in the sense that they take the winter gardens or the platforms that we introduced. I want to see why they decided to go for a similar solution. When we decided to do large, oversized housing, there is a clear position and intention behind that decision. This is what I push students to find in themselves—to develop this position, which is not just related to one project but is a general position towards architecture.

○ A decade ago, most teaching studios had been organized in a way that resembles traditional architecture competitions with students working separately on one and the same task. In your studio, students are encouraged to collaborate.

● **AL** When I studied, competitions were not that important; there were not that many. That was ten years after the '68 movement; everything was different back then. It was a time of opening up. Another few years later that changed back to a more traditional vision. But the first years at architecture school have been very interesting for me because we have been taught that, before developing ideas for a project, it is important to open your eyes, to go here and there, to document, to get to know and get behind the issue. I didn't perceive this as important while I was a student. It came years later that I understood that this method, which appears rather relaxed and not that organized, is extremely important. For me, a school of architecture is not about teaching and learning how to be a good professional. That is, of course, part of the education. But making architecture is so complex that it is important that, at the beginning, you understand very well what is demanded from a project. In the case of competitions, when a question arrives on your table, it has already passed through so many filters that the response is actually already there. You are just there to make a kind of an envelope. And if you are not satisfied with being placed into a project, where you don't understand what is behind the decisions that have already been made, you cannot be comfortable along the process. For me, I have to be sure that I have understood everything in order to define my position. This is what I like to practise with students.

○ This implies different formulations of a problem, different briefs.

● **AL** I never give students too precise programmes. Nowadays, especially within an urban environment, we are in the process of readaptation and transformation. Architects should be asked to analyse places, situations, or environments with regard to exploring and evaluating their potential instead of working with programmes.

○ I imagine that, when you design, then from time to time you experience incidents where you do something which you intuitively know is right. If that happens, do you then urge yourself to reflect on this instance in order to be able to provide a more rational explanation?

● **AL** Intuition is absolutely important. Architecture is special in that we have to deal with contraries, which are normally opposed in our minds. But that's wrong. Contraries are never opposed. They need each other. Intuition is not the opposite of rationality; it is something that allows you to start, to be in line with your feelings, with the way you have understood a problem, a situation. But intuition is not an argument, and design processes have to be explained. You must be able to explain the decisions that you made. It is important to have a serious and rigorous argumentation. It is very often the case that in the end you create a project that is rather close to your initial intuition. Intuition is always there. But during the process you have to make tests and analyse these in order to develop your arguments and to make sure that you take the right decisions. Rigour and intuition are absolutely not opposed—in the same way as generosity and economy are not opposed.

○ Especially if it comes to teaching, providing arguments and rationales is extremely important.

● **AL** When I first started to work as an intern, that was for a genius guy in an office in Bordeaux who always argued that making architecture is also an intellectual process. He often asked us: 'Do you think that your hand will give you the solution?' And then he would tell us: 'When you draw a line on your paper, you also have to think. You should be able to explain why your line starts here and why it stops there.'

○ On the website for your studio, you list a variety of books as references.

● **AL** We also provide students with a lot of buildings as references. Every semester we also give them a little booklet with a number of buildings of all periods, which we recommend them to look at very carefully. It's important to see what has already been done with respect to a certain topic. We never invent something new. If you study references, you see a lot of good ways of dealing with certain problems and issues, and you learn about various intentions.

○ Have you been taught to work with references during your studies?

● **AL** I don't think that I have been trained in analysing references for furthering an own project. It was much more about learning the history of architecture. But it is absolutely essential to carefully study the plans of references in order to learn about the intentions of the respective architects.

○ I always wonder why references in architectural design are not explicitly understood as an equivalent to the state of research in other disciplines—something that you have to consider and that you can build on.

● **AL** Maybe that has to do with the way that the work of an architect is still perceived: as a creation. You have a vision and then you pursue it. It is probably linked to this historical role.

○ To me it seems necessary that architecture has to become more systematic in relating to the state of research as well as with regard to archiving and imparting knowledge so that findings which have been generated through a project are adequately fed into the discipline and can be mobilized by peers in the future.

● **AL** I would say that ETH at the moment very much orients towards that, which is maybe why it is a good school.

Research for this volume was supported by the Swiss National Science Foundation.

3rd printing
© 2025
gta Verlag,
ETH Zurich
Institute for the History and Theory of Architecture
Department of Architecture
8093 Zurich, Switzerland
www.verlag.gta.arch.ethz.ch
verlag@gta.arch.ethz.ch

© Texts: by the authors

ISBN (Print)
978-3-85676-413-5
ISBN (pdf)
978-3-85676-450-0
https://doi.org/10.54872/gta/4550
Creative Commons License CC BY-NC-ND

gta Verlag

ETHzürich

Every reasonable attempt has been made by the authors, editors, and the publisher to identify owners of copyrights. Should any errors or omissions have occurred, please notify us.

The entire contents of this work, insofar as they do not affect the rights of third parties, are protected by copyright.

All rights are reserved. No part of this publication may be reproduced, stored in a retrieval system, or transmitted, in any form or by any means, electronic, mechanical, photocopying, recording, or otherwise, without the written permission of the publisher.

Bibliographic information published by the Deutsche Nationalbibliothek

---

The Deutsche Nationalbibliothek lists this publication in the Deutsche Nationalbibliografie; detailed bibliographic data are available on the Internet under http://dnb.dnb.de

---

Responsible person according to EU regulation 2023/988
GVA Gemeinsame Verlagsauslieferung Göttingen GmbH & Co. KG
Postfach 2021
37010 Göttingen, Germany
info@gva-verlage.de
+49 (0)551 38 42 00-0

Information · Imprint

EDITOR
Jan Silberberger

PROJECT MANAGER AND COPYEDITOR
Jennifer Bartmess

PROOFREADER
Christopher Davey

BOOK CONCEPT AND DESIGN
Brighten the Corners
(Frank Philippin, Billy Kiosoglou)

BOOKMARK-PHOTO
© Grazia Borrini-Feyerabend (see also footnote 18 in the introduction to this book)

TYPEFACES
Times New Roman, Helvetica Mono 821

PAPER
Munken Print Cream 15

PRINTING
Offsetdruckerei Grammlich

BINDING
Buchbinderei Spinner

Against and for Method · Table of Contents

INTRODUCTION
pp.1–16:
Jan Silberberger

PART ONE
Academizing Architecture

---
pp.18–38:
Design, Context, and Profession: Three Research Cultures in Architecture
Monika Kurath

---
pp.39–65:
Academic Research and the Design Studio
Johan De Walsche

---
pp.66–85:
Tacit Knowledge and the Politics of Architectural Design Research
Bernhard Böhm

PART TWO
Systematizing Design

---
pp.87–114:
Decision-Making in the Face of Uncertainty: Encounters between Design and Science in the Post-war Period
Claudia Mareis

---
pp.115–130:
Horst Rittel and the Discrete Identity of Design
Wolf Reuter

PART THREE
Design as Research

---
pp.132–141:
Can Scientific Research Be Designed?
Hans-Jörg Rheinberger

---
pp.142–169:
Contemporary Studio Teaching in Europe: Towards a Theoretical Framework
Kim Helmersen

PART FOUR
Knowledge Production in the Design Studio

---
pp.171–186:
The New Studio: A Mapping Controversies Experiment
Albena Yaneva

---
pp.187–204:
Referencing in Architectural Design
Jan Silberberger

PART FIVE
Review Practice in the Studio

---
pp.206–223:
The Crit: Constructive and Personal
Adam Jasper, Amy Perkins, and Jeremy Waterfield

---
pp.224–234:
Reimagining the Crit
Jan Silberberger

PART SIX
Practitioners' Views

---
pp.236–245:
Oriented towards Transparency and Comprehensibility
Interview with Dietmar Eberle

---
pp.246–254:
Objectivity and Rationality without Neglecting the Subjective
Interview with Elli Mosayebi

---
pp.255–261:
I'm Not a Rationalist, but I Like Logic
Interview with Momoyo Kaijima

---
pp.262–271:
Teaching from the Head Rather Than from the Belly
Interview with Adam Caruso

---
pp.272–281:
You Have to Know When to Stop
Interview with Anne Lacaton

INFORMATION
pp.282–283
Imprint

gta Verlag
ETHzürich

ISBN 978-3-85676-413-5